Understanding and Working
with
Parents and Children
from Rural Mexico

Understanding and Working with Parents and Children from Rural Mexico

*What professionals need to know
about child-rearing practices,
the school experience,
and health care concerns*

B. Annye Rothenberg, Ph.D.

**with
the views of twenty-seven Latino professionals**

The CHC Center for Child and Family Development Press
Menlo Park, California

This work was supported from 1992–1994 by a grant from the Center for the Future of Children of the Lucile and David Packard Foundation.

The CHC Center for Child and Family Development Press is not affiliated with the Children's Health Council (CHC).

Editor: Christine Johnson, San Jose, California
Text and cover designer: Detta Penna, Abbotsford, British Columbia
Printer: Sheridan Books, Ann Arbor, Michigan
Cover illustrator: Carlos Muñoz, Hollister, California

The cover illustration depicts the artist's view of a Mexican family that has come to live in California. The background represents Mexico (south of the border) and the U.S. (north of the border) and some salient features of life in both worlds for this family. Even the colors are different in their two worlds.

The CHC Center for Child and Family Development Press
(a subsidiary of the Banster Press)
P.O. Box 7326, Menlo Park, CA 94026
(650) 369-8032
www.bansterpress.com

Library of Congress Cataloging-in-Publication Data
Rothenberg, B. Annye, 1940–
    Understanding and working with parents and children from rural Mexico : what professionals need to know about child-rearing practices, the school experience, and health care concerns / B. Annye Rothenberg : with the views of twenty-seven Latino professionals.
        p.   cm.
    Includes bibliographical references.
    ISBN 0–9642119–0–4
    1. Mexican American families. 2. Mexican Americans—Social life and customs. 3. Social work with minorities—United States.
I. Title
E184.M5R64   1994   94–31386
306.8′0896872—dc20   CIP

Printed in the United States of America
10 9 8 7 6 5 4 3 2

*To the members of the Latino community who are
struggling to make their lives work
and their futures better
and
to the professionals who are
trying hard to better understand
and more successfully help them*

Table of Contents

Part III
Child-Rearing Practices—Up to the Teen Years

Part IV
The School Experience

Part V
Health Care Concerns

Conclusion   254

Appendices

Acknowledgements

The development of this book has truly been an exciting and rewarding experience. There are many, many people I would like to thank for their help and involvement in making this book possible.

The Children's Health Council (CHC), a child and family development and guidance center in Palo Alto, California, and its administration, staff, and Board of Directors, have been very interested in better serving families from ethnic minorities and enabling those from diverse backgrounds to feel welcomed and well cared for. The CHC has been very supportive of the preparation of this book. Most especially, I am grateful to Alan J. Rosenthal, M.D., Director, and Carolyn L. Compton, Ph.D., Associate Director, of the Children's Health Council for their long-standing guidance and friendship. We are particularly grateful to the Center for the Future of Children of the Lucile and David Packard Foundation, and to Program Officer, Deanna Gomby, for their interest in and support of this project.

The Latino community—the professionals and the parents—made us feel especially welcomed and encouraged us by sharing their heart-felt experiences and by giving generously of their time. We wish to thank each of them for all they have contributed. We are very indebted to the following individuals for allowing us to interview them and highlight their views in this book: Luz Agudelo, B.A., Maty Brito, M.S.W., Rosa Carreno, Juan C. Carrillo, M.D., Beatriz B. Cerrillo, B.A., Carmen P. Cortez, M.A., Amalia DeBord, L.C.S.W., Alice del Pinal, M.S., Rafael Diaz, Ph.D., Linda M. Espinosa, Ph.D., Flora Englund Fortis, M.S., Carmen C. Guedea, Jorge R. Gonzalez, L.C.S.W., Maria Felix Kramer, M.L.S., Reneé DeLeon Martinez, M.S., Ana M. Morante, M.S., Victoria J. Orozco, Rosalie Prado de Ramirez, R.N., M.S., Dolores Marie Ramirez, B.A., Rafael T. Ramirez, Ph.D., Maria R. Reyes, M.S.W., Raul Rojas, B.A., Josie Romero, L.C.S.W., Rita Rossi, Yolanda Ledon Torres, M.A., Gil Villagrán, M.S.W., and Graciela H. Ybarra, B.A..

Sheila Dubin, M.S., my long-time friend and colleague at the Children's Health Council, has been an important part of this project from the beginning. She interviewed many of the Latino professionals and, through her sincere, caring approach, developed trusting relationships that were so important in making the interviews meaningful. She and I were partners in several aspects of this project. Gail Hoben, M.A., another outstanding and dear colleague at the Children's Health Council, has made herself and her wonderful bilingual skills available to us every time we needed her to provide translation and sensitive observation.

Many other individuals and organizations enabled us to get to know Latino professionals and parents. We want to thank Joanne MacDonald, PHN, R.N., and her colleagues from San Mateo (California) Public Health Nursing Division—especially Judy Sencenbaugh, R.N., M.S., and Cynthia Pelich, PHN, R.N. We also owe our thanks to Jean Anthony, M.S., and her colleagues from the Family Focus for School Success Program in the Redwood City (California) School District—especially Silvia Renteria-Shing and Mercedes Otero. Our appreciation also goes to Larry Hammer, M.D., and the staff of the Packard Children's Hospital at Stanford, and the Human Investment Project of San Mateo, California.

Special thanks are due to the San Jose Mercury News. Through this newspaper's extensive coverage of ethnic minorities, we learned about many of the issues that are important to Latinos and found many people whose discussions with us added immensely to this book.

We also want to thank Kathy Merilo, R.N., M.S., and Francisco Padilla for their very helpful interviews; Karen Friedland-Brown, M.A., Becky Beacom, B.S. and Gail Hoben, M.A. for their helpful critiques of an earlier version of this manuscript; and Anita Abeyta, B.A., Maria Bryant-Coker, M.S.W., Vivian Estevez, M.A., Sara Valdez Macpherson, M.S., Esther G. Mota, B.S., Rosalie Prado de Ramirez, R.N., M.S., Elizabeth Solis, B.S.N., P.H.N., Larry Soto, M.S.W., Martha Guerrero-Soto, B.A., Gil Villagrán, M.S.W., and Marlene Zepeda, Ph.D., for their valuable critiques of this manuscript. Marlene Zepeda, Ph.D., and Rafael Diaz, Ph.D. kindly allowed us to include parts of their unpublished papers in this book. We are also indebted to the Child Welfare League of America and one of their authors, Elvia Krajewski-Jaime for allowing us to reprint an important article on folk healing.

Alison Desimone, B.A., the administrative coordinator of the Child Rearing Program at the Children's Health Council, has done an excellent job typing and assisting on this project. Joanne Mintz, M.A., also of the Child Rearing Program, has contributed enormously as a research and resource person. We also appreciate all the additional typing done by Mary Shepard and the photography by Phyllis Johnson. Christine Johnson has done a fine job editing the book. We especially want to thank Detta Penna for her excellent cover and text design, which includes the beautiful work of artist Carlos Muñoz.

Lastly, I would like to express my enormous gratitude to my son, Bret, for his wonderful ideas and advice at every stage of this project.

Foreword

Whatever else one can say about our society and world, this is a time of rapid and often dramatic change. Adaptability and coping with those changes are challenges which we all face on a daily basis. Among the most challenging is our rapidly increasing pluralistic society and how to address the needs of increasingly diverse segments of our population.

As physicians and mental health professionals, we face this challenge regularly. Our patients, particularly in public and clinic health care and child development settings represent a wide variety of ethnic, racial, and subcultural groups. The largest and fastest growing of these in the United States is the Latino population; in California most are of Mexican heritage. And as many immigrant and "minority" groups, they face significant economic, social, cultural, and other hardships in this country.

In our attempts to provide appropriate health care, mental health, and child development services to Latino individuals and families, we struggle and often are frustrated with differences in language, understanding, and cultural beliefs and values. "Why doesn't she take her medication? Why doesn't he keep his appointments on time? Don't they care about disease prevention and prenatal care? Why don't they comply with recommendations about infant care or follow through on referrals?" Certainly many individuals follow our recommendations and are helped by them. For many others, differences in cultural background and belief systems become barriers both to providing and accepting appropriate medical, mental health, and developmental care. While we often expect and hope for greater understanding on the part of our patients, it has been obvious for a long time that professionals as well need to develop greater awareness, sensitivity, and understanding of our patients from diverse subcultural groups.

One approach many of us have supported is the education and training of professionals from ethnic minority cultures who might relate more sensitively to patients of similar backgrounds. While this approach has had some success, it is clear there are not now nor will there be in the near future enough "minority background" professionals to provide health, mental health and child development services for our growing "minority" populations. While we need to continue and increase our efforts in this approach, non-minority background professionals need to develop our own multicultural awareness and sensitivity to serve our patients from diverse cultural backgrounds more successfully.

In an effort to close this "sensitivity gap," many of us have read about other cultures and have attended multicultural awareness workshops. For most of us these have been too theoretical, too general, and only marginally helpful. As clinicians, we need to understand the background, beliefs, values, and day-to-day living practices of our patients from diverse cultural groups. Personal experiences we have with individuals from particular cultural groups provide us with some information but obviously are fragmented, idiosyncratic, and may in fact lead to non-helpful stereotyping.

This book is different—in content and in style. This approach to "understanding and working with parents and children from Mexico" takes us back to their roots in rural Mexico to provide us with a historical as well as socio-cultural understanding. It covers issues of real practical value for the health, mental health, and child development professional: family structure and values, marriage, having children, pregnancy, infant care, machismo, male and female roles, the role of the church, specific child-rearing practices, views of education and special education, views about health care, physicians, and folk healing.

The style of the book in particular is unique. The author, while an experienced, talented, and sensitive clinician is not of Latino background and makes the point that she is in no way an expert in this area. Rather, the book provides a bridge for information gathered through extensive interviews with Latino professionals, and extensive observations in child care facilities and with Mexican families. Further, the information is conveyed through the eyes, with the words and feelings, and from the hearts of the Latino professionals themselves through verbatim quotes from their interviews. The book takes us on a journey of learning about rural Mexican culture and its influence on the Mexican family's adjustment in the United States. The information and topics covered, presented in the Latino professionals' own words, gradually unfold and build the story as one topic prepares us for the next in a natural progression. The book also addresses some very complex cultural issues for many Mexican-Americans who are at various stages of acculturation. While group values, customs and practices are identified, individual variations are taken into account and addressed. Some practices and customs are characteristic of individuals and families who live in poverty; others are strongly influenced by religion and thus overlap with practices derived from culture. The book addresses and differentiates these as well.

The book's author, B. Annye Rothenberg, Ph.D., has more than twenty years experience in developing and directing the parenting program at The Children's Health Council. She has authored two other textbooks on child rearing and parenting education, and has provided training for parenting educators, physicians and mental health professionals, child development specialists, and others on these issues. The CHC's Child Rearing Program, her textbooks, and her training activities have received national recognition and acclaim. Her interest and motivation in developing this book resulted from expressions of concern and frustration by physicians and mental health professionals as they attempted to address child development and parenting issues, health and mental health concerns of their patients. They did not have sufficient information and understanding, nor could they find it from currently available literature or workshops, of the cultural issues which influenced their patients' responses to health and mental health care interventions. This book is an attempt to address these issues more specifically. It is the first in a series of similar publications, each of which will focus on the day-to-day practices, values, and customs of particular subcultural groups in this country.

Hopefully, through increased understanding of culturally influenced day-to-day practice and custom, we can develop more sensitivity and awareness of illness and disorder in the context of our patients' personal history and culture, and develop our recommendations and interventions to complement these rather than conflict with them. As always, we must accept our patients where they are, with dignity and respect for their own beliefs and practices, and apply our services to support and build upon these to the extent we can. Through greater understanding and support of our patients, we can increase communication and follow through with our interventions, providing more personal satisfaction and enhancing their welfare.

We believe this book will help lead us in this direction.

Alan J. Rosenthal, M.D.
Child Psychiatrist and
Director, The Children's Health Council
and
Clinical Professor,
Department of Psychiatry and Behavioral Sciences,
Stanford University School of Medicine

Preface

In the southwestern states and California, hundreds of children from Mexican families enter our public and private schools and child development centers each day. They join the thousands of Latino children already in child care and school and they present an ever-increasing challenge to educators of preschool, elementary, and high school students.

Initially, we Anglo educators attempted to define this challenge as a language problem and designed programs to teach English as quickly as possible. As we grew more sophisticated, we recognized more fully the need to respect the cultural background of not only the Mexican families but all segments of our multicultural society, and incorporated study of cultural traditions, history, art and music, and holidays into our pluralistic curriculum. Whenever possible, we hired bilingual teachers and child development specialists and Latino personnel to work directly with children and families. When that was not possible we learned to use interpreters and translators to bridge the "language barrier."

But the challenge was always viewed as the need to acculturate the family as quickly as possible so that they would adopt our standards, our values, and our ways of doing things.

This book presents a different challenge—a challenge to Anglo professionals not only in education but in health care and mental health, child care, and parent education to learn more about families from Mexico, and to grow in our understanding of their values and customs and the ways they are incorporated into their lives in order to work with them more effectively. The challenge is to recognize and to appreciate the ways in which their beliefs and experiences affect the ways they view their children and rear them.

This book takes you on a journey, following families from rural Mexico to the United States, through the years of marriage, child bearing, and child rearing into the school experience. The content of the book is based upon in-depth interviews with Latino professionals; their direct quotes are combined into compelling descriptions of family beliefs and practices. Through the words of these Latino professionals you learn more about cultural values and the ways in which these values are taught through specific child rearing practices in

Mexican homes. You learn to understand and appreciate the struggles of the rural Mexican family as they enter and try to become a part of the education system with its very different Anglo values, and the confusion and the isolation which results. You experience the fears and frustrations which surround the special education system, the same fears and frustrations which all families of children with special needs experience, but made more painful by both the language barrier and the differences in cultural values and views of handicapping conditions. You enter the health care system with a family who may be more trusting of folk healers; you feel the confusion.

Understanding and Working with Parents and Children from Rural Mexico in its unique format and specific content succeeds in presenting a very personal perspective of the children and families we serve; it portrays in a thoughtful sensitive manner a description of the rural Mexican family structure, relationships, and child rearing practices.

The book is "must reading" for every child development specialist and teacher who strives to work effectively with every Mexican child and family in his or her care. If you can use the information in this book to observe one child more thoughtfully and understand his behavior more fully; if you can assess one child more carefully and objectively; if you can talk with one family more sensitively about their child's special needs, then Dr. Rothenberg and the twenty-seven Latino professionals she worked with will have achieved their goal.

Carolyn L. Compton, Ph.D.,
Learning Disabilities Specialist and
Associate Director, The Children's Health Council
and
Clinical Assistant Professor,
Department of Psychiatry and Behavioral Sciences,
Stanford University School of Medicine

Introduction

The long-held image of the United States as a melting pot where those from minority cultures eventually assimilate is vanishing. As we try to incorporate this change in attitude about minorities and their assimilation into our thinking, we find that this newer view makes it *our* responsibility to learn about other cultures in order to be effective in our relationships and in our work with them. We then find ourselves struggling with the reality that it is very hard to learn enough about a minority culture to feel that we really understand. Understanding the ways of people who come to the U.S. from other cultures does not come easily for most people—even when they are eager to learn. Those of us who are professionals in health care, education, social services, mental health, and special education, and many other service-oriented fields really *need to* learn. But learning about another culture requires both time and experience. Too often, we as professionals don't have enough of either.

By learning as much as we can about the cultures and beliefs of families we serve, we think professionals will be able to provide more welcoming, accepting, and satisfying service to the families. *This book was written to provide professionals with an introduction to the lives, culture, beliefs, and attitudes of families from Mexico, specifically from rural and semi-rural Mexico.** This pop-

*The majority of families coming to the U.S. from Mexico come from rural and semi-rural Mexico. Approximately 30% of people living in Mexico (total 1990 population: 81 million) live in rural and semi-rural areas with populations well under 2,500 in those regions. But at least 70% of those from Mexico who come to the U.S. come from these sparsely populated regions that exist throughout Mexico—north, central, and south. In the last 10 years, due to the 1980s economic crisis in Mexico, immigration from the cities of Mexico to the U.S. is increasing. However, at least 60% of the Mexican immigrants still come to the U.S. from rural and semi-rural areas. (Personal communication, Wayne Cornelius, Director, Center for U.S.–Mexican Studies, University of California, San Diego, August 5, 1994.)

1

ulation is often very culturally different than families from the cities in Mexico—partly due to the lack of access to education—and often harder for American professionals to work successfully with.

Why is it important for service providers to understand Mexican immigrant families? Latinos, of which Mexican origin families represent the highest proportion, have the highest fertility rate in the U.S. and their numbers in the general U.S. population are expected to outpace the national growth rate into the next century. Although Latino families are becoming an increasingly visible part of the social and educational landscape, our knowledge concerning development in this group is relatively limited.

Even though the Latino population is the largest and fastest growing minority population in California and in the U.S., our staff at the Children's Health Council (CHC)* as well as many of our colleagues at schools, clinics, and other agencies have long felt out-of-touch with the needs of Latino (and other ethnic minority) families. This has been true both in our direct work with families and in our training of professionals.

Through our work as child development and child behavior specialists, we have learned that a more detailed understanding of family and parent/child functioning is a requisite to successfully guiding and educating children and their families. Because culture plays a major role in all areas of life, understanding a family's culture is a necessary starting point.

Much has been written about the orientations and values of different cultures (for example, "individualism" vs. "familialism"). Though these writings tend to be very general, they have, at least, made information on various ethnic groups' values more accessible. It has also made us more aware of the outcomes of the different child-rearing practices in various cultures. But we need more specific information about the beliefs and practices in child rearing that produce these outcomes.

What will help us are details about the attitudes, views, and specific "building blocks" involved in the handling of infants and young children in areas such as crying, feeding, sleeping, playing, communication, limit setting, and language and motor development. *We need to learn more about the day-to-day and moment-to-moment roles parents from rural and semi-rural Mexico and their extended family take with their children and the decisions they make concerning their children and why.* This information will allow us to understand both the family's and the culture's contribution to a child's development. As

---

*The Children's Health Council is an interdisciplinary center for child and family development in Palo Alto, California. It provides child- and family-centered clinical services in mental health, special education, and child development through preventive, diagnostic, treatment, and community outreach programs.

we learn more about individual cultures, our guidance to families can be built on the beliefs they hold dear. Our education and guidance, of course, has to be based on the individual history and uniqueness of each family.

The Project

With the support of foundation funding, staff from our Center were able to spend nearly a year learning about families from rural and semi-rural Mexico. We wanted to learn about family life, child-rearing practices, and health care practices. *Far from considering ourselves experts on Mexican culture we saw our role as that of a conduit, or bridge, carrying essential information about Latino families to professionals, especially to Anglos.** As you will see, we interviewed the real experts on Mexican culture: the Latino professionals who will be speaking to you directly on these pages.

In gathering the information for this book, we kept one predominant question in mind: *What would be important for professionals, such as ourselves, to know and do when serving, educating, and treating the Mexican population in the U.S.?*

We began our learning through reading books, journal articles, and newspaper articles. We read in fields such as health care, child development, mental health, and education. These readings lead to contacts with national and local Latino organizations and with most of the Latino-focused parent education programs. We developed an extensive (75 item) interview that focused on the beginning years of family life to help us understand the building blocks of the Mexican parent/child relationship. (See Appendix A). The interview included detailed questioning in the area of infant, toddler, and preschool child-rearing practices because these years in a child's development and in parent/child relationships have such an important impact on a child.

Through our contacts, a list evolved of Latino professionals who work extensively with Mexican families in the United States, primarily from rural and semi-rural Mexico. This list included parent educators, home educators, social workers, early childhood educators, school psychologists, school principals, university professors, health care professionals, etc.—most of whom work in California and, as you will see, all were very knowledgeable and articulate.

---

*Throughout this book families from Mexico are referred to as *Mexicans, Mexican-Americans, Mexicanos, Hispanics,* or *Latinos.* The Latino professionals we met during this project suggested these and other possible designations but as with other minority groups, preferences for how they want to be referred to change with time. However, the terms Hispanic and Latino are both much broader than the term Mexican, and refer to people born in Spanish-speaking countries and to people born in Latin America, respectively. The words *Anglo, U.S.,* and *American* are used interchangeably to refer to the predominant or majority culture in the U.S.

We talked individually with the professionals to explain our interest, learn about their backgrounds, and let them review our interview questions—which they found very comprehensive. After our discussions allayed any fears they had about reinforcing negative stereotypes about Mexican families and adding to the barriers already experienced by Mexicans in the U.S., the Latino professionals all responded enthusiastically to our project.

As we conducted our initial interviews, new questions surfaced about areas we hadn't initially intended to include, such as what life is like in Mexico, why Mexican families come to the U.S., what adjustments and prejudices they experience in the U.S., and what the issues are for older children, teenagers and their families. We modified our interviews to incorporate the new questions and invited additional Latino professionals with expertise in these areas to join our project. Some of these professionals specialized in elementary, intermediate, and high school education; some worked with Latino youth groups; others focused on women's issues. With the additional interviews, we were able to broaden the scope of our work to include these and other related issues.

In all, we conducted interviews with 27 Latino professionals.*

All of these professionals have close family links to Latin America. One-third of our interviewees were born in Mexico. Most of these professionals moved to the U.S. when they were 10 to 15 years of age and have lived here for 15 to 35 years; a few came as infants. Another one-third of our professionals were born in the U.S. Most of these professionals had either one or both parents who were born in Mexico; the remainder, whose parents were also born in the U.S., had grandparents from Mexico. Except for one from Spain and one from Cuba, the remaining one-third of our professionals came from Central or South America. It is interesting to note that two-thirds of our Latino professionals are of Mexican heritage—consistent with the proportion of Mexican or Mexican-descent families among the Latino population in the U.S.

Most interviews took 1½ to 2½ hours and were conducted in person or, if the distance was too great, by telephone. The interviews were tape recorded and later transcribed. *The interview process was very difficult and emotional for nearly all of the Latino professionals.* They spoke candidly about their people, their heritage, and themselves, about both the joyful and painful aspects of Latino life. They did this with the hope that their efforts would contribute to a better life for Latinos. Some of their responses triggered a sense of despair in them. Almost every one of the professionals expressed a feeling at some point

---

*A list of the professionals interviewed, with information about their backgrounds can be found in Appendix B.

during their interview of being disloyal to their own people. This ambivalence, which is natural for bicultural individuals, is captured in these quotes.

To broaden our understanding and to compare our impressions with those of our Latino professionals, we surrounded ourselves with Mexican culture. Beyond our interviews and extensive readings, we met with groups of Latino public health nurses, parent educators, and social workers and listened to their views. We attended workshops (such as those of the Hispanic Women's Council) and accompanied public health nurses and parenting educators on visits to 15 homes of Mexican families who came from rural and semi-rural Mexico. The main focus of those home visits was on the parent-child interaction and the professional/parent interaction. (During these visits, the public health nurses and home educators translated for us.) We made additional visits to shared homes of single mothers from Mexico and to nursery schools and child-care centers that served mostly families from Mexico. We watched videotapes, movies, and theater about life in Mexico. We made observations at pediatric clinics, community centers, food markets, and department stores serving nearly exclusively Latino families (with dialogue translated by a Spanish-speaking colleague).

Each step of our learning process added detail to our picture of the issues facing Latino families. Each resource validated what we were learning from the others. *We were continually drawing tentative conclusions, checking them out, and modifying them.*

Our interviews with the Latino professionals were by far our most valuable resource and are the heart of this book. Throughout our interviews, we asked the Latino professionals for advice about what other professionals could do to make their work with Mexican families more successful. Most of their experience with Mexican families were with those from rural and semi-rural Mexico but they kept reminding us that families from large towns and cities in Mexico were quite different. The Latino professionals generously shared their ideas and their experiences. They gave us many suggestions about ways to make U.S. life, customs, and systems more understandable to Mexican families. And they told us of the need for Mexicanos to make certain changes as well. But the professionals worried about changes that Mexicans feel pressured by U.S. culture to make that might go beyond the necessary and interfere with values that they hold dear.

Our snapshot of life in 1994 for Mexicans in the U.S. who come from rural areas may be very different just a few years from now. We repeatedly heard about the many changes that had occurred and were still occurring.

Dealing with Difficult Issues of Socioeconomic Level, Education, Religion and Acculturation

When trying to learn more about another culture, we have to look at factors that can confound what we find.

Socioeconomic/Educational Level: In the U.S., the Latino population lives, on the average, at a lower socioeconomic level than the Anglo population. Twenty-nine percent of the 22 million Hispanics living in the U.S. live below the 1993 poverty level ($14,350 or less for a family of four). This is in contrast to 9% of non-Hispanic whites. About 30% of Hispanics have no health insurance, compared to 13% of whites. Interestingly, 80% of Hispanic men were in the labor force—a higher percentage than that of non-Hispanic white men (75%).* Significantly, although it continued to grow during the past decade, the percentage of Hispanics enrolled in higher education is still the lowest of all minority groups. In 1991, Hispanics had the lowest level of high school completion (51%) of all race and ethnic groups in the U.S. From these statistics, it is clear that many Latinos are poor and have little formal education. These statistics are descriptive of the Mexican segment of the Hispanics in the U.S.

All people with little education and low incomes have many experiences in common. *But this book is about rural/semi-rural/very small town Mexican culture and values, not about the culture of poverty.* The interviewed professionals and the authors were all keenly aware of this and quick to point out when an experience was due more to socioeconomic level than to Mexican culture.

At the same time, poverty and limited education cannot be ignored when trying to understand the lives of many Mexican families in the U.S. Both factors are a very important part of the U.S. experience for a significant number of these families. These are the families we see a great deal of in California and are trying to learn more about in this book. These are the families that come from semi-rural and rural Mexico, from small towns and poor farms. Many of the Latino professionals we interviewed come from this same background as well.

Religion: Much of the Mexican experience is almost inextricably tied to Catholicism. Ninety percent of Mexicans are Catholic. It is nearly impossible to separate out the influences of the Church from the influences of being Mexican. For most in the U.S., being Catholic is part of being Mexican. The group we are trying to learn about are mostly low income with limited education, from rural areas and very small towns of Mexico, and mostly Catholic.These are the Latino families that American professionals find so challenging that they especially need to understand better.

*Based on a 1992 national census report.

Acculturation: The interviews explore the changes that occur as a family becomes acculturated. *Acculturation involves more than the number of years lived in the U.S.* It is reflected in, among other things, an increased use of English in the family, increased interaction with people other than Latinos, and more schooling. It involves personal struggles about the conflicting values of the two cultures, Mexican and the U.S.. But *acculturation* does not mean *assimilation*. Acculturation is an acceptance of one's minority culture *and* of the majority culture and, through eventual adaptation, internalizing elements of both cultures. Assimilation generally means that the ethnic minority gradually loses its distinctiveness and becomes part of the majority group.

Many immigrants across the world as they come to new countries do not necessarily become acculturated, and certainly do not necessarily become assimilated.

Immigration Status

Although we all know that there are many illegal or undocumented immigrants among the Mexican population in the U.S., we generally did not ask our Latino professionals to differentiate between legal and illegal immigrants in their responses—they spoke about all the Mexican families they work with. When they did differentiate, it was because the specific question highlighted the difference in experience for the two groups. Because it is very common to have both legal and illegal residents living under one roof, the families we work with may well represent both kinds of residents. *No particular judgments about immigration status are being made in this book.*

Stereotypes

Trying to better understand any group of people is fraught with the problem of stereotyping—of describing a group as though they all thought and behaved alike. *Stereotypes can become so much a part of how one views another culture that they become barriers (often unintended) to getting to know and appreciate the people of that culture.* Stereotypes are most prevalent when interaction between groups is quite limited—especially when languages differ.

Stereotypes often have some truth to them, and some value; they help people simplify and classify but can also prevent people from getting to know each other and become friends and learn from each other. Too much trust in the stereotypes perpetuates them and perpetuates separation among groups.

In this book, we have tried to provide a foundation for more in-depth learning about families from rural and small town Mexico. Understanding the basis for, the reasons behind, the values of, the motivations, and the hopes of a people can have an important ameliorating effect on the ways we look at others. This is what is intended here. In Chapter 6, p. 36, on being a Mexican living in the U.S., we further explore stereotyping. It's important to remember that an individual's behavior, attitudes, beliefs, and character are governed by many factors other than culture. These factors include individual background and experiences, socioeconomic status, sex, age, length of residence in a locale, education, and the history of the culture's entry into the U.S. (including the impact of shifting immigration regulations)—each of which will have an impact on cultural practices as well.

In order to understand the Mexican immigrant as an individual, it is important to understand the variability that exists in this population. Although a great number come from small rural communities in Mexico, many do not. Although some already have family members residing in the U.S. to which they can turn to for support, many do not. Tremendous variability also exists in the quantity and quality of the schooling received in their home country. However, regardless of these differences, Mexican immigrants share the belief that economic and educational opportunity are better achieved in this country. Thus, they are willing to tolerate high degrees of personal and economic hardship to afford future possibilities for themselves and their children. Like most immigrants, this is why they come and this is why they stay.

Individual Differences

We all recognize that every individual and every family is unique. Of necessity, this book contains many generalizations. *These generalizations can be used as a starting point, but it is important that they don't prevent us from seeing the individuality of the person or family we are working with—an individuality influenced by their skills, temperament, upbringing, opportunities, stresses, etc.* This book contains many suggestions on how to identify the unique qualities of an individual or family.

Challenges in Preparing this Book

As you can imagine, the difficulties we experienced in undertaking this project and communicating what we have learned have been an enormous challenge. However, what we have learned from meeting with the many Latino professionals and Mexican families has been so insightful and, we believe, helpful that we have prepared this resource for your use and ours. Behind all of this is our underlying view that a lack of information about people who are different leads to discomfort, myths, stereotypes, and prejudice. It can also lead to inaccurate assessments, education, and treatment. All of these interfere with relationships among people of different cultures. It is our hope that the information provided here will enhance the quality of service and satisfaction experienced by Mexican families and of the professional in his or her work with the families.

Organization of the Book

This book is presented through the voices of the Latino professionals—the true experts. Sometimes the comments they make are not consistent with one another and that should be expected. Human beings, regardless of ethnic/cultural affiliation, will demonstrate differences in perspective. However, only those views that we heard expressed by many others were actually included. Even so, the Latino professionals we interviewed work in different milieus from each other providing different services. Each is at their own unique place in their acculturation, has a different background from others and different personalities. Some of the professionals have a more open, revealing relationship with those they serve and some have less. The comments, however, made by each Latino professional should be considered as well-founded. By reading the comments presented in this book, a clearer picture of what it means to be a Mexican immigrant will emerge in all its complexity and contradiction.

Understanding and Working with Parents and Children from Rural Mexico is divided into five parts, each containing topical chapters. The best foundation for understanding the family from rural and semi-rural Mexico will be gained by reading Parts I, II, and III sequentially before reading the remainder of the book.

Part I is about life in rural Mexico—an important starting point for a book chiefly about people from Mexico or of Mexican descent. Our experts talk about why and how Mexican families come to the U.S., the adjustments they have to make, and the issues of prejudice, Latino values, beliefs, and family structure. In Part II we learn about the beginning years of family life: marriage, infant care, and the roles of mothers and fathers. Part III focuses on child rearing practices up to the teen years, with special attention given to communication and limit setting. Part IV explores the school experience, both in Mexico and in the U.S. It also provides insight on issues of special education (including family involvement) and discusses critical aspects of the teen years. Part V, though speaking directly to health care issues, will be of value to all professionals. In this part, the Latino professionals offer suggestions on establishing an enhanced relationship with small town Mexican families and understanding and working more effectively with their folk healing practices.

In the Appendices, you will find resources to help you understand and become more comfortable with families from rural Mexico. The appendices include a map of Mexico (with all its 31 states and their pronunciation), recommendations for additional reading, a list of Latino parenting education programs and of a wide variety of other Latino-focused organizations.

This book is for the teacher, nurse, physician, parent educator, special education clinician, child-care provider, mental health clinician, social services staff, and others who want a better understanding of families from rural Mexico, the regions where well over 60% of those who come to the U.S. come from. *We hope you enjoy and learn from what we believe will be an interesting and helpful journey.*

PART I

LIFE IN MEXICO,
ADJUSTING TO THE U.S.,
PREJUDICE/STEREOTYPES,
AND LATINO VALUES

Chapter 1

Life in Rural Mexico

What is living in rural Mexico like?

Because most Mexican families in the U.S. came from rural or semi-rural Mexico, we begin here. These quotes paint a picture of life in Mexico that helps us better appreciate the world view of the families we work with, the lives they left behind, and the lives of their families and friends who remain in Mexico.[1, 2, 3]

As a general guideline, *rural Mexico* has been described as sparsely-populated areas of up to about 100 people who survive by living off the land; they have livestock such as chickens and pigs and raise corn and small amounts of other crops; they earn money by going to town to sell eggs, bananas, oranges, etc. There is usually no electricity or water in the house; no radio or telephone; water comes from the well or a river. School continues up to about third grade; schooling beyond that is not within walking distance. To get to church, usually you have to walk to town. *Semi-rural Mexico* often has as many as 1,000 people in an area; some survive off the land but often not totally. Many go to the nearest town to work as domestics. Homes often have

---

[1]Throughout this book, you will hear many voices and views expressed, some that even seem opposite to each other. We value the diversity and feel that the many quotes in each section provide a more balanced and rounded picture of reality for the Mexican families from many experienced perspectives.

[2]See Appendix C for a map of Mexico and its 31 states including a pronunciation guide to make it easier for you to know where in Mexico the families you work with come from. For further reading, see Appendix D.

[3]Comments by the author, such as this one, will be found throughout the book—usually at the beginning and/or end of a chapter. Those comments will be set off from the rest of the text for ease of recognition.

electricity but not phones. The area may have a little plaza with a church and one general store that sells beans, rice, bread, etc. From there, people take a bus to the towns. *Towns in Mexico* are very little cities with maybe up to 5,000 in population. These towns may eventually become cities. The streets are often not paved. There are usually some Catholic churches and maybe some churches of other denominations. The town would have businesses including for example, hardware stores, pharmacies, grocery stores and beauty salons. Schools would typically be available through junior high. High school would still be a bus ride away in the nearest city. There is usually a family doctor who goes to the rural and semi-rural areas.

Maria Felix Kramer, Branch Library Supervisor

Where I come from in one of the rural parts of the state of Tabasco, there is still only subsistance living. Many of my family still live there and I visit every year. The people there raise livestock such as chickens and pigs, and maybe cows if they can afford them, for their own consumption and to sell. They live in box-like one room concrete houses with a flat roof. There is usually one light bulb hanging in the center of the room. That is the electricity they have. There is no refrigeration. If they have any food, it's for eating at the moment. If, for example, there is some meat from an animal, they would boil it right away and eat it. Everything is boiled if they're going to eat it. Each day, they make tortillas by boiling and grinding the corn first and then making the tortillas. If any are left over, the next morning they may barbecue the tortillas and eat them with coffee and milk which is a typical breakfast. If you're lucky, you have some lard and salt on the tortilla and that tastes delicious when you haven't eaten for a long while. Preserving everything is done by boiling.

There is also one water pipe with a faucet just outside the house; there are no sinks or toilets in the house. The toilet is in a little shack outside and just has a seat. It's like an outhouse. When you go to the toilet, you take a bucket of water with you and throw it in the toilet after you've gone. Transportation is mostly by walking or by bus. The roads were paved once a very long time ago but are now just packed dirt and are very dusty. Buses take people to the cities with their crops to sell and they take children in the higher grades of school to the bigger towns for their education. Parents need to earn money for children's clothes and transportation to school. They might sell their pigs or chickens to do that. There are also vans that take children on more direct and faster routes to school but they cost much more.

Maria Felix Kramer, Branch Library Supervisor

In some parts of rural Mexico, life is dirt floors and dirt roads, mud, outhouses, having a lot of farm animals around, growing your own vegetables, and having your own *curandero* [koo·rahn·DEH·ro: folk healer].[4]

Graciela Ybarra, Resource Teacher

In parts of rural Mexico, they have only outhouses. Sometimes people don't even have that. In the *most* isolated parts of Mexico that haven't been reached yet by community health workers, people go to the "toilet" in their yards or in the field.

In much of rural Mexico, people can only bathe once a week. Water comes into the rural areas only once or twice a week, so people fill up their small pools with the fresh water to survive until more water arrives. (These "pools" are made of cement—like a water hole in the yard.) This water is used for drinking, bathing, cooking, and watering the animals.

Further south into rural Mexico, they wash at a local water hole. (The water hole is a bit like a river, but the water just sits there.) People wash their clothes by rubbing them on washboards. They rinse them and pound them on the rocks. Then they just hang them out on bushes to dry for a while before carrying them home.

Carmen Guedea, Parent Educator

There is a lot of poverty, even though the people work hard from early in the morning until sundown. It's a hard life because everything is far away and they don't have cars. Hospitals are long distances away. It's common to have to walk several miles each way to bring your children to school. It shows how important it is to the families that their children get an education. They are fighting against so many inconveniences.

Maty Brito, Mental Health Outreach Counselor

[4]Spanish words: The Spanish words used by the Latino professionals, all of whom were bicultural and bilingual, are included, followed by a pronunciation guide and a definition. These guides will appear at least the first time the word appears in each Part. Rather than use a formal pronunciation guide with phonetic symbols requiring special knowledge or references, we give an approximation of Spanish pronunciation based on standard American English sounds for the non-Spanish-speaker. The sound of the long "o" (as in "lone") presented some difficulty and will be represented as "o" or "oh" or "oe".

They raise their own food and have little contact with people other than their own family. So going to school or getting things that are not nearby is a chore. Their whole life is survival and their priorities have to be the things that are most important. There are no frills like we have in the U.S.

Dolores Ramirez, Multicultural Director

Life is hard for them. It's different than here. They have different customs. For example, some don't wear shoes because they don't have them. If they do have them, they only wear them to go to school.

Many of the rural Mexicans don't attend school beyond the third grade. It's not that they don't want to, but the schools are too far to walk to. After the sixth grade, schools are even farther away—mostly in the cities. And after the sixth grade, school isn't free. All the services are far away: schools, stores, hospitals, everything. You couldn't even get to where we used to live by car. It was three hours on a donkey to the nearest road.

Graciela Ybarra, Resource Teacher

There's an illiteracy problem. It's more important to work in the fields and get something on the table than to go to school. To go to school, you have to dress up, you have to be clean, you have to do what the teacher says. All you get is book knowledge, and that doesn't help you in the fields. This seems to apply more to boys than to girls. But many do have a sense that there is something better. Those are the people who come to the U.S. to better their lives.

Dolores Ramirez, Multicultural Director

Some homes have electricity and running water; others don't. The south area is more Indian and poorer.

Maty Brito, Mental Health Outreach Counselor

Rural Mexico has both very small towns and *ranchos* [RAHN·choes: ranches] and *ranchitos* [rahn·CHEE·tohs: small farms]. Some of the ranchos and ranchitos have electricity. It depends on how close they are to a town. Most of the people or houses in the small towns have electricity. Water usually comes from a well or a faucet, again depending on their distance from a town. Houses are made of adobe and brick in the towns and of adobe on the *ranchos*. They are usually built around a courtyard or patio. The houses don't always have glass in the windows and are often not open to the street or road.

Most families that live on *ranchos* or *ranchitos* live with extended family. The grandparents or older uncles may not work on the land anymore, so the younger generation takes over working on the land. Today, even people who live on *ranchos* may own a store or small eating place in town, if town is close by. Sometimes they own a store with a restaurant in the front. These stores mainly carry staples—tortilla flour, powdered milk, canned goods.

Government services are very slow in these rural areas. It may take up to four weeks for a letter to travel 500 miles from one small town to another. Many of the people living on ranches have to go into town to get their mail.

Not all people who live in small towns have phones. The services are available, but it takes a long time to get a phone hooked up. Whether or not a *rancho* has a phone depends on how close it is to town. If it has a phone, it would most likely be in the main house where the owner lives. The outer houses, where the workers live, may not have phones. Most *ranchitos* don't have telephones. But if there's electricity, people usually have a TV.

Rita Rossi, Librarian and Resource Center Staff

Most people coming from Mexico are from *ranchitos*. These are very isolated dwellings with no electricity, no running water, and no paved roads. The shock of moving to our urban areas is very great for them. Many are very intimidated by it.

Amalia DeBord, Clinical Social Worker

Preparing for a meal takes a long time. Some people cook on stoves. Depending on their economic status, some people cook on something that's a combination stove and barbecue pit. You have to put wood under it to keep the fire going. People who live closer to the U.S. have gas stoves. Northern Mexicans have more modern appliances because it's much easier to go over the border to buy and sell things.

Carmen Guedea, Parent Educator

Almost everyone from rural areas has somebody in the U.S.—whether it's a brother, son, daughter, grandchild, or cousin. The family members remaining in rural Mexico take care of the family's property, animals, and crops in Mexico. It's very common for the relatives in the U.S. to send $20 or as much as $50 to their families in rural Mexico; this will last the family two weeks. Doing this is very common.

My family lives in the U.S. nine months a year and goes back to Mexico December through February. During the nine months they are in the U.S., three or four young men in Mexico take care of their fields, their animals, and their house. My uncle sends the men money from the U.S. This helps feed their family. All through the year, these men also work with other people's crops. Usually they're paid with chickens and goats and things like that.

In rural and semi-rural Mexico, none of the women work outside the home. And the men are not working because there are no jobs. They may work annually at harvest time and make their own corn into corn meal. There are very few jobs for money. They don't pay taxes and they're not on any payroll.

I just came back from a week in Juarez, Mexico. Living in Mexico is so different. Mexicans take things as they come. There's less sense of direction. There is little emphasis on "what am I going to do today" or "what am I going to plan for the next month?" People do things more from minute to minute, hour to hour, with no preparation. People don't plan, for example, to go to the grocery store. Someone will say, "We need to go to the grocery store because we need to eat," and they go. They buy food like fruits and vegetables on a daily basis. If they can afford it, they also buy meat—again daily so it's fresh. If they don't get their milk and eggs from their own cows and chickens, they also buy milk and eggs daily. It's not like in the U.S. where we plan everything.

Carmen Guedea, Parent Educator

Chapter 2

Attitudes about the U.S.

Why do Mexicans want to come to the U.S.? What attitudes and feelings do Mexicans have about the U.S. before coming here?

In this chapter, we are looking at issues concerning the basic needs and hopes of people living in Mexico. We can see more clearly how important the U.S. is to them. We can also see some of the internal conflicts and fears they experience in their relationships with the U.S.

People from Mexico come to the U.S. because they want to improve themselves. In Mexico, they are working so hard trying to support their family, and they don't see any light. Even if both parents work, they only have enough money for the necessities—sometimes not even that. They come to the U.S. and believe they can improve themselves and have a more comfortable life. They're coming from a Third World country to a First World country. They expect to work hard, improve, and make money. They believe this will make them feel better about themselves and their lives.

Maty Brito, Mental Health Outreach Counselor

A lot of the people who come here come from the *ranchitos*. The rural people starve before the city people do, so you see a lot more rural people coming to the U.S. But we are also seeing a lot more people from the cities. It used to be that if you couldn't make a living in the rural area you'd go to the cities in your own country. But now that there is no work in either place, people are coming here.

Dolores Ramirez, Multicultural Director

Many of the Mexican immigrants who come from the cities of Mexico may have come from the great poverty found amidst the modern conveniences there of gas stoves and electricity. Although their lives are very different from those coming to the U.S. from rural Mexico, they, too are looking for ways to survive.

Gil Villagrán, Child Welfare Social Worker

Many families have come out of desperation because there is little for them in Mexico. At least in the U.S. there may be an opportunity. Some come to the U.S. and expect to stay. Some families hope to earn enough money here to go back home and buy a house, or fix up their house, or start a little business. It usually doesn't work out that way. They can't make enough money; they can barely keep it together here. And sometimes children don't want to go back to Mexico when they grow up.

Maria Reyes, Social Worker

Most Mexicans come from poor, agricultural communities. Life is very hard and they come here for economic reasons. Though they may live in very poor conditions by U.S. standards, it still may be much better than they had in Mexico. Even living below the poverty line in the U.S. is better than what they had in Mexico. So coming to the U.S. is a step forward.

Ana Morante, Outpatient (Mental Health) Case Worker

For some, the dollar is the big god. Many have relatives who were in a poor situation in Mexico and moved to the U.S. They had to struggle here, but in the end they achieved some sort of economic and social improvement. For them that is a lot. They think everything will be easier in *El Norte* [ehl nor´·teh: the North, meaning the U.S.]. They think they'll be able to make more money here than in Mexico. It's their dream that they can move to the

U.S., improve themselves, make money, then move back to Mexico. Their patriotism is very strong.

Maty Brito, Mental Health Outreach Counselor

The U.S. is seen as a place that is very rich—that you can pick money up off the streets, that it's easier to make a living. Some have grown up in families that have told them over the years, "When you grow up, you go north to make your life" (meaning they should go to the U.S.).

Maria Reyes, Social Worker

I feel that in general Mexicans look upon the U.S. as a place of opportunity. They see a lot of their own people successful in the U.S., so that means there must be opportunities here. They realize that it will be very different, that there will be conflict, that there will be struggle, that there will be prejudice. They realize that people don't want them here. But at the same time, they see people that are successful, they see people that have been here for generations that are successful, and they want that. So I think there is a conflict. They want what the U.S. represents, but at the same time they don't want to give up who they are or where they come from. So they bring that with them. It takes them a long time to give that up. I hear stories about children who were born here saying that when their parents came here they just came temporarily. The parents had their suitcase waiting; they were always going to go back. This was in their minds; that is how they survived. They felt they'd have to give up their culture if they stayed here. And it takes a while for them to know that they don't have to give up their culture. It is a beautiful culture.

Dolores Ramirez, Multicultural Director

Is there a mixed attitude toward the U.S. based on the history of Mexican-U.S. relations?

No one leaves a happy, nurturing parent, but in Mexico, the country is an "uncaring parent," and illness, starvation, and unemployment are the evidence. Meanwhile, just across a dry riverbed are our cousins, the U.S.A., our half-siblings, the California to Texas siblings who were kidnapped in 1848 by President Polk and "Manifest Destiny." Some of us feel that the U.S. is *our* land and we have a right to be here. There's a saying that I saw on a tee shirt that expresses this. It says, "I didn't cross the border; the border crossed me."

Gil Villagrán, Child Welfare Social Worker

The older generation used to talk about the fact that land that is now part of the United States used to be part of Mexico. But middle-aged Mexicans ("the younger generation") don't talk about that.[5] They're more concerned about whether they will make it in the U.S. and what impact life in the U.S. will have on them. They wonder, "Can I treat my wife the same way, or will she get educated? And will I be belittled by that?" They're afraid that the U.S. is full of loose people who have no values or morals, that it's a terrible place to live because kids talk back to their family members and ask questions when they're not supposed to. This is considered disrespectful and very unacceptable.

Carmen Guedea, Parent Educator

[6]

Many Latinos have very positive attitudes about the United States. They like it here; they want their children to do well; they see that there are opportunities here, and they feel a certain loyalty to the U.S. because they know they can have a better life here.

Most Mexicans don't feel negatively toward the U.S. Some have both positive and negative feelings. They know there are resources and agencies here that will help them in ways that were unavailable in Mexico. Some have had very good experiences with the police here. Some have found they can get help from the police in the U.S.—help they never got in Mexico. But there are also a few who got battered in a confrontation with the police here and were scared. They felt it was unfair, a big misunderstanding. And now they're suspicious of police.

Maria Reyes, Social Worker

[5]The United States and Mexico are, historically, geographically and economically intertwined. All of what is now the southwestern part of the United States and beyond was once Mexican territory. The continuing relationship between Mexico and the U.S. can be reviewed in books listed in Appendix D under "History and Current Conditions."

[6]Throughout this book, this symbol indicates the end of the responses to the preceding question and a return to the responses to the general questions listed in the Chapter opening.

Mexicans don't see moving to the U.S. as meaning that their children are going to grow up here or get married or get an excellent job or have an excellent education as much as, "My kids will eat and they will be bathed and warm and they will have clothes."

Some of those who came here see the U.S. as a source of income and know that if they have a child in the U.S., they'll qualify for public assistance. And the woman will have MediCal. This means she'll have some security if her husband leaves her. This is why they come. But, to them, nothing is more beautiful than Mexico.

Carmen Guedea, Parent Educator

I think some who come here know about the welfare system's benefits they or their children would qualify for. But many others would do anything— any type of work—before they would take a handout from the U.S. government. They feel taking a handout is a source of shame; all they want are opportunities.

Maria Kramer, Branch Library Supervisor

Many come because they think they can earn a better living here. They may have a friend or a relative that moved to this area and later went back to Mexico to bring them to the U.S. Most of the people worked as farm laborers when they were in Mexico. It's hard for them to get work here because they are not trained to do other types of jobs.

Amalia DeBord, Clinical Social Worker

The majority of the people who come here from Mexico come here for the exact same reason that the Pilgrims came and the Jamestown people came which is to make a better life for themselves.

Gil Villagrán, Child Welfare Social Worker

Parents want their children to learn and that's why some of them come here. They realize they need help in educating their children.

Victoria Orozco, Family Resource Specialist

I think 90% would say it's easier to live here as far as material things. That's why they feel satisfied living at what is a low level by American standards. At least here they have some shoes and some bread. They feel almost grateful to be here. But there is a big trade-off. They give up their spiritual side, their family, their villages. They have to work more hours, so they have less time with their family. Often, the working conditions are poor and the type of work they do is sometimes degrading.

Graciela Ybarra, Resource Teacher

Many of my clients remember how poor they were as kids in Mexico, so they try to give their kids as many material things as they can. This makes them grow further from who they are. They're from a culture that couldn't nurture them financially, and now they're here in a new culture that can give them a little more. Most of them have had to work since they were little; they've had to work hard—for survival. Many took care of younger siblings. They may have come from homes with no money, lots of alcoholism, and violence where there was not enough time, energy, or desire to parent the kids. The focus is just survival—survival now and in the immediate future.

Ana Morante, Outpatient (Mental Health) Case Worker

Here, at least children get to go to school, get free lunches (if they qualify), and get better medical care. Even if the family's living in a garage—and it can be pretty dismal—it's still better here. It's so hard in Mexico. It's even hard getting kids into a school. There aren't enough schools there and they're very crowded. A child may not be able to go to school some years. And some can't afford the registration charges and materials for school. Here the education is free.

Maria Reyes, Social Worker

As long as Mexico has the economic problems that it has (the lack of medical care, the lack of opportunities to get a good job or to get ahead), people will continue coming here— even if it's very hard here and not as good as it used to be. It's so stagnant in Mexico. There's so little opportunity.

Maria Reyes, Social Worker

Chapter 3

Coming to the U.S.

What is getting to the U.S. from Mexico like?

We now look at the journey across the Mexican border—at what is a dangerous and frightening experience for many Mexican families who come to the U.S., an experience that affects their lives for years to come. Their willingness to endure these hardships demonstrates how truly important coming to the United States was for them. The anxiety continues for the undocumented Mexicans who continually face the possibility of being deported.

Some people come on tourist visas. That's more expensive. And they don't go back to Mexico. Some fly or come in cars with relatives. Some walk across the border, across the hills at Tijuana. It's long, dangerous, dirty, and frightening, and mostly done with a *coyote* [ko·YO·teh: someone whom they pay to help get them across the border]. They might have to pay the *coyote* $500—if it's a long trip. If they own a little house in Mexico, they don't sell it because they hope to go back someday.

Maria Reyes, Social Worker

It's awful! It's horrifying! They come with a *coyote*. Sometimes women are used as *coyotes* because the border patrol usually doesn't stop women coming with children. There are both male and female *coyotes*. You have to get near to the border—Tijuana, Nogales, Juarez—on your own. *Coyotes* in the border towns say, "I'll charge you so much money to get you to the United States, to where you're going." And then they'll bring them. But to cross the border, some people have to cross the mountains. They have to go through tunnels; they have to sleep in the desert for days so they don't get caught. The *coyote* guides them to the U.S.—maybe to San Diego. And there's another border crossing in the middle of San Diego and Los Angeles, and they have to go through the desert again to get to Los Angeles.

Coyotes overcharge, beat the people up, rape the women, and mistreat the children. Sometimes they separate the children from their families because they need a child in another van to make a childless couple look better. This child goes through the torment of missing his family for three or four days until they're reunited.

Carmen Guedea, Parent Educator

They pay hundreds of dollars to get someone to get them over the border. Some of the stories that I've heard are horrendous. The *coyotes* will have a certain route where they'll take them across. The *coyotes* may be smuggling drugs. The Mexicans might be asked to carry some drugs as part of their payment to get across. If they bring small children with them, it's a hazard. Sometimes they have to run across highways that are very dangerous. Sometimes they come across through sewage pipes. Most come by land. Those are the illegals, of course. Those that come legally usually have family here, and they get papers. They have to pay bribes in Mexico to get these papers because there are long waiting lists. You can get illegal documents—it just costs money. It used to be that if one member of the family was documented, the whole family was legal. Now that's not the case. The government's talking about not letting families use services like school if the parents are not documented—even if their children are legal.

Dolores Ramirez, Multicultural Director

You pay the *coyote* half their fee at the border and the other half when you get to your destination—like Salinas. People are brought in semi-trucks, vans, station wagons, cars—whatever the *coyote* is driving. These people have no papers. If the INS [Immigration and Naturalization Service] agents find out about them, they put them in jail for a few days before busing them to Tijuana. From Tijuana, they only need $100 to cross the border again. If they've worked while in the United States, they might call a family member or someone they trust to pick them up and take them back to the U.S.

Mexicans come to the U.S. undocumented because they can't get in any other way unless they have a father or mother in the U.S. who will legalize them by getting an application. If they get documentation, they can just fly here.

Carmen Guedea, Parent Educator

Some people I've talked to say coming to the U.S. was easy. They just crossed the border and paid a *coyote*. It was harder for others because they had to pay a lot of money and were taken advantage of. Some had to spend all their savings to come here. That shows how important coming here was to them. You have to be strong to leave your stability and everything that is familiar behind you to come to another country. They can't speak the language, and they don't understand the culture. That is very hard. They feel a lot of pride about their heritage, their country, their music and folklore. Just by listening to them, you can feel their sadness about having to leave their country for economic reasons. They have to leave, but their heart and soul are still there.

Maty Brito, Mental Health Outreach Counselor

Chapter 4

Initial Adjustments

What are some of the adjustments Mexicans have to make when they move to the U.S.?

The adjustments immigrants from Mexico must make when they leave their rural lives in a Third World country and come to the more comfortable, prosperous, and technologically sophisticated U.S. are tremendous. Their culture shock is compounded by the foreign language, the need to find a job, and the changes in their family's way of life and in their children's education. An appreciation of the changes that permeate the lives of these immigrants will help us understand and respect the effort and the stresses associated with adjusting to life in the United States.

One of the biggest adjustments is living with strangers. Mexicans have such a close-knit community in their country. When they come here, they may know only one person. I know this one woman who lives with three families in one apartment, but she doesn't know the other families. Apartment living is an adjustment. They've never lived in that type of housing before. There's a lack of privacy. They feel suffocated. Most of the families here live in tiny apartments or with a lot of other families in one small house or apartment. There's one family that has six girls and lives in a one-bedroom apartment. The parents sleep in the living room and all six girls sleep in the bedroom. They also have to adjust to different foods. Transportation, too, is a big problem. In order to get ahead and get a good job, you need transportation, and most families don't own a car. Not knowing the language is a major problem, as is the attitude of Americans. The Mexicans feel discriminated against.

Graciela Ybarra, Resource Teacher

The first months are very difficult because families have to move in with a sister-in-law or mother-in-law or a friend that they trust. A couple or a family will all sleep in one room. This is an adjustment because, in Mexico, they may have two or three bedrooms. Husbands and wives don't sleep in the same room as their children. In Mexico, the boys usually have one bedroom and the girls have another.

The Mexicans that come here are worried about work; they need to get a job. There might be problems with the family they're staying with or renting a room from until they can get their own place. The children are used to much more freedom in Mexico. They're used to throwing rocks, running around with cows, etc., The children are not used to being "careful" because they don't come from places with costly posessions. Here the people they're staying with get worried that the children might accidentally do things like break their windows.

Carmen Guedea, Parent Educator

Families miss the open space. They want to plant and grow things and do many other familiar things.

Maria Reyes, Social Worker

There are many, many adjustments that they have to make. It begins with adjusting to a completely different culture. The ideas, the ways to act, the way to talk. Their view of the world is completely different; concepts are very different. It is hard for them to understand our laws. They don't understand the word "abuse" as it is defined here. If you grow up in a society where they punish you physically, what we call abuse seems normal. They don't understand how you can be put in jail for what they see in Mexico as the proper way to teach their child. And they don't know how to use the system to their benefit. It's so different in the United States and parents are confused by that. They're confused by the way mothers here raise their children to be independent and by the way that children have active roles in the family. Even the food here is different. They are used to eating natural foods. In the U.S., we have a lot more processed and packaged foods. And, of course, the language is different—even the structure of the language. In English we say "white house." In Spanish we say "*casa blanca*" [KAH·sah BLAHN·kah: literally, "house white"). Saying "white house" feels like you are talking backwards. They also have to adjust to the rejection they feel from society. They feel like nothing. They feel that they aren't doing anything here except making and spending money. They don't have relatives or land, and they feel that they want to go back to Mexico.

Maty Brito, Mental Health Outreach Counselor

The main problems are understanding the language and its idioms, trying to find a good job to get enough money to satisfy basic needs, and trying to understand the new culture and the environment around them. How do people behave? What are the values? Some of the values in the U.S. are very different from the Mexicans' values and beliefs.

Children naturally adjust faster than the parents. They're socialized in school, they meet children from other countries, and they learn the language faster than their parents. It's very important for parents and children to get adjusted to the new environment. Many parents are so busy trying to find resources to survive that they may not have any free time to spend with their children or to do something for themselves. Work is one of their strongest values.

Raul Rojas, Parent Educator and Community Outreach Coordinator

Mexican children are used to being told what to do by their family members. They come to depend on that. They don't question why something is, and they don't have a lot of analytical skills. So, for children, it's hard to act independently and to become independent.

Graciela Yburra, Resource Teacher

They have a very difficult time. A lot of the families are not here legally, and that creates a problem because some of them don't know how to get help. I deal with a lot of preschoolers who come here with all kinds of developmental delays. Not knowing how to get help becomes a problem. When the men can't find a job, the children suffer. I know a lot of families who have ten people living in one tiny apartment. The children don't have a permanent place to sleep and they are always tired in school. This kind of home environment can create problems for the children in school. It's not that they don't value education, it's that basic needs sometimes take precedence over education. When families arrive in the U.S., their focus is survival. They need to get acculturated: they need to get housing, they need to find out how to survive. School is not their priority. Once a child gets into school, it's not that the parents don't want to be supportive, it's just that they don't know how to be. Because they don't know the language, they believe they can't help their children. It's one of my jobs to tell them they don't have to speak English to help their children. They can help them in different ways.

Flora Fortis, School Psychologist

I think the first thing they have to adjust to is the language. That is why they congregate where there are a lot of Spanish-speaking people. They try to find a job where English is not a requirement. They also have to adjust to a new diet. The diet here is very different than they are used to. In Mexico, they had all fresh food but no refrigeration. Here they have refrigeration and all this convenience food, but they want their traditional foods. The educational systems, too, are very different. The Mexican system is more like the European system. There is a lot of respect for education and the teacher. The role of the teacher is to develop the mind; the role of the parent is to develop the soul. What a child learns is the teacher's job. How he or she behaves is the parents' job. Whatever the teacher says, the parents will follow. They will believe it and respect it and not argue with it, especially if they don't have much education themselves. When they come here they find that to get a good education for their children they have to be involved in the school—especially in the public schools. If parents have enough money, they will put their children in Catholic schools, which are more like the schools in Mexico. The Mexican parents have a hard time with taking a larger role in their children's schooling. There's a lot of conflict there. They want the best for their children, but they don't know how to deal with the system here or how to make an impact. They will try to blame the system and say that it's wrong because it doesn't work for them. Our school system is a big change for them. It's important that they get involved before their children get to adolescence and start to rebel. By then the parents don't know what to do.

Dolores Ramirez, Multicultural Director

I think we overlook the impact of parental loss. Parents grieve for their country, just as we in the U.S. would if we permanently moved to another culture. You don't just get there and think, "Hooray, hip, hip, hooray!" You go through a grieving process. It hits you that you may never return to your country. I don't think we look at the parents' grieving process in terms of not only their loss of country but also their loss of culture. Their kids become more American than Mexican as they grow up. And some of the American cultural ways are not very acceptable to the Mexican parents. We have to look at the parents' grief about the realization that their child is no longer a real Mexican child. We also have to look at parental anger and all the things that go with having to move and having to belong to this culture. Historically, there has not been a "good neighbor policy." And when you wind up being the low man on the totem pole in jobs and the economy and don't see things getting better in the future, it's a real struggle. The child has to cope with the parents' anger while trying to fit himself or herself into the school system.

Yolanda Torres, Child Care Consultant

There's a problem getting things done. You really have to know what you want in order to get things done in the U.S. Families need to learn how to go after what they want. It can be very demoralizing to stand in line for a day or two to get a job or temporary housing. They don't realize that they have rights as immigrants. They need to know how to get through the system. Because the Mexican population is not comfortable with asking questions and demanding their rights, the system is overwhelming. They have to deal with agencies that they never had to deal with in Mexico. This is especially overwhelming for people from rural areas, who had no contact with government agencies, or forms, etc. The rural areas in Mexico are much more isolated and rural than what most of us know.

Renee Martinez, Professor of Child Development

In rural Mexico, people don't wear watches. Time is important but not in the sense of knowing when it's exactly 9:00 a.m. or to be watching the clock every minute. It's important to know if it's early morning, noon, late afternoon or evening. When the sun is a certain height, parents in Mexico know it's time to get up and to start to get their children ready to go to school. But parents are not used to thinking that it's important to get their children to school by an exact time, say 8:25 a.m., as it is in the U.S.

Rita Rossi, Librarian and Resource Center Staff

There is an organized time in which to do things but it is not the ultimate drive to immediately accomplish it. There is a sense of organization but other priorities come into play and make us more flexible. We don't let time run us.

Rosalie Prado de Ramirez, Public Health Nursing Supervisor

I recently came back from visiting family in Mexico and began to better understand why I do certain things. There's an openness of the household. People can come over at any time. They really welcome you into their home. They have a real graciousness and an appreciation for everything that is done for them. The element of time is also very different. There is no hurry. "Take your time" is the way the Mexican culture looks at life. In Mexico, when you have a family celebration, you are expected to spend a whole day there. We, on the other hand, are run by the clock. At first it is a culture shock when you come to the U.S. Everyone seems to be rude. But as families live here longer, they get used to it.

Renee Martinez, Professor of Child Development

There is a love of life and a gentleness—a gentleness that is tied in with respect. There's a sense of celebrating the day.

Yolanda Torres, Child Care Consultant

To families arriving from Mexico, the U.S. does not have a warm, passionate culture. The people seem rude, cold, impatient, and prejudiced. And the language is hard.

Graciela Ybarra, Resource Teacher

When Latinos come here, they have to shorten their names to conform to the U.S.'s one first name/one last name tradition.

Ana Morante, Outpatient (Mental Health) Case Worker

Non-Latinos don't pronounce Latino names right, or they change them. Teachers, for example, may pronounce "*Jaime*" [HI·meh] as "Jamie" [JAY·mee]. Or they may say, "*Carlos.* Oh, that means Charles. Is it OK if I call you Charles?" What's a child supposed to say? It's demeaning to Latinos to have people not take the time and trouble to pronounce their names correctly; it's also demeaning when Anglos convert their names to an English version.

Yolanda Torres, Child Care Consultant

Chapter 5

Housing

Where do Mexicans live (house or apartment /own or rent)?
Who do they share their home with?
Is it a temporary or permanent arrangement?
Do they live in Latino or mixed neighborhoods?

When families come to the U.S., they usually live with relatives or with a friend until they can rent a place of their own. Most people rent apartments or houses. Life is much easier for them if they can move into a Latino neighborhood where the people are like they are, speak the same language, eat the same foods, and have the same values.

Graciela Ybarra, Resource Teacher

Most of the people that come here from Mexico know someone already living here. It makes them feel more comfortable to live in an area where people are like themselves. That way, when they go to the market, they'll see people that look and talk like they do. Most of them live in neighborhoods that are primarily Latino. They live in apartments or small houses—mostly with relatives or friends at first. They don't have the money to live by themselves. After they get a job, they can afford to get a place for their own family. They usually rent. I have never worked in a place where so many of the people are from Michoacán [mee·choe·ah·CAHN]. I like to say that the last person who left Michoacán had to turn off the lights.

Maty Brito, Mental Health Outreach Counselor

They move into primarily Mexican neighborhoods because of the language, the familiarity. Even though the children meet each other, the families don't often interact—except maybe at church. It's not necessarily a community. That's because all of the people are not from Mexico; they may be from different countries, and their customs and values may be very different. There is also a mixture of rural and city backgrounds. The language may be the only thing they have in common.

Dolores Ramirez, Multicultural Director

Chapter 6

Living in the U.S.— Prejudice and Stereotypes

How does it feel to be Mexican and live in the U.S. (prejudice, stereotypes)?

The extent of prejudice felt by Latinos is greater than many of us might realize. This prejudice has a serious impact on their self-esteem and may contribute to the downward spiral of their efforts and accomplishments. Latinos are painfully aware of many of the negative stereotypes about them. The prejudice they experience comes not only from the Anglo community but also from the Latino community itself.

It's very hard. Mexicans get ridiculed and laughed at because of their language. They feel a lot of prejudice. Even if the prejudice is not open, I think Mexican people feel it all of the time. In order to be "OK" here you have to be Anglo. A lot of Mexican people begin to have low self-esteem. If your accent is heavy, people speak to you like you are deaf or mentally retarded—even if you're educated. It really hurts. It destroys your self-confidence. Even the educated Latinos begin to feel ashamed of their language and their culture because it is not considered "good" in the U.S.

We need to feel better about ourselves. When there is no structure to let our people know what their rights are, they begin to feel less than human. A feeling of shame begins to develop. A grandmother came here from rural Mexico, worked hard, and bought a house. But she didn't want her children to speak Spanish. I know this is an English-speaking country, but what is wrong with speaking Spanish, with being bilingual? It's the shame they feel. They want to keep their culture, but it's very difficult.

Maty Brito, Mental Health Outreach Counselor

Sometimes the fear of being discriminated against holds us down. The reality is that more than 50% of our population will not advance. We don't have the skills to compete. The only way we can get the skills is to take a risk—a risk of being discriminated against and judged. It's very painful. For example, it was very hard for me to go through school. I was the only Latino who graduated from high school in my school of 500. None of the other Latinos graduated. Many were in gangs. I was in a gang. I was in jail by the time I was 14. Every one of my friends got pregnant. There was a lot of pressure from the Anglo community. They didn't have to say anything; you could feel it. I worked as a migrant farm worker with my family. One summer the owner's kids were out working with us in their bikinis. I felt like I was being mocked. Here we were having to do this work to survive, and they were being taught a lesson about money.

When you are the only Latino in a class, you have to think only of yourself, and that is very hard for Mexicans to do. Even now I get discriminated against. I just went to Safeway. I'm getting my master's degree. I don't need to be wearing a title, but the cashier asked me if I was going to be paying with food stamps. There was a blond, blue-eyed woman behind me, so I asked the cashier if she was going to ask her if she was going to pay with food stamps.

Now with Governor Wilson saying that these Mexican children don't deserve an education, people feel that the government is against them, too.

Graciela Ybarra, Resource Teacher

In this country, Latinos often feel anger and frustration. It takes years to learn how to deal with it, especially for those who don't have the language or the confidence.

When I talk on the phone, people hear my accent and think I don't understand. They treat me like I don't know what I'm talking about. And, in total frustration, I say to them, "Don't listen to my accent; listen to what I say!"

From a meeting of Latina/Chicana social workers
at a county social services agency[7]

---

[7]The following are the social workers who participated in that meeting (Fall 1993): Socorro Gutierrez, M.S.W., Celia Medina, M.S.W., Maria Oropesa, M.S.W., Maria Reyes, M.S.W., Julie Serrano, M.S.W., and Diane Soriano, M.S.W.

What stereotypes do Latinos think Anglos have about them?

Latinos think Anglos believe that all Latinos are in gangs, lazy, and don't like to learn; that jails are full of Latinos, that Latinos drink a lot, that they use drugs and are aggressive and violent, and that they don't know how to work together.

Raul Rojas, Parent Educator and Community Outreach Coordinator

There's a stereotype that Latinos are lazy, in gangs, and use drugs. Latinos are seen as second-class citizens that shouldn't have the same rights. Latinos also feel many negative things about American culture.

Ana Morante, Outpatient (Mental Health) Case Worker

Mexicans are lazy, they're not hard-working and are always late.

Mexicans are unskilled and on welfare; they're a drain on the economy.

Mexicans are stupid. Mexicans are just fun-loving, silly, like children.

Mexicans are gutless (agreeing to whatever you say).

Mexicans don't value education.

Mexicans drink a lot.

Mexicans fight a lot—knifing and shooting.

Mexican youth are often in gangs. They use knives and guns too freely and bring more violence to this country.

Mexicans won't learn English; they are less willing to assimilate.

Mexicans are only here for better wages; they have no real allegiance to the U.S.

Most Mexicans are here illegally, so they are "criminals" and should be found and sent back.

From a meeting of Latina/Chicana social workers
at a county social services agency

Latino parents in parenting classes were asked to write down ten stereotypes that others have about them. They came up with many more than ten.

Raul Rojas, Parent Educator and Community Outreach Coordinator

There's a stereotype that Latino children are in gangs. It's a problem that negative stereotypes come to the minds of people about Latinos. I'm trying to help parents to feel good about being Latino, to fight against stereotypes. Latinos have the same qualities, talents, and intelligence to do what we want to do as anyone else. We need to create a new image about who the Latino is.

Raul Rojas, Parent Educator and Community Outreach Coordinator

With lower-income people who come from Mexico, I see a sense of shame about their culture. It's because of what they hear from Americans about being Latino. When I ask Latino parents in my parenting class what Americans say about Latinos, they quickly give a long list of negative things. Mexicans feel Americans have a very negative image of them. When the dominant group looks down on you, the common coping mechanism is to become less like your group and more like the dominant American group. This makes you weaker.

Ana Morante, Outpatient (Mental Health) Case Worker

In our parenting class, parents were asked, "How do you feel about people thinking this about us?" They said, "I feel angry, uncomfortable, depressed. I feel bad about myself. I don't like people feeling this about us." Stereotypes are creating barriers that keep us from having a good relationship with ourselves, with other Latinos, and with other cultures.

We need to learn more about ourselves as Latinos, and then more about other cultures. It's hard to change some of these stereotypes. The pressure of the environment is heavy. It's something we are carrying for a long, long time, so we have to be very strong.

Raul Rojas, Parent Educator and Community Outreach Coordinator

Latinos have stereotypes of Americans, too. They see them as arrogant, pushy, boastful. This comes from their stereotype of how Latinos behave who have become very American.

Sometimes I think that the problem is not so much prejudice as it is a lack of understanding of how the system works. Because the system is not working for them, they figure it's because they are Mexican.

Dolores Ramirez, Multicultural Director

When you're Latino, you are always different. Your appearance counts a lot in the U.S. If you are very fair-skinned, then you can't be Mexican. Americans think that to be Mexican, you must be very dark, ignorant, and have a thick accent. They won't accept as Latino someone who doesn't fit that image. There's a lot of pressure from other Latinos to act like a Mexican and not be like the Anglo culture. There's also a lot of pressure from the Anglo community to act Anglo. You really have to identify yourself and be stable inside. You have to be American but retain what you want to retain from your culture. But you can't escape your appearance. When I was living in "redneck country," my kids got picked on because they were Mexican, and when we moved to Oakland, they got picked on because they were white.

Dolores Ramirez, Multicultural Director

It seems that we as Mexicans are aware from the minute we're born of the racism and the discrimination here in the U.S. I think it colors the way we raise our children or view our culture, and it gives us a false image of how we should behave. If there were no racism, would the Mexican family coming here have to act the same as they do now? I don't know, but what I do know is that there is a lot of anger and resentment toward Anglos for making people give up their culture in order to make it here. You are also angry at yourself—angry that this is the only way you can make it. I think the families sometimes hide their culture, and sometimes they exaggerate it. It colors the whole way you are. It always makes you feel that you're not part of the culture as a whole. There is both envy of and anger at the people who become more "Americanized" and make it in terms of that culture.

Yolanda Torres, Child Care Consultant

Families know what's expected of them in Mexico. But here it is not always clear what is expected according to the American culture. This is because of language and cultural traditions and economics.

Anglos tend to think that if they directly translate something written in

English into Spanish it will still make sense and be taken in the same context. But this is insulting to Latinos because the context has been left out. Literal translations are an insult in any language. Latinos begin to feel that *they* are the stupid ones rather than the person who did the translating.

Josie Romero, Clinical Social Worker and
Director of a Family Institute

Shame is a big factor in Latino culture in general. It's not just in the U.S. that Mexicans are oppressed. Mexicans have been taught at many levels that the closer they are to U.S. culture—the closer they are to being fair-skinned, blond, etc.—the better they are. It's thought that the more they think like Americans, the better they're going to be. Being Latino is shameful—especially for the Latino middle-class because it's hard for them to identify with the more traditional part of their Latino culture. Even though they will never be American, the middle class try to deny the part of themselves that is Latino. This rejection of their own culture makes them more vulnerable. They imitate things they are not, and the more they do this, the unhappier they feel.

Middle-class Latinos in the big cities of Latin America grew up with the American ideal. They didn't learn to be proud of being Latino, of having dark skin and dark hair. There's a big part missing there. They think they're different from other Latinos. Latinos can be so out of touch with their own culture. They've lost the richness. They've lost what there is to have pride in.

Latinos who are middle income, educated, and from big cities in Latin America will be much more like Anglos than like Latinos in how they were raised, how they think, and in their values. They try to be more like Anglos and look down on more traditional Latinos. When they come here and feel discriminated against, they may feel negatively about themselves. Children might feel shame if their parents don't speak English well.

There's a high level of discrimination among Latinos. Those more in touch with Western society will look down on people who come from small towns and tend to be more traditional and have less income and less education.

Middle-class people in Lima [Peru], where I come from, try to be "American." We have a shame about ourselves and believe that everything that comes from us must be bad. You hear it everywhere. Of course, what can you expect in Lima where there are long lines to stand in to buy things made in the U.S.? What's made in Peru is considered not good enough. This is the feeling of many middle-class Latinos who have been exposed to the West. This is true in the other Latin American countries, too.

It's no solution to try to be "American" because you never will be—no matter how much you strive. It will always make you feel like a second-class people. Latinos feel shame from the negative ideas that Americans have about Latinos. Sometimes two Latinos will talk to each other in their accented English because they are ashamed to be Latino.

Latinos carry a baggage with them of racism, sexism, and oppression. There's the trauma of alcohol, drugs, and violence at home (intra-familial trauma). In Latino culture, alcohol is promoted as something fun, something to do. There's not the health-consciousness about alcohol that there is in the U.S. Alcohol plays an important role in the Latino culture. Violence is also an important part of the culture. This has something to do with *machismo* [mah·CHEES·mo: see Chapter 22, p. 97].

Latinas [lah·TEE·nahs: Latino females] in my women's workshops see many positive things about American culture: the organization of the culture, the clean country, the system that works a little better. I advise them to take the best of both cultures, to respect both cultures and not put down either of them. I try to help them understand that we should not feel lesser because we're Latino, and we should not feel more important because we're Latino.

Ana Morante, Outpatient (Mental Health) Case Worker

I feel very concerned about my community. I want to let people know that we are a population that wants to grow. We want to break up the stereotypes. We are human beings with intelligence, like other people, and we need opportunities to grow. We need to demonstrate that, given the opportunity, we might be very successful. As a community, we're going to try to continue working hard to adjust to this new culture, to understand more about it, and to learn to live healthy in this new culture. It requires a lot of energy to grow healthier in this country.

One of our responsibilities as Latinos is to educate ourselves first. And we have a responsibility to try to get to different economic and political levels, to have more decision-making power on the issues that affect Latinos. We need to work with our kids to encourage them to stay in school, to do things for themselves, and to provide a healthy environment where our future will be better than it is now. But we need time and patience. Things are changing now. There are more Latino professionals now than in the past, but we still need more professionals for this fast-growing population. I hope we will have a better life in the future for our kids.

Raul Rojas, Parent Educator and Community Outreach Coordinator

Chapter 7

Latino Values

What are some of the key values of traditional Latino families?

The values of Mexican families differ from those of the dominant Anglo culture in the U.S. These value differences are reflected in family relationships, relationships with others, gender roles, expressions of emotions, and the role of the children in the family. The following quotes will provide some clues about these values and their expression that can help build a bridge to better communication, understanding, and respect. We need to respect their values. At the same time, we can support Latinos in their efforts to incorporate aspects of U.S. culture that may enhance their success and acceptance.

Excerpted from "Some Thoughts about the Implications of Latino Child Development for Early Childhood Professionals," an unpublished paper (1993), Marlene Zepeda, Ph.D., Assistant Professor, Child and Family Studies, California State University, Los Angeles, California:

Latinos hold certain values and beliefs that are important for childhood socialization. The following is a simplistic overview of important core values and beliefs that will vary in individual families depending on their acculturation level, their socioeconomic standing and their ethnic loyalty. It is very important to see these core values as broad generalizations subject to adaptations to local conditions.

Familialism

This value is viewed as one of the most important culture specific values of Latinos. *Familialism* refers to strong identification and connection to the immediate and extended family. Behaviors associated with familialism include strong feelings of loyalty, reciprocity, and solidarity. Familialism is manifested through the following: (1) feelings of obligation to provide both material and emotional support to the family, (2) interdependence on relatives for help and support, and (3) reliance on relatives as behavioral and attitudinal referents.

Respeto (respect)

Associated with familialism is the cultural concept of *respeto*. The cultural value of respeto is an extremely important underlying tenet of interpersonal interaction. Basically, respeto refers to the deference ascribed to various members of the family or society because of their position. Generally speaking, respect is accorded to the position and not necessarily the person. Thus, respect is expected towards elders, parents, older siblings within the family, and teachers, clergy, nurses, and doctors outside of the family. With respect comes deference, that is, the person will not question the individual in the authority position, will exhibit very courteous behavior in front of them, and will appear to agree with information presented to them by the authority figure.

Bien Educado (well-"socialized" or well-"mannered")

If a person exhibits the characteristics associated with respeto then they are said to be *bien educado*. What is important here is that the term education is not formal education but the acquisition of the appropriate social skills and graces within the Latino cultural context. For traditional Latinos, a person could have honors from Harvard University, but if they did not conform to this system, they would be considered as badly educated.

Incorporation of important cultural values and beliefs into the practitioner's interpersonal conduct provides families with a semblance of cultural continuity and maintains feelings of self-respect. The practitioner can accomplish this by demonstrating high degrees of courtesy and politeness, understanding that indirect communication on the part of the child and the parent is a reflection of "respeto" to those who are authority figures, and viewing the broader family configuration as an important resource for understanding Latino family dynamics. Within this general framework the practitioner must accommodate individual differences and local community conditions.

Excerpted from "Latino Gay Men and Psycho-cultural Barriers to Aids Prevention," an unpublished paper (1993), Rafael Diaz, Ph.D., Associate Professor, Stanford University School of Education, Stanford, California:

Simpatia

Simpatia expresses the importance of smooth, conflict-free, and non-confrontive interpersonal relations as another very important value of Latinos. Simpatia emphasizes the need for behaviors that promote smooth and pleasant social relationships. Simpatia moves the individual to show a certain level of conformity and empathy for the feelings of other people. In addition, a person with simpatia ("simpatico") behaves with dignity and respect towards others and strives to achieve harmony in interpersonal relations. Researchers have operationally defined simpatia as a general tendency toward avoiding interpersonal conflict, emphasizing positive behaviors in agreeable situations, and de-emphasizing negative behaviors in conflictive circumstances.[8]

Familismo

The importance of family relations and the actual close involvement of families in the lives and affairs of the individual members is not considered a temporary situation of youth, but rather a life-long commitment that connects individuals, even after marriage, to a relatively large and supportive social network of caring and concerned human beings.

Latinos are highly aware and proud of this shared cultural value. For example, when Latinos talk about themselves in comparison to the Anglo mainstream culture—they often refer to the distance and coldness of relations among Anglo family members, and about their puzzlement at how Anglos "leave their families behind when they turn 18" or how "even some of them talk badly about their parents."

Membership in the extensive and resourceful social network of grandparents, aunts, uncles, their children, more distant relatives and the compadres and comadres provides individuals with a sense of security and social connectedness that protects them from both economic hardship and social isolation or loneliness. *Familismo* provides a natural support system that protects individuals from both physical and emotional stress. For Latinos in the U.S., social support within the family system constitutes one of the most important protective factors against the health risks posed by poverty and minority status.

---

[8]This courteous behavior does not in any way imply that the person is in agreement with what was said or will do what was asked (i.e., accept what was said).

Every culture has its values that are valuable. When a family can articulate their values, they usually use them in their child-rearing practices. The child is usually indoctrinated with those values. In my family, the value of respect was important—respect for your elders, for yourself, and for others. The other important values for us were the value of knowledge, the value of education, the value of flexibility, the value of honor, the value of faith, and the value of the family. Those values were pounded into us. We were taught to protect and defend the image of the family to the outside world.

Josie Romero, Clinical Social Worker and
Director of a Family Institute

Your culture gives you strength to face challenges. The deeper the roots, the stronger you're going to be. In the parenting classes I teach, I try to awaken the sense that our culture is very important and has many positive elements that we need "to make ours" again. We need to take pride in our culture, not let it go.

Ana Morante, Outpatient (Mental Health) Case Worker

Many parents are working hard to keep their values, but at the same time it's important to adjust to this new culture. It's hard to keep these values. It's like a negotiation, a balance between your own values and those of this culture. It's hard for parents to change, but they want their kids to negotiate with this new culture. They know the children are more in touch with this culture, more socialized.

Parents are still thinking nostalgically about the traditions in Mexico, about how they were raised and educated, and how the extended family helped the nuclear family. Many are trying to provide these values to their kids at the same time as they're trying to teach their kids to live in this new culture and to appreciate its values.

Raul Rojas, Parent Educator and Community Outreach Coordinator

Except where noted, the following is the author's summary of the values mentioned most frequently during the interviews with the Latino professionals. Quotes from the professionals are included when relevant.

Values of Families from Mexico

• Close-knit families (includes aunts, uncles, grandparents, cousins, comadres [ko·mah·drehs: godmothers], compadres [kohm·pah·drehs: godfathers], etc.), with lots of time together—talking, eating, celebrating.

• Caring about the family, the extended family, and friends; a spirit of cooperation and loyalty rather than one of individualism or competitiveness. (A Mexican child raised in the United States may be seen by his family as becoming too selfish and self-centered.)

> Latinos living in the U.S. miss their families in Mexico *very* much—their mothers, uncles, cousins. When someone becomes ill in Mexico, people make huge sacrifices to get the money so they can go to Mexico to be with them, especially if the family member is ill or dying. They want to go so much.
>
> *Maria Reyes, Social Worker*

• Friendships and being helpful to others; how you treat people is very important.

• Character development—a balance of dignity, trust, respect, love; having good values.

• Listening to the family and its advice.

• Respect toward adults, toward elders, toward relatives. Respect toward teachers and school. Respect for yourself. (To show respect, Latinos are less direct than Anglos about what they want or need. They see Anglos as saying whatever they want to say.)

> When Latinos go to college, get positions, and get money, they start to think of just themselves. A lot of this caring about family disappears. They don't have time for families or family parties. The warmth decreases and families feel badly about it.
>
> *Victoria Orozco, Family Resource Specialist*

> In the U.S., money and materialism are too high a priority.
>
> *Graciela Ybarra, Resource Teacher*

In the Latino culture, a sense of cooperation is promoted rather than a sense of competitiveness. The more you are in the U.S. culture,

the more you consider yourself before considering those around you.
It's easy to lose your sense of cooperation.
Ana Morante, Outpatient (Mental Health) Case Worker

• Religion—faith, spiritualism (respect for the Church)
• Spanish language—It's very important for children to learn English, but
parents also want to keep speaking Spanish so they don't lose their language
and so their children will always know Spanish well.
• Valuing traditions—food, music, art, storytelling (teaching about the culture's meaning and messages through stories passed on through the generations)

Food is very important in our culture. You may have no furniture,
no possessions of any kind, but if you have food to have a feast and
you invite friends, you have wealth. Ideas such as these are very strong.
Amalia DeBord, Clinical Social Worker

• Distinct male and female roles
• *Machismo* [mah·CHEES·mo]. It originally meant being brave, honorable,
and strong, with the courage to face obstacles and protect and provide for the
family. It included protecting the women (mothers, sisters, etc.) and having
honor (including protecting and defending the image of the family to the outside world). *Machismo* had many positive components. (See Chapter 22, p.97
for more information.)
• Education/knowledge
• Hard work—If you work hard at honest work, you'll have something—
even though it may not be much
• Being warm, passionate, feelings-oriented

Latinos are feelings-oriented all the time. It goes with their personalities and goes back generations to the culture. The Spanish people are very warm and they hug. We never mind showing it. We laugh,
cry, and scream a lot. The feelings are strong. It's important to understand feelings. Latinos express them more. But we also have to learn to
control them.
Victoria Orozco, Family Resource Specialist

• Love of children (touching; emotional nourishment)
• Children should be seen and not heard—when with adults. It's expected
that the child should be well-behaved—quiet and not aggressive or assertive.
(Latinos feel that children in the U.S. are expected to be aggressive.)

Children are part of the social circle. They are there to learn and
observe and to help in social tasks as required. Children are respected
but opinions are only accepted when they have been requested.
Rosalie Prado de Ramirez, Public Health Nursing Supervisor

Chapter 8

The Role of the Church

The Church plays an exceptionally important role for many Mexican families. That role is, arguably, both positive and negative. In this chapter, we look at the positive influences of the Church. Other parts of this book, especially in Chapter 23, p. 101, address some of the Church's more negative influences.

The Catholic Church is the unifying force in the family.

Dolores Ramirez, Multicultural Director

For traditional families, everything that happens in their lives is because God wanted it to happen. The Church is very important, and whatever the priests say is so.

Maty Brito, Mental Health Outreach Counselor

Even when families don't go to church, they are often very religious and have deep religious convictions. They have a lot of faith, and they have a great belief in special prayers. They may go to church to light candles; they may pray to a particular saint. It's common to promise in your prayer that you will do a particular thing if you're given the blessing you're praying for. Some families have altars in their homes with a little candle.

Carmen Cortez, Associate Director, Parenting Program

For most Latinos, the Catholic Church is their place of worship and plays a very important part in their lives. They see the priest as a counselor. They go to him to talk about family problems, about illness and death. The lives of many Mexican people are centered around the Church. For the more educated population, some of the teachings of the Church (like birth control) are hard for them. For many Mexican families, faith and the Church helps them endure the hardships in their lives. People ask for miracles and offer to sacrifice something in exchange. For example, "I won't cut my hair or my son's hair for a year if I can buy a house." If they get the house, they'll fulfill their promise. Or they may offer to sacrifice money or not eat certain foods or go back to Mexico and walk 10 miles to the nearest cathedral. After families cross the border into the U.S. safely, they may go back to Mexico in December to give thanks for their arrival. They crawl to the altar on their knees as a way of showing gratitude.

Carmen Guedea, Parent Educator

The Church meets some very important religious needs. It's a safe place and your traditional values are reinforced there. It's also a place to socialize, a place to have little fiestas, carnivals, holidays, and other celebrations like baptisms, first communions, and marriage.

Dolores Ramirez, Multicultural Director

The Catholic Church provides a culture and strong moral values and tradition for the families. It also provides ritual. The Church is changing, but perhaps not fast enough for a lot of people. It provides moral guidance for people. For many, without the Church there is no guidance. It is so much a part of our heritage. Many of the people we work with have little or no formal education or knowledge of the greater world. It would be hard for them live their lives without the Church's guidance.

Maria Reyes, Social Worker

Chapter 9

Family Structure

Who commonly lives with the parents and children?
What is the role and influence of the extended family?

Unlike the traditional U.S. nuclear family, the Mexican family is an extended family. Mexican parents and children may live with grandparents, uncles, aunts, and cousins. Recognizing the important role that members of the extended family members play in the lives of the Latinos we work with might encourage us to offer opportunities for the extended family to be included when we work with parents and children.

Most families live with a lot of relatives. I think we are famous for our large families. Many grandparents are here, too, and often live with their children and grandchildren. If relatives come here from Mexico, it's assumed that they'll live with the family members that are already here.

Maty Brito, Mental Health Outreach Counselor

Lots of extended family are living together—especially if they have financial problems and can't pay rent. Sometimes four generations live in a home. It's very common for many extra people to be living together.

Carmen Cortez, Associate Director, Parenting Program

Most families do not live as nuclear families. If they do, it's not for very long because there are many relatives and friends who will live with them for at least a while.

Linda Espinosa, Professor of Education and
Former Director of a Parenting Program

Latinos live with extended family, such as grandparents, uncles, cousins, even friends. Large families are the norm. Many of the members of the extended family who are living with them are temporary. It's very common to help others who are coming to the U.S.

Dolores Ramirez, Multicultural Director

Latino families are very close. There is usually some relative around. They are very protective of each other. Older brothers always protect their sisters. Children may live with their families until they get married, no matter how old they are.

Maty Brito, Mental Health Outreach Counselor

There is an understanding of mutual agreement and assistance. Blood and "who you are and who your family is" is strong in our value system; help from outsiders is looked down on in terms of accepting assistance.

Rosalie Prado de Ramirez, Public Health Nursing Supervisor

We want to be very careful of stereotyping because it's very damaging to everyone. Every family is unique, and the uniqueness is going to be based on their generation and the ethnicity or culture that they come from. In Santa Clara County [California], there are 17 Latin American cultures represented. While the language may be the same and some of the culture, they are very different. The uniqueness also has to do with their level of education and the child-rearing practices that the parents received.

There are, though, some commonalities in a Latino home. For example, there are the dynamics of the extended family. In the Latino family, every one of us is given implicit authority to discipline not only our children but also our nieces and nephews and grandchildren. The grandfather, grandmother, uncles, and aunts will sanction or disapprove of a behavior. It is part of being a family—except for those families that have over-acculturated and feel that they should go it alone. Latino families sometimes give up a support network when they come to the U.S.

Josie Romero, Clinical Social Worker and
Director of a Family Institute

Grandparents are more traditional and more authoritarian. They are considered knowledgeable and wise and it's hard for them to give up their traditional ideas. It's hard to break away from grandparents. It's hard for parents to go another way. Even the father in a family succumbs to his mother or mother-in-law. This is due to respect. Grandparents believe in disciplining for the good of the child. They feel his future depends on this. Some grandparents think they were too harsh; they wanted more enjoyment. But it's most common to continue the authoritarian tradition.

Dolores Ramirez, Multicultural Director

Grandmothers provide a close-knit family. They help the child develop values. Siblings in a Mexican family have a close relationship. This is very important. There's lots of physical affection.

Rafael Ramirez, Elementary School Principal

There's not much disagreement between generations. There may not be a whole lot of changes from one generation to the next, because they live with their extended family—maybe with their grandparents. There might be four generations in one house. Even if they're educated, their respect for the older generation comes out, though not as strongly. Dad still has the last word.

Carmen Guedea, Parent Educator

PART II

THE BEGINNING YEARS AS
A FAMILY,
BECOMING PARENTS,
EARLY INFANT CARE,
ROLES OF
MOTHERS AND FATHERS

Chapter 10

Views About Marriage

Views about the basis for marriage in traditional families are expressed in this chapter.

Marriage is a strong priority.
Carmen Cortez, Associate Director, Parenting Program

Marriage means unity and the extension of the family.
Rafael Ramirez, Elementary School Principal

Marriages may just be ones of convenience. When young men who have been working in California go back to Mexico from December through February (during holidays and when some kinds of work are more scarce), young women may be so eager to move away from Mexico that, after a brief courtship of maybe a month, they'll get married.

Men from Mexico with very little education may feel threatened by a woman in the U.S. who has an education and can speak both languages. So he may be more inclined to marry a woman he's met in Mexico who has not lived in the U.S. It's important for many men to feel they have control over the woman.

Carmen Guedea, Parent Educator

Once she's married, a woman takes on the traditional roles. This means she's going to have the children God gives her and she is not going to have relationships with other men.

It's common in traditional families for females to start having children at age 13, 14, or 15. Females start having children just after they're married. There used to be a strong sense of shame for women who became pregnant and weren't married, but this has diminished over time about as much as it has for the Anglo population as a whole.

Carmen Cortez, Associate Director, Parenting Program

Virginity is so important to a *macho* man. If he has sex with her and finds out that she is not a virgin, he may run away without saying anything—maybe leaving her pregnant.

Maty Brito, Mental Health Outreach Counselor

Chapter 11

The Meaning of Having Children

Here we learn what having a child means in a marriage. The responses also touch on men's and women's views. Chapter 23, p. 101, elaborates on these.

It's OK for a man to get a woman pregnant here and not marry her, but it's not OK for a man to go to Mexico and get a woman pregnant and not marry her. In my experience, if a woman in Mexico gets pregnant, her family will send her to the U.S., maybe to California.

Carmen Guedea, Parent Educator

Their roots in the Catholic Church are very strong. The Church believes in marriage with one husband and one wife, and everything is for the family.

Dolores Ramirez, Multicultural Director

The Latino woman wants to have a husband when she has a child. Being married before having children is very traditional, but there is less of a stigma now for single mothers.

Largely because of the seasonal patterns of going back and forth to Mexico each year, many men develop relationships with more than one woman after marriage. They may have several groups of children.

Dolores Ramirez, Multicultural Director

Girls from about 15 to 20 years old are expected to get married. They're expected to have their first baby within a year (but not in less than 9 months).

Carmen Guedea, Parent Educator

For the woman, having a child is an act of independence: "I'm a mom now."

Dolores Ramirez, Multicultural Director

For the woman, a child means responsibility and the expected completion of the beginning of the wife's role. Having a child also means identifying with the husband's family. You almost have to have a child to become part of the family.

Carmen Guedea, Parent Educator

For men, having kids is part of *machismo* [mah·CHEES·mo: see Chapter 22, p. 97 for more details]. Once there are kids, the man feels proud, manly.

Dolores Ramirez, Multicultural Director

For a man, a child is a symbol of the marriage. He wants his first to be a boy. It is assumed the wife will be responsible for the child. Having a child doesn't mean the husband and wife are in love or monogamous or have a strong relationship with each other.

Carmen Guedea, Parent Educator

A Mexican or Latino woman dreams of being a mother. That's what you're raised for, especially in the Mexican culture.

For the man, it's a *macho* thing that he have kids. The more kids he can have, the better he feels.

Rosa Carreno, Community Health Worker

To the woman, having babies is her role in life. It means that she is a woman. For a man, it is a reaffirmation that he is normal. It is part of his virility.

Maty Brito, Mental Health Outreach Counselor

Families from Mexico feel that children are a blessing.

Dolores Ramirez, Multicultural Director

Family Planning

The traditional Latino views about birth control are strong and closely linked to their culture. A poor Mexican family in the U.S. that wants to have large numbers of children can present a cultural challenge for the U.S. professionals who work with them. Approaches used by Latino professionals to teach parents who have children about birth control are mentioned.

In Mexican families the babies are not planned. My guess is that about 90% are not planned.

Rosa Carreno, Community Health Worker

Children are never planned.

Carmen Guedea, Parent Educator

Feelings about pregnancy and birth are strongly rooted in Catholicism. The influence of the Church pervades their feelings and beliefs about relationships, male/female roles, pregnancy, and birth. Hispanic families have internalized the dictates of the Church over many generations.

Women are not supposed to be informed or knowledgeable about family planning, so it's up to the man. For men, it's not consistent with their male role to use condoms. The Catholic religion opposes and prohibits birth control in any form. Having many children is the norm.

One of the common mores about Catholic *Latina* [lah·TEE·nah: a female Latino] teenagers is the need to be virtuous. This means you don't know about birth control and sexually transmitted diseases. If you become knowledgeable about how to prevent pregnancy and you come prepared, you're in a category of girls that is not respectable or marriageable.

Linda Espinosa, Professor of Education and
Former Director of a Parenting Program

It seems to me that they relate pregnancy with the Church. If they get pregnant, that means God wanted them to have a baby. I hardly ever hear from my clients that they use any type of contraceptive or that they plan the family. It's against their religion and their ideas. It's hard to tell them that there are many ways to prevent pregnancy. Pregnancy is something that happened to their mother and grandmother. It's just considered natural.

They don't think about the future, about what kind of education they can give their children. I think it has to do with religious ideas again. If they get pregnant, they'll get by somehow. There is a saying in Spanish that God is going to give. "God wanted me to have this baby, so we're going to have everything; we don't have to worry." They have so many immediate problems—mostly economic—that I don't think thinking about a child's future is a priority in their life.

Maty Brito, Mental Health Outreach Counselor

In the past, men would have extra-marital affairs as a form of family planning so that their wives would be able to rest from being pregnant so often—especially if he could afford keeping two households. Men were expected to support both families equally. Sexual abstinancy or separate beds were the other methods of family planning.

Rosalie Prado de Ramirez, Public Health Nursing Supervisor

Are women more apt to ask men to use condoms now that there is more talk of AIDS?

The younger generation of women are beginning to take more responsibility, but the older women are not. There may still be a fear of being harmed by the male if they hurt his ego. Also, they may be in denial about the possibility that their partner might engage in other sexual activities. If they ask him to wear a condom, it's likely to seem that the woman is accusing him of other relationships.

Renee Martinez, Professor of Child Development

Teen pregnancies are kind of normal. They don't believe in any kind of birth control. Even now with AIDS. The way they see AIDS is that it's a homosexual illness. You have to explain to them that it's not just a homosexual disease.

Maty Brito, Mental Health Outreach Counselor

A woman believes that her husband will take care of her. The husband says to the woman, "I don't want to use any birth control, I will take care of you."

Rosa Carreno, Community Health Worker

Latino *macho* men won't use condoms. They don't believe that it's their role. They believe it's a woman's role, and many of them don't want their wives or their women to use protection. They don't like it. Many believe that it's an American idea and they don't want any part of it. If a woman gets pregnant and the father doesn't stay, the woman thinks it's her role in life to be a mother and take care of the child. Men think the same thing. It's like it's a woman's problem, and if she gets pregnant she has to take care of her future. Many of my clients get pregnant at a very early age, 15 or 16. If the father stays with her, they'll raise the baby together.

Sometimes I talk about abortion and the women get offended. They are living in real poor conditions (some are still on welfare) and, even though they say they don't want to have the child, they don't want to hear about abortion. It's something bad, something evil. They have real, real deep beliefs in having as many children as they can.

I don't think that most people will talk to doctors about adult problems such as sex. In many of the Latino cultures, sex is taboo and is not talked about. You don't talk about sex with strangers.

Maty Brito, Mental Health Outreach Counselor

If women want to talk about birth control or sex, they would rather talk to a woman doctor. If a male doctor talks to them about birth control or sex, they get nervous and forget what he says. And the man wants to go to a male doctor.

Issues such as sex and any kind of abuse are hard to talk about. It's important to have someone to talk to in their own language.

Rosa Carreno, Community Health Worker

A woman may have a lot of children and wish her husband would do something about birth control. But he won't have a vasectomy—it's not his problem; it's unmasculine. Condoms are not accepted either. Men reject these ideas. The most acceptable idea is that of a woman having her tubes tied. If they have six, seven, or eight children, he might be persuaded about this. An unwanted pregnancy can't be imagined. Women have to be taught about contraception.

Dolores Ramirez, Multicultural Director

Once you're having sexual relations, if the man says you can have an IUD or use birth control pills, then you can do it. Otherwise, the woman won't take precautions. She'll count on him to either raise the issue or not, and she'll follow his advice. Men don't run the household on every issue, but they do on this one.

Carmen Cortez, Associate Director, Parenting Program

Planned Parenthood wants to discuss contraceptives with its clients. If a woman's pregnant, Planned Parenthood discusses options, including abortion. This is shocking for Latino mothers. It's very unacceptable. They have a very strong objection to abortion.

Dolores Ramirez, Multicultural Director

Younger women get taught by Planned Parenthood and the federal Women, Infants, and Children [WIC] program to try to consider holding off another pregnancy until their baby is a year old. Planned Parenthood and WIC ask, "Have you considered birth control?" It's widely believed among the mothers that if you're breast feeding you won't get pregnant. WIC and Planned Parenthood try to explain with statistics. If you explain often enough, they'll begin to learn. For example, they might realize that breast feeding is not enough, that you have to use something else to prevent pregnancy.

Carmen Guedea, Parent Educator

I address the myth of "If I breastfeed, I can't get pregnant" right away. I ask, "Do you want another baby? What are you doing about it? Do you know about condoms? Is your husband comfortable with that?" I ask basic questions. I found that if I ask the father those questions, it's very embarrassing. They don't want to hear these questions, so I give them a brochure in *español* [ehs·pahn·YOHL: Spanish] with pictures and drawings that describe the different methods. That way, when they go to the clinic they can ask questions. Otherwise, they feel they have no information of any kind. After I give them this brochure, they know what's available.

Women may discuss birth control, but that doesn't mean that they do anything about it. They don't want to upset the apple cart. What *is* becoming popular among the women is Norplant. Mexicans are very resistant to family planning. It's a very strong culture for *machismo* [mah·CHEES·mo: see Chapter 22, p. 97 for more information]. I really understood what *machismo* was when I worked at a factory. This was back in the '70s. I worked with a Mexican woman and her husband. She told me that she was pregnant. She told me that she came to this country to earn money for her six children that were in Mexico and that this pregnancy was unplanned. I told her that in this country she had some options. The next day the father came to have lunch with us. He addressed it with me. "No, we cannot consider abortions." Why? Because it is very important that his wife be impregnated every year so that the rest of the group knows that he is *macho*. I had no idea about this.

Amalia DeBord, Clinical Social Worker

The only birth control we sometimes see is the male condom, because Norplant and birth control pills are not accepted. Men don't want to use a condom. Those with more formal education are more likely to accept the use of condoms. But the less educated use nothing.

Carmen Guedea, Parent Educator

Norplant is pretty high in popularity right now. You have to give women a lot of information. I really recommend that somebody who talks about birth control with a woman be fluent in Spanish.

Rosa Carreno, Community Health Worker

In talking to women about birth control, it's very important to involve the man. Then we can make some progress.

By the time women get married, they're already pregnant or have been involved in sexual activity. It's not planned. It just happens. The more educated they are, the more likely it is that the child will be planned—or at least that the mother will be on some type of contraceptive (either birth control pills or an IUD).

Carmen Cortez, Associate Director, Parenting Program

The longer they're in this country, the more likely it is that they will "plan" having a baby. The Latino family view is that it's a blessing to have children and that "children come."

Dolores Ramirez, Multicultural Director

In the past twenty years I have seen a change in the women we work with in the community. We have started talking with the mothers and grandmothers to encourage their acceptance of birth control. The church influence has also changed. There are more women now using some type of birth control. Often time, the husband and the rest of the family are not aware of it.

Rosalie Prado de Ramirez, Public Health Nursing Supervisor

I encourage my staff of parent educators to advise mothers to keep the numbers of children down. This puts some of my staff (all of whom are Latino) into a real cultural conflict. Men view children as a testimonial to their virility and their manhood. When women started to have some independence and financial decision-making power, there were issues between men and women (including my home educators and the parents they served). This upset the dynamics of men who expected to always be in charge and to always have the financial upper hand. This created tension and stress. Our staff had to figure out ways to help women have more choices without alienating their husbands.

Linda Espinosa, Professor of Education and
Former Director of a Parenting Program

Chapter 13

Problems Getting Pregnant

Although described as a rare problem, it's interesting to note where Latinos place the responsibility for infertility. The subject of folk healing is also introduced—a subject that will be expanded on in Part V.

I don't see the population I work with getting tests or getting fertility guidance. The woman in the Latino culture is the one who is blamed if she can't get pregnant; it's never the male. But infertility is rare.

Carmen Guedea, Parent Educator

Women use teas with herbs that they believe will increase their fertility. They believe that it's a stigma not to be able to become pregnant. It's something that they don't want people to know about. They take some kind of homeopathic herbs, natural things. I have heard that there is a belief that before your period you have to take some kind of teas with garlic and other herbs to become more fertile.

Maty Brito, Mental Health Outreach Counselor

They have teas for anything and everything. They ask around and go to the *botica* [bo·TEE·kah: drugstore] for teas that help them get pregnant. It's passed down in family lore. In San Antonio, it's easy to go to a *botica* and ask for tea for a specific problem. They'll advise you. The *botica* also has candles, special kinds of soaps, teas, and things like that.

Carmen Cortez, Associate Director, Parenting Program

If a woman's having problems getting pregnant, she might go to a *curandera* [koo·rahn·DEH·rah: folk healer] to get her uterus massaged. Massage is used because it is believed that the uterus has fallen and that massage makes it go back into place. It's her responsibility to get pregnant. The woman might be given herbal teas to drink and a shot of medication. The woman believes these things will help her get pregnant.

Carmen Guedea, Parent Educator

Usually, a woman will go to the healer and the healer will give her a massage. They give good advice. They give chamomile tea to help relax them.

Rosa Carreno, Community Health Worker

The problem is worse if it involves the man. Men never admit they might have infertility problems. They feel less *macho* if they can't make a woman pregnant.

Maty Brito, Mental Health Outreach Counselor

Infertility is always viewed as the woman's fault. It's very hard for a man to accept that it might be his fault. A man might leave his wife if he's in a childless marriage. It's very important that there be children. The more educated they are, the more likely that they'd go to a doctor for help or consider adoption.

Dolores Ramirez, Multicultural Director

Chapter 14

During Pregnancy

When a woman becomes pregnant, what is she expected to do differently?
What are people around her expected to do for her?
Does she typically get prenatal care?

The roles of men and women in traditional families emerge more clearly here, as do some of the barriers to early prenatal care—an issue of considerable concern for many health care professionals.

She will get lots of encouragement from family and close friends. You're not supposed to lift things or bend over or hang clothes (that is, raise your arms). You're supposed to take care of yourself, *but* the house should be clean and the meals should be made. You're expected to continue with your ongoing responsibilities.

Carmen Cortez, Associate Director, Parenting Program

The pregnant woman is not expected to do less. But she is expected to eat well, take care of herself, and get enough rest. She gets a lot of advice, but she's expected to take care of this herself.

Dolores Ramirez, Multicultural Director

When a woman gets pregnant, she watches the kind of food she eats and tries to get the best diet. They feel that they are responsible for the child that they are going to bring into the world, so they try to do their best.

Maty Brito, Mental Health Outreach Counselor

In Mexico, foods, milk, etc., are delivered fresh. Here they have to get used to the refrigerator. The further they get from traditional eating patterns, the more health problems they start to have. Here, they tend to change from corn to flour tortillas, which are not as nutritious, and use convenience foods and frying.

Dolores Ramirez, Multicultural Director

Most will eat more because they believe they should eat for two. Many gain too much weight. The pregnant woman's household responsibilities remain the same. Women don't typically go for monthly clinic visits or use vitamins. Our parenting program has to push them to go to the clinic. Most women get no prenatal care. Many don't take care of themselves at all. They go to the hospital emergency room to deliver the baby—that's their first and last visit. Generally, they don't do anything special when they're pregnant.

Carmen Cortez, Associate Director, Parenting Program

The grandmother will tell her to rest and not lift heavy things. Through our county public health services, we have to push prenatal care. It's not their first priority. They often wait until they are five or six months pregnant, until they show, to get care.

Rosa Carreno, Community Health Worker

Some women go for check-ups. The husband will take her the first time, and a family member will take her after that. Prenatal check ups are required by WIC. If a woman goes to WIC after the second month of pregnancy with proof of pregnancy, she gets milk, cheese, beans, etc., and then goes regularly for a check-up. The husband encourages this because of the food supplement.

Carmen Guedea, Parent Educator

In our parenting program, we find it useful to make women aware of their bodies, how you get pregnant, what happens when you give birth, the growth of the fetus, the importance of nutrition and vitamins, and how easy it is to go to the clinic to get vitamins. Doctors are not used a lot during pregnancy; they cost money.

Carmen Cortez, Associate Director, Parenting Program

Although the word is starting to get out to the women that you should go for medical check-ups when you are pregnant even when nothing is wrong, we have a long way to go in educating families about the benefits of preventive care. Even when things don't seem to be going right during a pregnancy, the pregnant women turn first to their families. When there is no nearby family, they'll look for an experienced, wise woman in their building or neighborhood. Incentives like MediCal applications being taken at the clinic or women needing a physician's form to get on WIC are the most helpful in bringing pregnant women in for prenatal care. This is particularly true of those coming from rural and semi-rural Mexico and from very small towns. Those from larger towns and cities are often more used to the idea of prenatal (and other preventive) health care.

Amalia DeBord, Clinical Social Worker

Pregnancy is viewed as a physiological function of the body and is not seen as a "sickness" for which you need a physician. Therefore the concept of early prenatal care does not have a major significance. Being healthy means you will have a healthy baby.

Rosalie Prado de Ramirez, Public Health Nursing Supervisor

Dads do not have a big role—other than financial. It's unusual for a woman to take a childbirth class, but if she does it's even more unusual for the baby's father to attend it with her. Most of the Latino families we work with have no health insurance or medical coverage.

Linda Espinosa, Professor of Education and
Former Director of a Parenting Program

Women are supported by advice from family and friends during pregnancy. Women need to be much more informed about prenatal care. Money is a big problem in getting this care.

Dolores Ramirez, Multicultural Director

In some of the communities here, the neighbors are close and when a woman gets pregnant they help her. They bring food and treat her like she is a queen. I notice that in our town the neighbors are real attentive to the pregnant woman. People bring things that they've made for the baby. Sometimes I think that women get more support from outside the home, from the neighbors or relatives, than from their own husbands.

I've been working with a lot of alcoholic men, and they don't change when their wives become pregnant. They still want their wives to serve them. She is the woman and women have to do the home chores. A lot of women feel it is their duty to do the chores, even when they are pregnant.

Maty Brito, Mental Health Outreach Counselor

The man's role during his wife's pregnancy is just to bring home the paycheck to pay for a roof over their heads and food on the table.

Dolores Ramirez, Multicultural Director

It's expected that the marriage relationship remain the same during pregnancy. But the husband should cater to his wife if she gets a craving. He doesn't take over her work or the kids. He doesn't baby her.

Carmen Cortez, Associate Director, Parenting Program

During his wife's pregnancy, the Latino man has a role of support and hope. Families come together in a very special way. Latino families love children and respect the period of child bearing.

Rafael Ramirez, Elementary School Principal

Labor and Delivery

Where do most births take place?
Are fathers usually present during birth?
What do men and women expect the birth
experience to be like?

In this chapter, we learn more about births in the Latino families and, particularly, the beliefs of the mother about the birth process.

Most babies are born in a hospital—mostly in the emergency room. Usually the father or the parents and sisters are in the waiting room. But they don't take Lamaze classes, so they're not in the delivery room.

Carmen Cortez, Associate Director, Parenting Program

In this area, babies are mostly born in hospitals. In Michoacán [mee·cho·ah·KAHN] where many of our families come from, the births take place at home. Fathers don't attend births yet or go to childbirth classes, except those who are more educated. Traditionally, it's not very common.

Rafael Ramirez, Elementary School Principal

I've hardly heard any of my clients tell me that their husbands have been with them in the delivery room.

Maty Brito, Mental Health Outreach Counselor

Only the more educated take childbirth education classes. It's uncommon for Mexicans to take childbirth classes, even though WIC gives you an appointment card for childbirth classes and waives the fees.

Carmen Guedea, Parent Educator

Lately, you find fathers attending the birth—especially first-time fathers.

Rosa Carreno, Community Health Worker

Having a doctor is very necessary because the woman is out of her culture (she doesn't know midwives, etc.).

Dolores Ramirez, Multicultural Director

Pregnant women are usually on MediCal. They need a doctor in the U.S. and they usually go to a community hospital.

Carmen Guedea, Parent Educator

I've noticed that women don't ask for any anesthesia. It's like they have to feel the pain. It seems they've heard that if you have a baby, you have to feel a lot of pain, that you will be a better mother if you feel the pain. A lot of women don't really know that there are options.

Maty Brito, Mental Health Outreach Counselor

A woman is expected to be strong. They expect that it will be a hard time, a hard labor. There's a lot of screaming, and maybe cursing. There are no inhibitions.

Carmen Cortez, Associate Director, Parenting Program

Having a hard labor is an expectation; that's what most older women have told young women from the time they have started their menses. Often this warning is used as a method for the prevention of pregnancy for the young girl. It is also believed that hard labor makes you into a strong woman. That way you will know how to take pain and deal with it.

Rosalie Prado de Ramirez, Public Health Nursing Supervisor

Women never ask if it's going to hurt or if they're going to get any drugs. They expect the birth to be natural.

Rosa Carreno, Community Health Worker

Most Mexican women don't take drugs unless they're having a C-section [Caesarean section] or unless they're more educated. Women from Mexico are against drugs. I also feel that 90% of the time, women from Mexico don't even drink alcohol; it's the opposite for the Mexican men.

Carmen Guedea, Parent Educator

Chapter 16

Early Days of Post-Partum Care

What is expected of the mother in those first few weeks after the baby is born?
How are others expected to help the mother?

This chapter explores cultural expectations about the mother's care—and some of the changes in expectations that are being seen. Mothers' views of how they are "supposed to feel" after childbirth are also mentioned.

You're supposed to feel really happy and joyous about having your baby, but the reality is that a lot of times the mother doesn't feel good—she's tired and has the blues. But culturally you're supposed to feel good about yourself and the baby and be all right. Women hold back a lot on what they really feel (bad, tired, etc.). There's not a lot of information for these women on how their body works and how their emotions are affected. We talk to them about these things in our parenting classes. We explain it and show diagrams and pictures. Once the mothers know it's normal, there's a sigh of relief. It makes them feel more comfortable with themselves. They will only discuss it with others who have heard the same information that they have. Relatives wouldn't understand.

Carmen Cortez, Associate Director, Parenting Program

A mother is expected to breastfeed or bottle-feed her baby. For 40 days she is to do none of the usual cleaning or cooking. If there's no one with her, she has to do her usual cooking and cleaning. She's supposed to bundle up to stay warm. If she takes a shower during the first week, or if her breast milk falls on the floor, she believes her breast milk will dry up. There are lots of old wives tales. Lots of taboos. They believe touching a cold floor gives you air in your tummy.

Carmen Guedea, Parent Educator

After a woman has a baby she takes real good care of her diet. If there's a grandmother around, she takes good care of the new mother. During the time before she gets her period again, some won't drink anything that has acid in it.

Maty Brito, Mental Health Outreach Counselor

Acid is avoided so that the postpartum flow will not cease. Women have been taught that acid clots the blood.

Rosalie Prado de Ramirez, Public Health Nursing Supervisor

The mother is expected to hold, feed, and comfort the baby—nothing else (like cleaning). The mothers want to follow the tradition of staying in bed for 40 days. The more the new mothers have been exposed to working women and education, the more they are aware that you can get up right away and go on with your life; you don't have to stay in bed and have female relatives do things for you. The tradition is slowly changing, but I still see women mostly staying in bed and not doing housework, just taking care of the baby.

I feel the 40 days gives the mother time to regain her strength. Our parenting program is putting women through ESL [English as a Second Language] classes, GED [high school equivalency] courses, and community colleges. Two of our new mothers were back in classes a week or two after giving birth. I wonder if we're actually helping them by pushing them to be super women.

I assumed *Latinas* [Latino women] would have less children after they got more education. With more education, they would be able to get better jobs.

But it's not happening. They're still getting pregnant. But they are going on with their lives sooner after pregnancy. Now, it's often less than a month before they go back to normal activity.

Carmen Cortez, Associate Director, Parenting Program

It takes the mothers a very short time to recover from childbirth. They are usually very healthy.

Maty Brito, Mental Health Outreach Counselor

Our parenting program encourages mothers to go for a six-week check-up to get inoculations for the baby. They need encouragement to use the medical system.

Carmen Cortez, Associate Director, Parenting Program

Forty days is the cultural expectation during which a woman has been given permission by society to take it easy. The mother (grandmother, sisters, or some female member of the family) comes to her aid. You are not supposed to use the broom, mop, etc., although you do not necessarily need to stay in bed. Remember in the *old* medical post-delivery follow-up, all women were kept quiet or in bed for six weeks! Postpartum mothers are fed well to help them recover their strength.

Rosalie Prado de Ramirez, Public Health Nursing Supervisor

The women are considered fully recovered in 40 days. These 40 days are very important. A Mexican man will have sex with his wife during those 40 days if he wants to. Some women get pregnant during those 40 days. A one year age gap between children is very common among low-income Mexican women. There is a greater gap for women who are more educated—maybe a year-and-a-half.

Carmen Guedea, Parent Educator

The mother takes care of her baby. If the baby wakes up in the middle of the night, it's the mother's responsibility. But there are some men who do take care of their wives after she has a baby, especially men from the younger generation.

Maty Brito, Mental Health Outreach Counselor

Mexican men are not involved with the house, with the kids, with the kitchen. They don't go to the shopping center or change diapers. When I go on visits to patients' homes, I try to involve the father. I just say, "Here, I'd like to see you bathing the baby; your wife is sick; she just had a C-section; there's nothing wrong with your doing it." I have to push them through it, but they do it. You have to tell them the good part of it. You have to tell them, "Forget about looking funny. Your baby is going to like you." The fathers come to like it, but you need to be there to help them try it.

Rosa Carreno, Community Health Worker

Chapter 17

Early Infant Care: Milk Feedings

What do families think about breast feeding vs. bottle-feeding?
Which is the most common way to feed a baby?

Here we see what is common when beginning a new baby's milk feedings.

Mothers believe that breast feeding is another part of pregnancy. It is just a natural part of mothering. Mexican mothers typically breastfeed their babies. People think there's something wrong with a man who doesn't get his wife pregnant. People think there's something wrong with a woman who doesn't breastfeed her children.

Mothers are so worried about their babies. Mothers are always trying to feed their babies—many times they overfeed them. The mother and the community think she is not doing her job if the baby is not round or if it's not interested in eating. Sometimes the baby is crying for other reasons, but the mother thinks, "Oh, he's hungry."

Maty Brito, Mental Health Outreach Counselor

Mothers typically choose breast feeding. We try to get the mothers to breastfeed for at least a month before they start following family advice on supplementing the feeding. The father wants the baby to grow up to be healthy. But if breast feeding interferes with sex, he doesn't want his wife to breastfeed.

Carmen Guedea, Parent Educator

There is still a strong value about breast feeding, as there is in Mexico. It's the natural way. But bottle-feeding is common, too. If the grandmother is in the house, she'll urge breast feeding—usually feeding on demand.

Dolores Ramirez, Multicultural Director

Some women feel they cannot afford to eat well; therefore it is cheaper to bottle feed. There is a myth regarding breast feeding that one may expose the children to too many stresses of the stomach because when the woman is upset she also upsets the infant. For example, it is believed that if you eat and have an argument or see something that frightens you, it will be carried through the milk and upset the infant as well.

Rosalie Prado de Ramirez, Public Health Nursing Supervisor

Many years ago, Mexicans were brainwashed into thinking formula was better. Middle America showed people that formula was the modern way. Soon people in poverty believed that bottle-feeding with formula was the better way. Still now in San Antonio, 99% of second- and third-generation, low-income Mexican-American women don't breastfeed. They use formula. However, the more educated mothers in our Latino community feel breast feeding is the better way. Our parenting program is trying to talk poor mothers into returning to breast feeding. A lot of these women are under stress and they don't eat well. Even if they breastfeed, we wonder if their babies will get good nutrition. Now the mothers almost have to learn the art of breast feeding again. It's no longer natural. There's a lot of uneasiness and discomfort about breast feeding. These women's mothers didn't breastfeed either. First we have to teach the mothers that it's OK to breastfeed, then we can go on to discuss that breast feeding "is better and cheaper."

Carmen Cortez, Associate Director, Parenting Program

Chapter 18

Early Infant Care: Other Feeding Issues

What is a baby usually fed?
What kinds of feeding issues come up and who do parents talk to about them?

Learning what babies are fed can help professionals work with women on feeding issues. Suggestions are made—suggestions that can apply to areas of working with Latino families other than feeding. This chapter also mentions some common folk healing methods and what Latino professionals think of them.

We try to encourage mothers to breastfeed for at least the first month, without supplementing with a bottle. After that, someone in her family usually says that the baby keeps crying because he's not full and she should add a bottle. By four months, most mothers we work with are just bottle-feeding because she is expected to have a clean house, dinner on the table, and be ready for whatever her husband wants.

We encourage them not to feed the baby cereals or solids during the first three months. By the fourth month, they often give cereal (sometimes out of the bottle) because they think "the baby will sleep better."

Carmen Guedea, Parent Educator

Mothers put baby cereal, like Gerber rice, in a bottle at a very early age. They believe the baby is not getting enough to eat, that he must be hungry. So they give him more to eat. They give them mashed beans, mashed potatoes, mashed rice, and egg very early—by a few months of age. They also use a lot of soda and Kool-aid in the bottle or teas, such as *manzanilla* [mahn·zah·NEE·yah: chamomile], for colic or stomach problems.

As for soda and Kool-aid, when we notice mothers are giving these to their babies, if the mothers haven't gotten to that lesson yet in our parenting curriculum, we talk to them about it in private. We can't say, "You're doing something wrong; that's bad. Stop it, now!" We have to go about it very carefully and in a very caring, nurturing way. We have to make sure they still feel in control of what's happening to their children. Parents don't give things like soda and Kool-aid intentionally. A lot of times, they run out of formula and don't have milk or juice. These cost more than Kool-aid. They may have only soda at home. They also give the baby bread soaked in bean soup (*sopa* [SO·pah]). It's soft and the babies suck on it.

Carmen Cortez, Associate Director, Parenting Program

Many mothers breastfeed every time the baby wants to suck. We have many problems with that. They just feed the baby on demand and the baby may gain too much weight too quickly. Parents say, "My child doesn't like the pacifier" and "The baby keeps crying." We teach them how to use the pacifier and how to calm the baby.

If the mother has to go back to work, she mixes formula-feeding and breast feeding. You have to be careful about how they use the formula. Some use it straight, without diluting it; some dilute it too much.

If the mother listens to the grandmother, she will feed the baby fruits, beans, and broth. They give it a little taste of everything. Some people even give it chili. They expect the baby to eat a lot of food. They always think the baby is crying because it's hungry, so they overfeed it.

Rosa Carreno, Community Health Worker

The new mother goes to the grandmother for advice if her baby is having feeding problems. If the grandmother isn't around, the mother may go to an older woman in the community. Sometimes rice water is prescribed by the grandmother (or the older woman). They always suggest natural things. Rice water is given for diarrhea. You put rice in boiling water for 15 minutes, then let it cool and drain it. This is used especially for babies. In the Latino culture we believe in medicine, but we believe even more in the natural things because they have been working for centuries.

Maty Brito, Mental Health Outreach Counselor

Giving herbal teas is part of the culture. They give it to help the baby sleep better and to reduce colic. During the first few months, giving herbal teas to a baby is very common. But they don't usually give juices to babies. If a baby is on formula, they might give it herbal teas every second or third day to clear its digestive system in order to avoid constipation.

In my extended family, we are given teas for upset stomachs or constipation. It seems to help. Babies are given tea or rice water to avoid diarrhea. It's rare to give Pedialyte. *Manzanilla* tea helps the baby sleep longer. *Rosa de castilla* [RO·sa deh kah·STEE·yah: rose] tea helps the baby sleep longer and helps colic. *Yerba buena* [YEHR·bah BWEH·nah: a type of mint] tea helps an upset stomach. I gave these to my baby because my mother gave me this advice while she was brainstorming with me, asking me, "Have you tried this? Have you tried that?"

If the baby is on breast milk, I tell mothers I don't think they should give teas. I tell them that breast milk should be enough if the baby is latching on often enough. I think they accept this advice from me because I'm Hispanic.

Carmen Guedea, Parent Educator

When a baby has stomach ailments or colic, the parents talk to everybody. It's very stressful because of all the crying. The parents feel very frustrated. They give *manzanilla* tea, or olive oil and a few grains of salt, or they rub the stomach with shortening and other ingredients. Other problems related to feeding include respiratory reactions to formula. There are lots of ear infections. Many kids are hospitalized for pneumonia.

Carmen Cortez, Associate Director, Parenting Program

It's rare for a baby to have feeding problems. If the baby is under six months, they'll take it to a doctor. If the baby is over six months, the mother and the extended family encourage it to eat. A *curandero* might advise something—certain kinds of milks or teas. If the baby is over one year old and the doctor says it's overweight, the parents ignore his advice. But during the first year, the parents want to be on target. If a baby is underweight, they give the baby vitamins and hope he'll eat better. They believe that the grandmother and the relatives on the father's side often know more about feeding than the doctor.

Carmen Guedea, Parent Educator

Mothers don't go to a doctor about feeding issues. They don't go to the doctor unless the child is really, really sick. They don't go for regular check-ups and they don't call for phone advice.

Carmen Cortez, Associate Director, Parenting Program

Typically, it is the aunt, grandmother, and great-grandmother who would be around and give the mother advice on what the proper thing to eat is—the amount, etc. Parents don't read books or manuals. Our home educators don't get involved with a mother's first baby, because in our program their focus is on preschoolers. A home educator might be involved with a new baby only if it has siblings that are preschoolers. Parents feed babies too many sugary, watery things. Parents lack the knowledge they need about how that affects the baby's development, his teeth, and so on. Lots of teeth are ruined by the time the child is three or four years old because the child has had too much sugar, cakes, and Kool-aid. Parents use these sweets as a way to quiet and pacify the baby. Information on what babies should eat is handed down within the family by female relatives. They give advice on how to keep the child quiet and happy and make sure he doesn't lose weight.

Linda Espinosa, Professor of Education and
Former Director of a Parenting Program

It is important to teach from what the parents know. In most cases, it is alright for them to provide the traditional teas. This helps to reinforce a mother's self worth that she is providing good care for the infant. Nutrition-ally, the teas are hydrating the infant and many are rich in Vitamin C.

Rosalie Prado de Ramirez, Public Health Nursing Supervisor

The first thing I do with a Hispanic mother is talk to her about how she's doing. I ask her questions like, "Are you sleeping?" Because her husband had to sleep at nights, one mama was trying to make her baby sleep during the night by keeping him awake all day long. I had to explain that the reason the baby had to wake at night was that his tummy was small and emptied every two hours. So the baby was going to be hungry and was going to cry when he was hungry. I also had to bring the father in and explain it to him.

Because most of these parents don't ask questions, you need to ask *them* the basic questions. They won't offer the information or ask the questions first. Once you verbalize it, they can deal with it. I don't talk with them about the future—even about two months from now. I talk about the here and now and how to solve the problems they have now. I show them pictures of how to do things with their baby. I ask them to show me how they burp the baby, and then I show them three positions for burping the baby. They walk out of here feeling more secure and confident. I use my position as an authority to help them. But I also say, "Correct me if I'm wrong. This may not be happening to you or your baby." Then I give them the information.

Amalia DeBord, Clinical Social Worker

Mothers try to give solids early on because they believe crying means the baby's hungry. Mothers don't listen to their doctor's advice on feeding. Our parenting program is trying to get families to listen to the doctors. We tell parents that what the doctors are telling them is good, sound advice. It's helpful to engage the parent in a discussion of what they're already doing and build from that. It's not helpful to assume they've started the baby on formula and cereal. When you ask if the baby has a lot of colic or what kind of bowel movements he has, the mother begins to understand that there's an association between how she is feeding her baby and what's happening to the rest of his body, including how the baby is behaving or feeling. Parents have to be able to relate the information you give them to what's happening to their baby right then and there.

People who have had a lot of children—mothers-in-laws, grandmothers—have a lot of opinions. Because parents get so much advice from their families, in our parenting program we say, "I know we all grew up thinking certain things, especially about how we were fed. But there's a lot of new information about children. Our families' intentions were good and, living in rural areas, didn't have access to things that we do now. So maybe we need to start changing what we were brought up with and what our extended family tells us and begin to think of new ways to do things. Some things are good and work well, but maybe we could do better on some things. Maybe we could change things so our children have it better than we did." The mothers we work with want to do well with their kids and have their kids be successful.

Carmen Cortez, Associate Director, Parenting Program

Chapter 19

Early Infant Care: Crying /Comforting

What is the general understanding about babies' needs?

How are babies involved in family interaction in the early months?

How is crying viewed by the parents?

How and when do parents respond to a baby's crying?

The way a family interprets a baby's beginning expressions of its needs can have a lasting impact on both the child and the parent/child relationship. Understanding the beliefs that underlie the behaviors can help professionals help families.

From my experience, Mexican mothers don't carry their babies around a lot, except when they're crying. The father and grandmother and others say, "You're going to spoil it if you carry it around too much." If the baby's hungry, the grandmother might hold the baby while the mother fixes the bottle.

Carmen Guedea, Parent Educator

Parents expect a baby to cry. They believe crying helps the baby's lungs develop better. A first-time mother will pick up and hold her baby a lot when it's under six months old. A second-time mom will walk up to the baby and talk to it, but she'll leave it where it is—in the carrier or in bed. When comforting a baby, the mother says, "Mama's here, Mama's here; don't cry. What do you want? What can I help you with? What hurts? Does your tummy hurt? Why are you crying? You don't need to cry." They'll hug the baby and kiss it and try to get it to smile.

Carmen Guedea, Parent Educator

Babies are wrapped very tightly. They keep a lot of clothes and blankets on the baby. And they hold them.

Linda Espinosa, Professor of Education and
Former Director of a Parenting Program

Babies are carried around a lot and comforted. They're wrapped a lot because they're easier to hold and makes it easier for older siblings to carry the baby. It's also more protection if baby is wrapped."

Rafael Ramirez, Elementary School Principal

Everyone in the family will carry the baby. Even the eight-year-olds will carry a one month-old baby.

Rosa Carreno, Community Health Worker

I find babies are bundled up a lot. It makes them sleep all day *and* be immobile. I try to help increase the mother/baby interaction, especially in how mothers comfort babies. I encourage mothers to take the blankets off their babies. I want them to be face-to-face, to talk to them and be with them.

From birth to five months, the parents don't spend a lot of time with their baby. They just walk by. They talk to it while feeding it, but they expect the baby to just lie there and listen to the radio. They just put the baby in front of the TV in an infant carrier. Other people may interact with the baby a little, but the mother is too busy. The mother often spends very little time actually interacting with her baby.

The baby's hands are covered with mittens so he doesn't scratch himself. There's a belief that if you cut a baby's nails, he'll go blind. Instead of the baby holding things, the mother will hold the rattle and shake it. I try to encourage mothers to give their babies things to hold, but the grandmothers will warn them against cutting the baby's nails so the baby has to wear mittens.

Once a baby is over four months old, it is introduced to the rattle. The baby will put things in its mouth and drool. Some fathers think the baby will get sick if it puts things in its mouth, so some parents discourage babies from doing this. This can be very frustrating for the baby and it interferes with the baby's learning.

Carmen Guedea, Parent Educator

Typically, it is thought that children should be quiet, well-behaved, and obedient. For babies, that could mean just lying and gurgling—being good. The mother holds, rocks, and sings to the baby. The overriding need of the parent is to have a child who is quiet and easygoing. If a child has a more demanding temperament, there could be a problem because that isn't how a baby is supposed to behave. Parents wouldn't know what to do about it.

Linda Espinosa, Professor of Education and
Former Director of a Parenting Program

When babies are awake they can be anywhere in the house, except the kitchen. Mothers are usually cooking, cleaning, and doing the laundry. They are usually very busy.

Maty Brito, Mental Health Outreach Counselor

Family members will pick up new babies when they cry. But their attitude that picking up a baby will spoil it surfaces when the baby is only a few months old.

If a baby cries, unless it's because he's hungry, it's looked on as something negative and parents tend to just let it cry. The family's attitude may be that the baby's spoiled and that he wants to be picked up all the time. We try to teach that a baby should be attended to if it's crying. Lots of parents have grown up thinking that picking up a crying baby is doing him a disservice, that it's not raising him right.

A baby may just stop crying because he gives up and knows no one will come. This can lead to a poor self-concept, a feeling that you're not important enough to be picked up. Or the baby may resort to other things to get attention—especially as he gets older. This could just make the situation worse; it's negative attention. All this can lead to a failure to thrive and to emotional problems.

It's hard for families to see that crying is a sign of the beginning of communication, that it's normal and natural for babies to cry, that it's part of establishing oneself in the world.

As the infant gets bigger and louder, the parents feel that the child is accountable for his actions, that there's some purpose in that crying and that purpose is to be picked up and get attention. The parents don't want that. They believe that if they pick up the baby too much when he cries, he will become a discipline problem when he gets older.

Carmen Cortez, Associate Director, Parenting Program

Babies are carried very little. When they are carried, it's either by the parent or by whoever is around. Babies are either kept in their beds or bassinets or in umbrella-type strollers. And they stay there for long periods of time. Some are kept in infant seats. Parents will put the baby on a blanket on the floor once it starts crawling. A baby who is carried around a lot is looked upon as being spoiled. They think that a baby who gets used to being carried will want to be carried forever. They feel they're doing the right thing by not letting the spoiling start. This belief leads to limited parent/child interaction because there isn't much physical closeness.

Carmen Cortez, Associate Director, Parenting Program

Throughout this chapter, Latino professionals expressed their concern that the beginnings of really responsive parent/infant interaction may be thwarted almost from birth because of the parents' belief that attentiveness will spoil the baby. These Latino professionals feel that parent/baby or adult/baby interaction may be far too limited and might have a significant and negative impact on future patterns of parent/child communication. They are also concerned about the effect it might have on the infant's feeling of effectiveness, of being heard, and of later self-esteem.

Chapter 20

Early Infant Care: Sleep Schedules

Are babies put on a schedule?
Where do they sleep?
What if parents think the baby is not sleeping
*   enough?*

Most babies don't have schedules. Because there's a lot going on in the family, babies just kind of fit in. The babies are fed, of course, but there's not much thinking about organizing a schedule around a baby's eating or sleeping patterns.

Linda Espinosa, Professor of Education and
Former Director of a Parenting Program

Most parents make no real attempt to get a child on a schedule. Educated parents might try.

Carmen Guedea, Parent Educator

Babies usually sleep with the mother. It's thought that the baby will be cold if they don't have their mother's warm body next to them.

Rosa Carreno, Community Health Worker

Lack of finances prevents mothers from buying a crib until the infant is a few months old; also if she is breast feeding, it is easier just to reach over in her own bed and put the baby to her breast.

Rosalie Prado de Ramirez, Public Health Nursing Supervisor

Babies usually sleep with their mothers, fathers, or with another sibling because of the lack of space. If a baby misses his nap time, the parents will try to keep him up so he'll sleep through the night. If a baby has a hard time sleeping, the mother will try to sing to it or rock it or maybe feed it.

Maty Brito, Mental Health Outreach Counselor

A mother will give the baby mint or chamomile tea to help it sleep.

Rosa Carreno, Community Health Worker

Chapter 21

Baptism

What is the importance of baptism for the family and for the baby?
When do babies get baptized?

This chapter shows the significance that baptizing a baby into the Catholic Church holds for the Mexican family. A major family celebration accompanies the baptism. Among other things, the celebration is a time when a child's godparents are announced and their very special relationship to the child and his parents is formalized.

For Latino families in the U.S., baptism is very important. They have a strong faith in the Catholic Church. If the child is not baptized, they believe his spirit will be in limbo—which means he won't go to heaven after death.

Rafael Ramirez, Elementary School Principal

Baptism is like a gift. It's a way to confirm the baby to God and to say "thank you" to Him for giving you the baby. Families try to baptize the baby within the first six months after its birth.

Maty Brito, Mental Health Outreach Counselor

Catholics practice infant baptism. Culturally, it's a very important event because parents select the godparents and have a big celebration. Part of it is the naming of the child, expressing plans and dreams for the child, bringing him for friends and family to see. It's a ceremony and the baby gets a lot of gifts. The *comadre* [ko·MAH·dreh: godmother] and *compadre* [kohm·PAH·dreh: godfather] will be responsible for raising the child if something happens to the parents. Historically, there was a much greater likelihood that something would happen to parents and they needed to make sure someone would raise their children. The tradition of godparents still continues in this country. Godparents are a family's very best friends. They're very close, practically family. Godparents come to all family events. You can borrow money from them and you're never alone. With Anglos, the role of the godparents is far less important.

Dolores Ramirez, Multicultural Director

Babies get baptized around three months to one year. A family may hold off until they have money for a party. Baptism is important because most Mexicans are Catholic.

Carmen Guedea, Parent Educator

The real meaning of baptism is that it's a ceremony of welcoming the child into the Catholic/Christian family. Now, it's sometimes just an opportunity for adults to get together and drink or to receive presents for the kids. Some of the meaning has been lost.

Ana Morante, Outpatient (Mental Health) Case Worker

There's a huge family celebration with the baptism. The family buys new clothes and spends much more than you think they would. Baptism is the baby's introduction to the Catholic religion. Usually the baby is about six to eight weeks old. Baptism is part of the Catholic religion and is very important for the baby and the family.

Linda Espinosa, Professor of Education and
Former Director of a Parenting Program

Babies get baptized when the families can afford it. That's another cultural thing. Even though the families don't have a lot of money, a baptism signifies bringing the child into the world. We want to share it with our friends.

Food is important in the Latino culture. If you make a party you have to have food. They have rice, beans, tortillas, meat, and lots of other food—no matter how poor the family is. It's important to them to take care of their friends and relatives. One way to do this is to feed them.

Maty Brito, Mental Health Outreach Counselor

The *comadre* and *compadre* are very close to the parents and are expected to assume the role of parent in case something happens to them. At the baptism, a mother will select close friends or even relatives who support her, in good times and bad, to be her child's godparents.

Carmen Cortez, Associate Director, Parenting Program

Baptism is of social and cultural importance because it formally introduces the newest member of the family to society. It officially recognizes who are the "second parents" of the child. To accept this role, there are certain obligations. You help to pay for the officiating of the priest, the child's christening clothing, and for part of the food to be served at the welcoming party.

Rosalie Prado de Ramirez, Public Health Nursing Supervisor

The *comadre* and *compadre* are very important. They will be close and highly-trusted family friends. They are people the parents share responsibility with, someone they will take criticism from (for example, "You're not treating your wife well," "Be careful," "Let's talk about wife beating," or "Don't hit your child so much.").

Carmen Guedea, Parent Educator

Chapter 22

Understanding *Machismo* (Being Macho)

What is machismo?
Are there positives as well as negatives?
How did it develop in the Latino culture?

Here we learn more about the origins and the original and more complete meaning of *machismo* [mah·CHEES·mo]. We also hear about why and how *machismo* is being perpetuated in the Latino culture. Many Latino professionals are quite concerned about the problematic effects of the negative aspects of *machismo* and are helping families to make some changes in the way they raise the next generation because the negative aspects of *machismo* are seen as damaging to the emotionally healthy development of both males and females and their relationships with each other.

The true and original meaning of *machismo* has been misinterpreted over time, especially in non-Latino cultures. The real meaning is a man who protects his family and provides them with what they need. A man who is *macho* is very faithful; his word is one of honor.

Ana Morante, Outpatient (Mental Health) Case Worker

Machismo refers to masculinity, maleness. Originally, the man who acts like he's *macho* was seen as protector, leader, the one who takes care of everything. Things were patriarchal. The man was the leader of family groups, government groups; he was courageous and strong. Men had to have all the attributes of leaders; these were positive qualities. It's how women were protected. About this man, people would say, "*¡Que hombre!*" [keh OHM·breh], meaning "What a man"—a courageous man.

Unfortunately, abuse of that system lead to the negative aspects of *machismo* such as domination, self-will, self-satisfaction, the "my needs are greater than yours" ideas. Yet a woman wants a man who is *macho*. Women have to be subtle and manipulative to get what they want from such a man because a woman wouldn't want a wimp. They feel women shouldn't crush the macho ideal. In fact, women build it up.

During the Mexican Revolution, women were being raped; there was no defense for them; they were slaughtered. If men didn't protect women and the family, it was much harder for families to survive. A father displaying *machismo* (being protective of those who can't protect themselves) might not permit his son-in-law to beat his daughter. In the U.S., *machismo* becomes sexual or anti-female. We focus only on the negative aspects of *machismo* like being dominant and cocky. In this country, *machismo* has been misinterpreted to mean something negative ("He's being macho"). But even in the U.S., there are those who are weaker and need protection in order to speak out and fight for what's right. This aspect of *machismo* has to be in the hearts of people. Some of it is ethics and morality. We shouldn't throw the entire concept out; we should keep the good parts.

Dolores Ramirez, Multicultural Director

The negative side of *machismo* is when a person suppresses the rights of women and children. The man makes all the decisions at home; women do not have the opportunity to make decisions or to contribute to the decision-making process in the family. The positive side of *machismo* includes doing things that are risky, going beyond the call of duty. There has to be a balance in *machismo*—a balance in your values and your own expectations as a man.

Rafael Ramirez, Elementary School Principal

To what extent and how is machismo being perpetuated among Latino families?

I am writing about AIDS in the Latino community and about the silence of sexuality and *machismo*. I am challenging the cultural values a lot. I need to understand what is behind these cultural behaviors. I see that behind some of this is the idea that Latino men have to prove their manhood, that Latinos are very passionate and cannot control their sexuality.

The rates of infection of AIDS in the Latino Gay community is rising very rapidly. I wanted to understand this from a socio-cultural perspective. I found that one of the factors is *machismo*. It's very hard to pin down. We usually talk about *machismo* in relation to the effect it has on women, but it has a lot of effects on men, too. There's a double-bind message: Young Latinos are told from very early on that being male is the most wonderful thing. The explicit and implicit messages are clear. Families take so much pride in a boy's maleness. There are a lot of positive things connected to their maleness and masculinity that are ingrained in the culture and in families. But at the same time, boys are given the message that they have to prove their manhood, their masculinity. Boys are confronted with a very high standard of masculinity and are told that they're not a man until they prove it.

Rafael Diaz, Professor of Education

Is how you are to prove it explicit?

Yes, it's very explicit, especially in the culture of elementary school kids. They are aware of who beats up who. And you can't show any aspect of "womanhood": crying, household chores, any kind of sensitivity. And then, of course, there is sexual prowess. Sexual penetration is the royal road to manhood. Latino males are encouraged from a very early age to really show their masculinity. Kids talk a lot about having girlfriends and doing this stuff. And a lot of it may be boasting, but it is encouraged in the culture. It is very clear that risk-taking, low sexual control (giving in to the passion), and having multiple sexual partners are all a part of how Latino males have to prove their masculinity. In a culture where you have such high standards of what being a man is, the male ego gets wounded very easily. So there's an incredible investment of energy in order to continually restore the male ego. A lot of the *macho* behavior is really coming from a feeling that you have to prove something. And it's a terrible burden for men and boys to always have to prove themselves. And, of course, it victimizes women, and a lot of women become objectified.

As boys are socialized as Latino males, they come to believe that they have to prove their masculinity. That masculinity is threatened by the incredibly high standards of what a man is supposed to be. It creates a lot of self-esteem problems. A lot of men become very disconnected from their hearts. Their hearts go one way and their sexuality another. They can't have sex with the woman they love, and they can't love the person they have sex with. Sex goes downhill in marriage. Men love their wives like the Virgin Mary, so they have their sex outside the marriage because they cannot connect the two. The fear men have of their own femininity and anything that reminds them of it is responsible for a lot of the abuse of women. The stereotyping goes on from day one. A baby is immersed in this way of making sense of sex roles.

Rafael Diaz, Professor of Education

What is the woman's role in machismo?

It is very important to understand what the women's role is in this. It is very important for women to have a man that is very strong and very *macho* and very masculine. It's important to have someone who can protect you. That is the good part of *machismo*—the protective part. So even though there is so much disruption connected with the negative aspects of *machismo*, the women conspire. There is a lot of support for *machismo* from the women. If women take over and become assertive, they are diminishing the masculinity of their partners. Women who can run the world, who take responsibility far beyond what their husbands can do, assume this submissive posture because it is very important to have a man who, in the eyes of others, in the eyes of the man himself, seems strong. This is because the more weak a man feels, the more *macho* he will act. This whole dynamic in the Latino needs to be fixed. It is very, very strong. (There are some historical accounts of why this is the case. There's an Arab influence and there's a connection to the Aztecs.)

In Latino communities, *machismo* is very prevalent and has far-reaching effects. If you offer a Latino mother in the U.S. assertiveness training with the idea that she will become more assertive in the schools and in her children's education, you cannot expect her not to be assertive in other domains, too. So a lot of men may not allow women to take that training.

Rafael Diaz, Professor of Education

Chapter 23

The Roles of Mothers and Fathers

What are the common roles of mothers and fathers and the advantages and disadvantages of the roles?

What struggles do mothers and fathers experience with regard to these roles?

Traditional Latino roles for mothers and fathers are still the norm for many Latino families. There are powerful pressures from the Latino community to maintain these traditional roles. This chapter poignantly describes struggles for Latino men and woman and presents some lesser known strengths of Latino women. Through excerpts from a book on Latino women, we gain additional insight into the issues facing women in the Latino community. Chapter 32, p. 156, looks at boys' and girls' roles and inspires us to think about some changes for the next generation.

The father's job is to work all the time, to earn money. If the mother works outside the home, it's her responsibility to come home, get the kids ready, bathe them, make dinner, feed everyone, watch some TV, and get the kids to bed. Then the parents go to bed. No one turns off the TV or reads to the kids.

Carmen Guedea, Parent Educator

Even if women are working outside the home, they are still expected to keep up with all the work at home. This is hard. The men don't have to do this additional work. But the husband only agrees to let his wife work outside the home if she promises to get all the other work of the home done, too. The women continue to work because of the recognition they get from their peers and supervisors at the workplace. It's a boost to their self-esteem. They don't get this recognition at home.

Beatriz Cerrillo, Family Resource Specialist

If you come from a traditional family, the woman will find her self-esteem in the way the rest of the family idealizes her. This makes her valuable and gives her a central role in the family.

Ana Morante, Outpatient (Mental Health) Case Worker

I feel that my husband should have a day off because he works so hard and does so much. I sometimes feel sorry for my husband, even though I have no days off and am in charge of all the housework. I feel so proud of my contribution to the household work that I don't want to leave any part of it for him to do. If I ask him to help, he'll do it and he doesn't mind. But I feel very proud that he is, for example, able to watch TV. I like my role. I feel I'm better off than the younger women who complain or feel like victims. What I do doesn't seem like extra work to me.

Victoria Orozco, Family Resource Specialist

The more traditional the family, the more typical the mother's and father's roles. The more westernized and educated the Latino family is, the more they tend to be egalitarian.

Ana Morante, Outpatient (Mental Health) Case Worker

When the family's level of education is a little higher, mothers are involved more in decision making. But in families without much formal education, the decision-making is mostly done by the father. It has been in the culture for years and years that the father has the role of decision-maker and protector of the family. After the family has been in the U.S. for a while, it is like the mother wakes up one day and says, "Come on, I can make these decisions, too. I count." But for families that have just come here from poor rural areas, the father makes all of the decisions. The mother follows whatever the father says. They don't even bother to explain "why" to the kids. It's just "Dad said so," so they have to do it.

Maty Brito, Mental Health Outreach Counselor

The roles are traditional in rural areas of Mexico. There's no such thing as a woman working outside the home. A woman should be at home taking care of the house and children. But I like to think those things are changing in this community. There's still the *machismo* idea that a woman should be home cooking and taking care of the family. Many members of this community came from rural areas.

Rafael Ramirez, Elementary School Principal

The father is the hard one with respect to discipline ("Wait till Dad gets home"). The kids might get a beating. The mother is easier. If the problem is really bad, she'll threaten and follow through. A Mexican mother and father don't discuss punishment, etc., the way Anglos tend to (for example, "Your mother and I both feel the same way about this.").

Carmen Guedea, Parent Educator

Daily discipline is the mother's role. The father may discipline, too, but only after the mother fails and only with the serious things. The mother will say, "Wait until your father gets home."

Dolores Ramirez, Multicultural Director

The father overrules the mother. His decision is always final. He listens to the mother's point of view, but the father makes the final decision on everything—not just child rearing. She asks him, "What do you think?" The father might say the opposite of what he said just a minute before. But the mother doesn't go against what her husband says. In more educated families, there's more compromise.

Carmen Guedea, Parent Educator

In Latino families, there is a hierarchy and a structure where older people have more authority over younger people. And males will have more authority over females.

Ana Morante, Outpatient (Mental Health) Case Worker

The children are taught to show respect to adults in general, but there is more of a reverence to the patriarchs in the family. That is a real struggle that the Mexicans have to deal with in terms of sexual and physical abuse. The perpetrator knows that you will not reveal who did the abuse because of respect. So we have to place more emphasis on respecting oneself and not so much on exposing the other person. When you are a girl, you are not allowed to talk about sex with anyone. As a girl you have to be an innocent, chaste virgin. They go so far to keep a girl's virginity that boys will have anal sex with them. A lot of rape is done this way. There is a real denial in older women about the fact that their husbands are having sex with other women. This denial helps them keep the family intact. That is the wife's major role.

Renee Martinez, Professor of Child Development

Domestic violence is typical throughout Latin America. There, fathers hit mothers, mothers hit kids, boys hit girls. The churches there support the subservience of women. Mexican women are jealous of other women. Men are often flirtatious and women fear abandonment. A Mexican woman who has no husband and children is not fulfilling her role, so she's not a woman and loses respect. Women have been culturally conditioned to act like servants at home to be valued. A woman appears as a slave to keep her role.

Graciela Ybarra, Resource Teacher

In many Latino families, the man can do what he wants. He can wake up his wife at 4 am when she's six months pregnant and have her make him a full course meal. He could be plastered; he could take another woman. Men are insensitive and egocentric, like five-year-olds. This contributes to the woman's low self-esteem. The husband beats the wife up behind closed doors. She cries quietly. He hits her with a belt and his fist. The husband embarrasses the wife in front of others. Boys get to discipline their sisters. The parents say, "Go get her," and the brother will drag his sister by her hair and dress. This embarrasses and hurts the girl.

In our home educators program, we find that wives won't even take the phone number of abuse referrals. If they do take it, they won't use it. Some men will tell their wives that they don't want the home educators in their homes. I always try to make another appointment. I have to win the husband over first before having a home educator is comfortable for the wife.

Carmen Guedea, Parent Educator

On our radio call-in show, women complain most about domestic violence and alcoholism. The women are very intimidated. They have nowhere to go and they don't work, so they think it's almost better to stay with their husbands where they have economic security than to have nothing. They may leave when their husband starts beating the children. That's their breaking point. With alcoholism, they want to be educated about how to live with it and who to get in touch with. We try to educate them against the *machismo* in the culture that allows men to beat women. If the husband won't get help, the woman calls our radio show because she wants to know how she can get help.

I got a letter from an institution that helps battered women saying that my program has helped over 200 women in this area, that through the program these women were able to realize that they were not alone and that they could reach out and get help. They felt heard for the first time.

Luz Agudelo, Radio Call-In Show Hostess

Even younger families who have been here for a while fall into the same patterns. If a man starts to help his wife, his brothers will step all over him with, "You're letting her tell you what to do. Who is the man in this house? Who wears the pants—you or her? I can't believe you're letting her tell you what to do." This creates big problems in the household. If he doesn't show he's *macho*, his brothers-in-law, etc., will almost disown him. They'll say things like, "If you beat your wife tomorrow, she'll stop being so demanding, and she'll stop nagging you." If your brother doesn't tell you, your father will. Women from the U.S. are harder to keep quiet when you beat them up. U.S.

women have control over themselves. They know what they want. The man has little power over Americanized Mexican women and the men don't want to share power.

Carmen Guedea, Parent Educator

Some Latinos feel that to be more *macho* you drink more. Then you can be the boss in your house and run everything.

Ana Morante, Outpatient (Mental Health) Case Worker

The young man is egged on to hit his wife or girlfriend by his young male friends coming from Mexico who don't want him to have a girlfriend or wife who is influential.

Maria Reyes, Social Worker

Latino women are taught to take physical abuse from men. Men have a lot of jealousy. They are taught that women are their property, that they can do whatever they want to women and that women are not supposed to do anything about it. Women accept this as how it is. They accept that men have the right to be jealous and possessive. In Mexico and other Latin countries, it's a joke to talk about reporting abuse to the police. What are you going to report? There are no laws that protect the woman and no child-abuse laws. So, the police aren't effective. Over there, you can solve many things if you know some important people or if you pay some money.

Latino women are very strong emotionally. There is an unspoken rule that fathers will be the disciplinarians, but the mothers often do most of the disciplining. Traditional mothers are very good at protecting each family member's role. They'll leave certain things to the husband, like the discipline of boys, in order to protect the father's role and self-esteem. This helps keep the balance. The mother has a lot of power in the family. Mothers are jealous of their role and want to be able to perform their whole role—without help. Many women, especially single parents, are overwhelmed. It's hard for them to let the kids do some of the work. Women will protect their realm if they're at home and the husband is working. This perpetuates a rigid division of labor.

Ana Morante, Outpatient (Mental Health) Case Worker

In the Latino culture, we have a very autocratic process. The father has the last word, even though the mother has all of the power. Only the mother knows how to work with the father so she can get what she needs. In the U.S. culture, it's "We're all going to decide." That doesn't happen in the Latino culture because a father feels very vulnerable if it seems he's losing power and control. It makes him feel very irresponsible. He feels he's leaving his children without guidance and discipline and boundaries. Unless you give a father another way of replacing the power and authority, he won't give it up.

In public, fathers will always have the last word. But at home the mother will have some say, even if the father has the last word. There's an implicit agreement that the mother will always make the father look good and the father will always defer to the mother—with the implicit understanding that he has given her the authority to decide whether to grant permission on something. There is a sharing of the authority, but the father always looks like he has the last word. If you are going to teach the mother to do things differently, you're not going to get anything done unless you get the father to understand why it's important. The mother is not going to risk violating the implicit rule in the Latino culture that the man is the authority.

Josie Romero, Clinical Social Worker and
Director of a Family Institute

Hispanic men don't traditionally have experience being friends with a woman, so women are either sexual objects or wives and mothers who you maintain control over. If I were to strike up a conversation with a man who was close to my age, it might be seen as sexual. If I'm of a different social class, they'd see me as superior and someone they couldn't relate to. But if I were a "tramp," they might badger, flirt, or talk with me. They have no history of equality in relationships with women.

Linda Espinosa, Professor of Education and
Former Director of a Parenting Program

It has always been thought that the Latino man is the head of the household, that he's the one who gives the orders. It's been thought that the Mexican woman is passive and accepting. Perhaps this is how it used to be. What people didn't know was how strong women can be and how many women are the force in their families. The women let the men do the talking, but the functioning of the family appears to depend on the competency of the mother.

When families come to the U.S., the mother is still the strength in the family. But she will turn to the man first to see what he wants and what he decides. It's different in every family. In some families, the one who is the leader is the one who has the abilities. The family will flourish if partners can work cooperatively.

Some men are more *macho* than others. They want to have their way and are more abusive. It depends on where they come from and their degree of education. Getting angry may be the only way a man knows how to deal with problems. Sometimes the woman sees that she can have some protection in the U.S. if she calls the police, that maybe he won't be able to keep beating her up. Sometimes the man will accept it and change once the police come.

Being in the U.S. also demeans our men. They often have few skills and are illiterate. The roles here are reversed: the woman works, perhaps as a motel maid; he stays home and watches the kids since he can't find employment. Mexican men are extremely hard working. Their way of showing their love for their family is through their work and their ability to provide. That's part of being *macho.*

I've seen some very strong, intelligent, capable women. They can keep their families together. But even these women have the self-effacing attitude that they're not good enough. There isn't much out there telling women that they're capable. Society here doesn't tell them. Mexican women come here with a better sense of identity than those who are second and third generation. Those who have grown up in the U.S. have gone through discrimination and prejudice and uncertainty. They don't have ties to Mexico or to the U.S. But they have brown skin and black hair—they can't get away from that.

Maria Reyes, Social Worker

For a man, there is a definite pride in and emphasis on having a family, even when family life isn't working. He would maintain the marriage and maybe have another relationship. The role of the male is not only that of breadwinner but also one of always having to say that things are OK, even when they're not.

I think that the male always has to have the last word. There are a lot of really strong Mexican women who rule the household but let their husbands save face by appearing to be in charge.

Renee Martinez, Professor of Child Development

A lot of the women were much more isolated than our parent education program and home educators had expected, given the tendency for the extended family to live together in the house. There's very little true emotional support for a woman's development as she moves through her adjustment to Anglo culture and its many options. In Mexico, these other options would not have come up.

A big issue for us was how to help the mothers move forward so they could be more competent with their children and function more independently. We had to teach some of the mothers how to use the bus and the bus schedule. Even the woman's going out might create tension in the family. We help them go to the library, get a card, check out books. We help them use community resources. As women began to get that ability to be independent, there were some problems in the family. So the man would start being home when our home visitor came. He wanted to know what the home visitor was saying to his wife. "What ideas are you putting into her head? What are you telling her to do?"

Home educators may be having some problems with their own cultural beliefs. They were selected because they had very similar backgrounds and could relate to the mothers. So they, too, have to deal with cultural changes. Socialization in the U.S. means that women function in very different ways than *Latinas* are used to.

Family members are a woman's greatest source of advice and support if they live close by. In Mexico, aunts, sisters, or grandmothers would be available to give the new mother some help and they'd be around during the birth of the child. We found many of the women in our program to be pretty isolated. They don't have their traditional support systems, even among other women. Many of the families come to depend on the home educators for just about everything because they have no one else. Their home educator will go to their family celebrations like a best friend.

Pursuing a non-traditional path may prevent a woman from getting good advice and support from her closest family members. They want her to do things traditionally so as not to upset the male hierarchy. For example, families typically tolerate an abusive situation in the home—a husband hurting his wife or children, or someone renting a room in the home who is selling drugs. Women are not supposed to take action or make the situation known. They're supposed to play a passive role and nurture the children. Many of the mothers in our program didn't want to challenge that. They were oppressed by it and they didn't like it, but there was no way they were going to do anything about it. They wouldn't even do anything about physically abusive situations. Abuse was what they expected, and they couldn't envision another kind of life. Even one college-educated mother from Mexico who was married to a college-educated man from Mexico wouldn't take the steps necessary to break out of the abusive situation.

I'm surprised by what women will put up with to have a man in the home. Our parenting program had workshops on domestic violence. It's not just Hispanics. It's very widespread, and it takes so much for women to break out of these situations.

Linda Espinosa, Professor of Education and
Former Director of a Parenting Program

The husband will have a problem with having a male professional talk to the Latino woman at her home. Some Anglo professionals think Latino women can make the decisions about children, etc., alone. They don't realize that the husband needs to be there. I sometimes counsel professionals about this issue.

Rafael Ramirez, Elementary School Principal

Though the degree depends on whether a father is first, second, or third generation, fathers still expect to have a traditional, strong authoritarian lifestyle. There's a mixed message there because the traditional father in the old Mexican family is supposed to support the family. But in Mexican families in the U.S. who are at a low-economic level, it's not unusual for the woman, even without education, to have a job instead of the man. So the dependent role that women had in Mexico when they didn't work outside the home changes here. We are seeing the divorce rate go up, and we're seeing more violence toward women because men are having a hard time handling these changes. Also, in the traditional Mexican family the woman is trained to be co-dependent. She enabled the male to do whatever he pleased, and she accepted that as her role. But this is changing in the U.S. There are a lot of mixed messages about these roles. There is also more homosexuality now, for both males and females.

Renee Martinez, Professor of Child Development

The family plays a very important and central role in Latino life. The mother is seen as the one who brings the family together. This role has been idealized because it's been equated with self-denial and abnegation. The mother expects to do a lot of self-sacrificing. This is thought to make them more in tune with other people's needs, and mothers are supposed to provide nurturing at home.

There's a division of roles. The father has more instrumental functions, like disciplining. The mother has more expressive functions, like nurturing. Taken to the extreme, this role makes it hard for women to get in touch with their own needs. The more she does, the more the family idealizes her, and the more obligated she feels. Girls are raised to have motherhood be their main role in life.

There's a big conflict for women who want to have careers. They usually choose to put their careers on hold or on the side. If they don't, they'll be criticized and feel guilty. There's a lot of pressure on women to provide emotional support for their families. They bring the family together—the mother (or the grandmother) is the spirit of the family. Women have a lot of skills, but they have to learn that the skills will do them no good if they don't get anything for themselves.

Ana Morante, Outpatient (Mental Health) Case Worker

The following views from a new book (written by a Latina for Latinas) provide a current glimpse at the Latina woman. Bettina Flores, described as the Betty Friedan of the Latina woman, wrote the book, *Chiquita's Cocoon: The Latina woman's guide to greater power, love, money, status and happiness,* to help Latinas realize that there are ways they can change their lives—lives that may make them feel trapped in a cocoon, not knowing a way out.

Bettina Flores says that Latinas have many self-defeating behaviors that are holding them back. These behaviors result from religious and cultural conditioning. She looks at the emphasis on marriage, having children, and accepting a subservient role to men. She also highlights the attitude toward money, developing oneself, and staying surrounded by only other Latinos.

She notes that Latinos tend to stay immersed in their culture, near those who believe as they do. She feels there is pressure to avoid becoming acquainted with non-Latinos. She thinks Latinas fear standing up to family and friends for things they believe in and need. A Latina breaking away from the home roost may be labeled a "loose woman" rather than someone seeking independence.

Flores says that Latinas get married at a very early age and look forward to it because they are taught to believe that "real life starts and culminates with marriage." Worst of all, says Flores, "the Latina does not even imagine there is anything else but marriage. She goes directly from the domination of her father to the domination of her husband," with almost no time in between for herself.

> [Women] are religiously, culturally and traditionally conditioned to having many children. . . .The practice of having more children than [women may] want, or can manage or afford, strongly diminishes the Latina's opportunity for anything more than a life of motherhood. . . . Latinas assume that being pregnant is one of the greatest things that can happen to them and, therefore, they should be thankful.

Flores feels that women who are not the homemaker type are "likely to be in the coma of depression common to many Latinas."

"This happens because [Latinas] don't see [themselves] as important or deserving enough to give [themselves] the same privileges" as those they nurture. "The more children [they] have, the harder it is to [treat themselves well.]" Flores believes that "raising children is one of the hardest jobs in the world and it's time to admit it. When we face this fact, perhaps we will learn to have fewer children."

Flores notes that "*machismo* is rampant within Latino marriages. *Machismo* is that subtle but very strong force that keeps a Latina 'in her place.'"

> Macho men want to rule. ["I'm the boss here and you will obey me."] They want all their needs—physical, emotional, psychological and spiritual—met at all times by "their woman." . . . Machismo attitudes extend from the kitchen to the bedroom and to the children; they persist unchanged generation after generation. . . .

> [A husband will tell a wife] she's not to go anywhere during the day unless she gets his permission ahead of time. Meekly the Latina accepts her husband's authority, and the control/obedience cycle begins.

> Macho husbands are mean, jealous and possessive. To cover up their insecurities and jealousies, they prey upon their wives by instilling fear in them. . . .

Flores also says:

> Traditionally, most Latinas are loyal, practicing Catholics. . . . We accept the church and its teachings the same way we accept our tradi-

tional and cultural practices—wholeheartedly. Our church and our culture have this in common: They both require *obedience*. . . .

No wonder the Latina can't make it in the competitive outside world. She is conditioned to follow orders. Somewhere, somehow, sometime, the Latina must become aware of all the forces paralyzing her mind. . .

. . . . Many Latinas are convinced that while you are on Earth you are not worth much because you are just earning the greater glory of heaven. These teachings give *you* a negative self-image but give the church a hold on your thinking, your behavior and your happiness. . .

There's a visible, obvious correlation between being Catholic, being Latina and being poor. Why this is so should be examined and questioned by every impoverished Latina. Lack of education and lack of job skills are some of the causes of poverty, but religious beliefs can be even more damaging. Psychological attitudes can make the primary difference in winning the war against poverty, especially cyclical poverty.

In her book, Flores encourages Latinas to have courage—courage to face self-truths, to want to change, to act differently, and to attain self-actualization—but not give up the wonderful parts of their bountiful cultural legacy.

What are Mexican-American women struggling with?

There is a lot more desire among the Mexican-American women to get ahead. I know there is a greater need for Mexican women in college to have support groups or mentors than there is for other students. Sharing and knowing that other women are experiencing the same things are very important to Mexican women. Though education is the norm for third- and fourth-generation Mexicans, first- and second-generation Mexican women do not have that support. But they do recognize that, on an economic level, it's important.

Renee Martinez, Professor of Child Development

When a woman learns there are things outside the family and aspects of herself that can be developed in different ways, there's a conflict with her previous image of how she should be. The path you take depends, in part, on how you identify with the Latino and Anglo culture. Beyond that, it's a very personal thing that depends on many factors. The best you can do is take the best of both worlds. You shouldn't go against your own desire to develop yourself as a mother, even if the Anglo culture says you should. But if you have other skills, you may want to try to develop them. It is extremely difficult and time-consuming for a Latino woman to try to develop herself while she is busy building the family.

The extended family can provide lots of roles for different people. If we can rely on them more, it will free us from our exclusive commitment to our family and our inability to do anything for ourselves. But the extended family is not as strong or as large in the U.S. as in Mexico.

Ana Morante, Outpatient (Mental Health) Case Worker

For many women who don't want to work outside the home, things are still fine in the Latino family. These women are comfortable with their role, and their role is not working against the family.

Beatriz Cerrillo, Family Resource Specialist

Latino males are discovering that they have to be supportive of what Latino women are trying to accomplish, supportive of women's changing roles. Men can't be role models for women. We are recruiting Latino women to be role models for Latino girls. There is still the traditional value of women being passive.

Traditionally, Latino women have not been supported in their efforts to get a better education. There's a new way of thinking that supports women who choose to have fewer children and get a better education. But the Latino men are going to have to decide, and the women have to be awfully strong and speak up for what they need and what they believe.

Rafael Ramirez, Elementary School Principal

PART III

CHILD-REARING
PRACTICES
—UP TO THE
TEEN YEARS

Chapter 24

Children's Play at Home

What are young children expected to do when they're awake?
What do children need for their play?
What role do parents expect to have in their children's play time?

Looking at children's play and the parent/child interaction helps us understand how a child's learning evolves at home. The Latino professionals express their concerns that certain aspects of the early learning and play patterns of babies and young children can have a negative impact on a child's readiness for school. Parents who understand this impact may be more motivated to make some small changes to help their child succeed in the U.S. Professionals who recognize why parents often take the roles they do in their children's early learning will be better equipped to support those parents. Remember that these changes should not detract from the basic fabric of Latino family's important values (e.g., respect for the parents, the extended family).

Parents perceive a child's ability to do things in terms of the child's size. When the baby is little, they will not expect it to do much. They don't realize how much a baby is learning, until it's pointed out that a baby changes each month. They expect the baby to just stare and look around. When he's able to sit and crawl, they expect that he will get into things. They'll expect that he'll learn to walk, holding onto things, and they want him to learn early. The

116

entire family encourages it. While parents expect the physical motor skills to emerge, they aren't aware of the cognitive development that's going on. They don't realize that a child needs stimulation of all his sensory needs—visual, auditory, etc. Whatever stimulation their child gets comes accidentally, including language stimulation. Most babies are not talked to—other than in affectionate terms when playing. There is no specific dialogue or communication directed to the child. Yet these are not quiet households. There's lots of language around the child, but it's not directed to him. The baby isn't involved in the language.

When babies get to be toddler age, they are generally expected to be in a little world by themselves. They are not looked upon as being a partner with their parent in doing things. They're supposed to just play ("Stay out of my way and don't cry.") They feel toddlers should do their own thing as long as they don't get into trouble. They will be around older children and around older siblings. You can see the whole little gang of children from youngest to oldest. They stick together. That's where the fun is.

There's also a lot of imaginary play going on. They do wonders with what's in their yards and houses, and with each other. The type of play children do tends more to stimulate their physical development.

If the parent has money, the children will have the same types of toys as you'd see anywhere in the U.S. But they don't have many toys. They will get what's on TV—guns, dolls, balls, and tricycles. They don't have puzzles, manipulatives, crayons, paste, paper, and coloring books. They don't have a lot of toys that stimulate thinking and reasoning skills.

In our work with preschoolers, which includes screening with the Denver Developmental Test, we consistently find that the language level of the Latino children is very low. They give short responses, without a lot of descriptive language. They seldom ask how, why, or when questions. The kind of language they are used to responding to is commands by their parents. They mostly ask what and where questions. Our parenting program teaches the parents how to stimulate language and cognitive development in their children through making and using toys and other things with their children.

The lack of cognitive stimulation children get is associated with some of the difficulties that Latino children have when they go to school. They don't have the solid foundation for learning, which includes language development, that children exposed to a lot of stimulation would have.

Carmen Cortez, Associate Director, Parenting Program

Mobile babies are put in a walker. Parents don't want the baby to crawl. And families are not knowledgeable about child-proofing and safety in their homes. Babies pull cords or their walker gets caught in a cord or they hurt themselves on the floor heater.

Families don't give babies very much that is exciting to do. Some might get a little batting toy. One- and two-year-olds play outside a lot. They play with cars, toy guns, dolls, and maybe a hairbrush and fake jewelry. They go for a walk with their mothers and go to the store a lot. Mothers eat with their child and talk as they eat, but, afterwards, the children are shooed out to the backyard. They watch *Barney*, etc., on TV. They don't have a lot of coloring books, paper and pencils, scissors, or a lot of those things. They basically play outside—running around a lot, riding bicycles, throwing rocks at cats. So they get good gross motor development; but they're not offered a pencil. This is the way the parents grew up. "If I wasn't given a pencil, why do my kids need one?" No Play-doh, paper, puzzles—not a lot of educational stuff. Its considered too messy and takes too much time to clean it up. I advise parents that they don't have to buy toys, that children can use plates, measuring cups, etc. I suggest mothers let them cook with them—like measuring things, grating cheese, and peeling and mashing the avocados for guacamole.

Carmen Guedea, Parent Educator

When children are young, and if the parent can afford it, a lot of parents try to give their kids whatever they want—especially food. But if a child asks for a lot of things, he's considered spoiled or too demanding. The expectations that parents have of a child at a given stage can be very unrealistic.

Carmen Cortez, Associate Director, Parenting Program

Parents don't show their love by playing with children and talking to them, but, rather, they may, for example, take them to the jewelry store and have their ears pierced. It's too materialistic now. There are one-year-olds wearing gold earrings and bracelets.

Carmen Guedea, Parent Educator

In this country, Latino parents tend to replace touch and emotional nourishment with material things and TV.

Graciela Ybarra, Resource Teacher

Children do a lot of free play—balls, guns, dolls, fantasies with siblings and cousins, and some fighting. They learn to compromise and bargain ("If you give me that, I'll give you this."). The mother and father don't interfere or show a child what they want him to do. Children have to learn to help each other out and share with siblings and cousins. Parents interfere only if there's a "dirty" fight with biting, slapping, pulling hair, or doing something underhanded; then everyone usually gets a spanking, no matter who started it.

Carmen Guedea, Parent Educator

There's a certain amount of normal fighting among siblings and cousins. But the children have been conditioned to share and play by a young age (by two to three years of age). They get along in group play, partly because they have been forced to get along. They are punished and spanked at home if they don't get along.

My experience is that the younger or smaller child will win out when a parent comes to mediate—even if the child's just a few months younger. The older one is supposed to give in to the younger one. Children are constantly told that and they just learn it.

Carmen Cortez, Associate Director, Parenting Program

It's difficult to explain how parents give their kids time. For example, when the father comes home, he has dinner, asks the kids what they're doing, then turns the TV to the Spanish station. If the kids say, "Dad play with me," he might say, "Go play with your brother; go do what your brother wants." Or he might go check on something the child wants to show him, say, "How nice," then go back and sit in front of the TV. There's not a lot of communication between parents and children. The parents focus more on themselves and don't understand that kids have special needs, that they like to be read to, etc. It's assumed that kids will learn in school, that at home they'll just play and shouldn't get into trouble. I work with parents on interacting with their children, on making time for them. I teach them how to talk to their children.

Carmen Guedea, Parent Educator

Parents don't do much talking, playing, or reading with their children. Families at a low economic level don't do much of this. (There are some who will read to their kids because they really enjoy it, but that's unusual.) Parents often won't play with their children because they feel the child won't respect them if they go to their child's level. I'm teaching parents to make changes.

Dolores Ramirez, Multicultural Director

One of the things I notice in Latino families is that they don't play a lot with their kids. They just put a bunch of toys on the floor and expect the kids to entertain themselves. Sometimes they say, "This kid doesn't like toys." We have to teach them to put a few toys out at a time. Sometimes they don't buy the right kinds of toys. Most of the parents I see don't have the appropriate toys for their child. They give the kids toys that the adults like.

Rosa Carreno, Community Health Worker

If parents do buy toys, they will take the preschoolers to stores and buy toys that they see on TV—action-hero toys, like GI Joe, for boys, and cute dolls for girls. They're not very expensive, but they hold a high appeal for children. There's lots of sibling play as opposed to interacting with parents. The expectation is that the children will amuse themselves with those kinds of toys and that they will play with each other. In general, parents don't know how to select toys that would have some educational value for children.

Linda Espinosa, Professor of Education and
Former Director of a Parenting Program

The parent's job is to keep children clean, clothed, and fed. The children have free play. The day isn't structured to allow a child to have reading time or to do things that prepare them for school-type activities.

Beatriz Cerrillo, Family Resource Specialist

Parents expect toddlers and preschoolers to just play outside. They are left unsupervised to roam, wander, and play. The child is free to experiment. But the environment may not be safe (cut glass, trash, etc.). When Latino children are indoors, as in a child care center, they are much more physical than other children because their language is more limited. They've had less language stimulation and communication growing up. These children may go through the whole day like a tornado. They haven't learned the social skill of how to sit down and play with an object and take care of it. If they have emotional problems, it's worse. It's hard for many preschool Latino children to be in a formal, structured environment. It's a real hard adjustment.

Carmen Cortez, Associate Director, Parenting Program

Depending on the family, some fathers will play with their children or take them for ice cream. It is difficult for many families because so many fathers are out of work. There's no money. There are a lot of worries that keep fathers and mothers from playing with their children. Parents want to do their best. They may want to play with their children, but many don't have the time or the energy. Many children don't have a lot of toys because there is no money. Sometimes they will borrow toys from other people.

Maty Brito, Mental Health Outreach Counselor

If there is time, a parent provides for their child's physical needs. If the child is right there and you're in a good mood, he'll get a lot of affection (kissing and hugging). It's automatic. There's not a conscious effort to give the child some individual time. To make that kind of time would ask a lot of the mother.

Carmen Cortez, Associate Director, Parenting Program

Parents feel they should be clothing, feeding, protecting, and providing shelter for their children. They don't think it's their job to play with them. If the kid wants to play, the mother will call another kid to play with him. Parents don't read to their children. People say, "I don't know how to read," but they read enough to read a story book.

Rosa Carreno, Community Health Worker

It is not common for parents to play with children because of the amount of work that parents have to do. It's also because there are clear lines between parents and children. They don't try to be their pals or playmates. Play is not seen as part of the educational process. They believe that education happens at school.

Carmen Guedea, Parent Educator

Parents feel children should spend their time playing. Children don't have a lot of toys, and parents need education about choosing appropriate toys for their children—toys that won't break and have to be thrown away. Parents just let children play. They want control of their kids, but they don't structure their play at all. Parents are amazed in our parenting classes when we tell them what their children learn from play. Parents think children start learning when they start going to school. Parents often don't see what children are capable of or what their needs are.

In our classes, parents are asked to remember joyful and painful things from their childhood. What comes out of these memory exercises is how little children need to make them happy. And parents realize, "We can do that."

Dolores Ramirez, Multicultural Director

There is little written information for the families in *español* [ehs·pahn·YOHL: Spanish]. Most of the parenting information I give is verbal. Many of the parents don't read. I have one beautiful book that covers parenting up to age two. The entire book is in simple illustrations and pictures. They are very simple pictures of things like what a baby does and how to hold a baby. That works, especially for giving such messages as "You don't have to spend money for toys; you can make toys." I don't give written information. If the parents are very poor, they don't read. They often come back and talk to you about the same things. So I give them homework. I tell them, "This is homework. I'm going to help you, but you need to do A-B-C and bring it back to me." I do problem-solving and set demands, and I tell them this is how they're going to survive in the system. And it works. I exercise authority. And I don't hesitate to do that, because it works. These parents are very isolated. They don't have their mother or grandmother to give them support, and using authority can be one way to give support in the Latino community. They look to older people in the family to give them orientation, and I take that role easily. But I *don't* underestimate their intelligence.

Amalia DeBord, Clinical Social Worker

Our parenting program does some exercises to help parents reflect on how they feel about themselves. We ask things such as, "What would you have liked to have happen when you were a baby or a child? What was your relationship with your mother and father?" This elicits a lot of strong emotions and a lot of crying. It's like a cleansing process about what happened in their past. And we tell them, "Now you have to move on with the future. There's new information and it's up to you to use it." Parents are open and willing to be exposed to new things that will improve their lives, as long as you approach them in a way that doesn't embarrass or demean them.

Carmen Cortez, Associate Director, Parenting Program

Overall, the Latino professionals felt that parental involvement in children's learning during infant, toddler, and preschool years is minimal. They noted that talking with the children and having materials such as coloring books and puzzles and activities such as reading are rare. These may be important factors in making some Mexican children ill-equipped for success in U.S. schools. Latino professionals have had success in helping parents learn why they should try to make some changes, what their children are capable of, and some new ways to involve their children in conversations, reading, etc.

Chapter 25

Television Viewing

How is television used by Mexican families? What do parents think about their children watching television?

In this brief chapter, we get a glimpse of the meaning and use of television for the family. Considering what is known about the effects of extensive television viewing on motivation, aggression, activity level, and weight control, this is a potentially important area of information for Mexican parents to have.

There is a lot of TV watching. I think it's the only time mothers have to do their chores. Latinos seem to love the TV; there's no talk of the TV being too violent.

Maty Brito, Mental Health Outreach Counselor

Latinos don't give TV a lot of thought; it's on a lot. Whatever the parents are watching is what the child is exposed to. The parents don't realize the pluses and minuses of TV until someone points them out to them. We try to discuss this in our parenting classes, assuming that if they learn about some of TV's negatives, they'd make an effort to take more control over the TV their children watch.

Carmen Cortez, Associate Director, Parenting Program

They all watch TV together. They watch the Spanish station and watch *novelas* [no·VEH·lahs: soap operas] in the evening. It's whatever the adult is interested in. There's not an issue of what's appropriate for children's TV. They're not really worried about what kids are watching; they use the TV like a baby-sitter. Toddlers and preschool children watch cartoons in Spanish in the mornings.

Carmen Guedea, Parent Educator

The Mexican families we work with use TV quite a bit and, in the community where I directed a parenting program, they watched several Spanish-language channels and even some English channels. TV is used for entertaining the kids; it's used as a baby-sitter. Children might be watching TV for hours, including late at night, and falling asleep in front of the TV. I don't think the parents have considered the effects of what a child watches on his development. We included this as a topic in our parenting curriculum's new information for parents.

Linda Espinosa, Professor of Education and
Former Director of a Parenting Program

TV is a problem. They jut let their kids watch TV. They have no idea what their kids are watching.

Dolores Ramirez, Multicultural Director

They don't have a lot of choice about letting their children watch TV. They live in these little condos, so where are the children going to play? They also don't have the appropriate toys for the kids. So the children watch too much television; they jump around the house, jump on the furniture. There's not much parental control in the families that I visit.

Rosa Carreno, Community Health Worker

With older kids, TV/Nintendo keeps them at home. That's better than being on the streets. At least the kids are not causing problems in the streets. It's better to have TV as the sitter (although it should be used more thoughtfully) than to have the children get into trouble (drugs, etc.). I think, though, that it's better for children to read or do sports.

Victoria Orozco, Family Resource Specialist

Chapter 26

Sleep

Where do young children sleep, with whom, and for how many hours each night?

Look at the issues of routines, amount of sleep, and co-sleeping arrangements. The Latinos' cultural emphasis on familialism and cooperation rather than on individualism and competitiveness is reflected in the sleeping arrangements.

Children are expected to sleep a lot when they're small and most of them do. They start sleeping through the night when they can go without a feeding. There's not much problem with ignoring a baby's crying during the night; the baby will go back to sleep. I sometimes worry that the foundation babies need for emotional stability during the first year is not developing the way we think it should. Mexican parents love their children. They ignore them because they think that's the right thing to do. Our parenting program suggests that they use all that love they have to pay attention to their child so the child will feel better about himself or herself when he or she grows up.

Carmen Cortez, Associate Director, Parenting Program

Mothers give their babies a bath every night. They believe it helps the baby rest better and sleep longer. Babies usually sleep through the night around the third month and are expected to be sleeping a lot day and night. After three or four months, they keep the baby awake a lot during the day so they will sleep better at night. They like the baby to take a nap in the morning and afternoon, but not in the late afternoon.

Children often sleep in the same room and same bed with the other children. If there are two bedrooms, the baby sleeps with his parents and the other kids (siblings and cousins) sleep in the other bedroom. A baby might sleep with his parents until he's about two years old, or until his mother becomes pregnant with her next child.

Carmen Guedea, Parent Educator

When more than one family is sharing an apartment, the kids are all jammed together and sleep all over the place. If the parents are making a reasonable salary, they will have a boys' bedroom and a girls' bedroom.

Dolores Ramirez, Multicultural Director

There is not a set bedtime. Bedtime is whenever they fall asleep watching TV, etc. If the mother is not working, she'll carry them to their room asleep. If the parents are working, there's much more of a schedule. The children all bathe together, then the entire family will go to bed at the same time—maybe 9:00 or 9:30 in the evening.

Typically, the children sleep about eight hours at night. Toddlers and preschoolers usually get an early afternoon nap, but often the children are still tired. They'll whine and be fussy and harder to get along with. When their parents are working, some kids may have to get up at 5:30 am to go to their sitter's house and are not picked up until 6:00 PM.

Carmen Guedea, Parent Educator

Mothers try to put kids into routines where they sleep at certain times of the day. All the children go to sleep at once. Babies sleep on big beds and sofas; they share beds with their siblings.

Carmen Cortez, Associate Director, Parenting Program

The parents say, "If you're not good, the bogeyman is going to come." They scare the kids a lot. I grew up like that. "You have to be good or somebody will come and take you." They are usually in the same room as the parents, so they stay quiet.

Rosa Carreno, Community Health Worker

Chapter 27

Eating

What and when do young children eat?

Toward the end of the first year, the baby may be fed two or three spoon-fuls of cereal, *fideo* [fee·DEH·oh: pasta] with tomato sauce, chicken soup, and beans. They're not fed Gerber's or other baby foods because they're too expensive. After the first year, the toddler will eat everything the family eats—pinto beans, perhaps soup, pieces of flour tortilla.

Carmen Guedea, Parent Educator

By one year or even earlier, a child eats pretty much what others eat. Toddlers eat whatever everyone else is eating, regardless of whether it's good or bad. Sometimes the pieces of food that children eat are so small and hard that they can cause choking. Our parenting program has been trying to teach about these dangers and beginning to introduce new diets with fruits and vegetables that cost no more than what parents are spending now.

Carmen Cortez, Associate Director, Parenting Program

Mashed table food is offered as soon as the first teeth erupt. Due to the cost and the lack of transportation, fruits and perishables may not be eaten as often during the week. Weekends are different, however. In Latin American countries, fruits and vegetables are nearby and often in abundance and cheap.

Rosalie Prado de Ramirez, Public Health Nursing Supervisor

When mothers aren't working outside the home, breakfast is usually about 11 am—unless the child is really hungry. The meal is usually fixed whenever the mother is hungry. She'll feed the child a lunch of beans and rice or noodles about 2 PM. She'll prepare dinner about 4 PM, because that's when the fathers and others who are working come home. If both parents work, the child will get breakfast at school. Most families qualify for free lunches whether the parents are working or not. If a child asks for food during the day, the mother will give him cookies or ice cream—anything he asks for. They don't do a lot of talking, like "If you eat this, it will take away your appetite."

Carmen Guedea, Parent Educator

Food is available. Children are given what they want, when they want it. It's not restricted.

Linda Espinosa, Professor of Education and
Former Director of a Parenting Program

Mothers don't wait for children to ask for food. They are always offering them something to eat. It's important for the mothers to have good food for their children.

Maty Brito, Mental Health Outreach Counselor

Chapter 28

Toilet Training

How and by what age do parents potty train their children?

Look especially at the approach parents take to toilet training. You'll note similarities to the approaches to limit setting discussed in Chapters 30 (p. 136) and Chapter 31 (p. 146) on limit setting.

Kids are usually potty trained by the time they are two. If a child is not trained by age three, the parents would typically worry that something was wrong with him. Children get trained by being put in underpants and getting a swat every time they wet. The mother does this, though the father may help, as will the grandmother or aunt if they're living with them. The parent just sits the child on the toilet until he goes. It typically takes a few days to a month to train a child. It depends on the child and on how scared he gets.

Carmen Guedea, Parent Educator

Toilet training has been a serious problem. I've seen parents start to potty train very early—from the time children can sit up and support themselves, as early as six months. The parents do the training. The parent will sit a child on the potty-chair with the idea that he's going to do it no matter how long it takes. Most kids start being trained by age one. I've seen a lot of parents use a floor-standing potty. Parents watch and catch the b.m. (bowel movement) in

131

the potty. Some parents get real rough—spanking the children, giving them harsh reprimands, not letting them get up. Because of this training, many children are in underpants and trained by the time they're two.

Carmen Cortez, Associate Director, Parenting Program

Having a baby toilet trained at an early age is part of being a good mother. Sometimes they punish the child as a way to teach them to use the toilet, but most of the time it's done in a good way.

Maty Brito, Mental Health Outreach Counselor

Chapter 29

Temperament, Personality, and Uniqueness of Each Child

Do parents see babies and children as unique and, if so, in what ways?

Do parents feel they can influence the kind of person their child becomes?

If so, what could a parent do to make a difference and in what areas?

Understanding how parents see children as unique and whether parents believe they can influence who their children become is a necessary starting point for some of our behavioral guidance with parents and their extended families.

I think they do think that babies have different personalities. They point it out to you, "This one is very quiet, this one is very intelligent." The mothers tell you which baby is good and which is bad.

Rosa Carreno, Community Health Worker

Mothers compare babies a lot, especially with regard to their development. For example, they'll say, "My older child crawled at five months; what's wrong with this one?" They don't compare personalities much. They might say one talks back, or is quieter, or one babbled more than its siblings.

Carmen Guedea, Parent Educator

The uniqueness they recognize is how much a child is like its family members—its mother, father, grandmother, or grandfather. They identify uniqueness as being a family trait, believing everything about a child is inherited. Therefore, it is not the child that is unique. If a child is talented in art when no one else in family was, the family would ignore the talent.

Dolores Ramirez, Multicultural Director

It's a double-edged sword. Parents realize that children are all different in terms of their personalities and temperaments. Yet, they treat all the kids the same whether they are shy or boisterous. Sometimes behaviors are attributed to a child ("We expected it because he's like so-and-so").

Carmen Cortez, Associate Director, Parenting Program

Our parenting program tries to teach parents about temperament. As part of our teaching we use a videotape showing children with different types of temperament. It helps the parents make sense of something they may not have considered before.

Linda Espinosa, Professor of Education and
Former Director of a Parenting Program

I've seen many parents who want to control, not influence, their children. They try to get their children to behave, to be obedient. An obedient child is a good child and reflects that the parent is doing his job. They believe they can have influence over whether their child becomes a "good child."

Dolores Ramirez, Multicultural Director

Some parents really like to teach their kids, to help their child's growth and development. They ask questions about ways to teach their children. But these are not the parents from rural areas, from the *ranchitos* [rahn·CHEE·tohs: small farms]. Those are the people I see.

Rosa Carreno, Community Health Worker

Sometimes they believe that they can make a difference in their child's life. It just depends on the person.

Maty Brito, Mental Health Outreach Counselor

It may be related to the Catholic influence, but there's a sense of "what will happen will happen." It's not a culture with a lot of history in organizing, planning, or trying to influence the future—especially among the rural, poor, uneducated population. That population uses a more day-to-day approach. With education, people become more future-oriented and start becoming more oriented to planning, organizing, and influencing what happens.

Linda Espinosa, Professor of Education and
Former Director of a Parenting Program

Chapter 30

Limit Setting with Infants, Toddlers, and Preschoolers

How are children expected to behave?
What do parents think the reasons are for very
young children misbehaving?
How do they teach their children not to
misbehave?
How does a young child know when his parents
are annoyed or pleased with him?

Limit-setting styles can provide important insights into children's behavior and the parent/child relationship. This chapter helps us understand how parents want their children to behave and the methods they use to achieve this. It sheds light on how parents talk to and listen to their children, on the parents' attitudes toward autonomy, and on teaching respect to children.

When babies do things they shouldn't, they're seen as being mischievous. Parents don't realize that children are naturally curious. Parents expect children to act like adults in terms of judgment (like not touching something that's breakable). So, if he does something he shouldn't, he'll probably get an ugly reprimand in a strong voice and a spank on the hand. Some parents say, "Get away from there! Don't touch that!" in a strong voice. Some will curse or call the child a demeaning name like "stupid" or whatever comes to mind.

Parents use a lot of commands rather than explanations. They also remove the child or the object. If the child keeps going back to the object, the parents believe the child is deliberately trying to make them mad. So the parents get angrier and there's more yelling and more hand slapping. Parents expect a child to behave and make judgments about right and wrong.

Carmen Cortez, Associate Director, Parenting Program

Safety is a big problem. The homes are not child-proofed. A child could take pills out of his mom's purse. Parents are sometimes harsh when they teach their children not to touch things. Children are not well-supervised and mostly get attention when they do something bad.

Dolores Ramirez, Multicultural Director

Parents feel that kids are doing something they're not supposed to be doing because they're bad. They're told, "Stop it, stop it! Leave it alone!" There's yelling and swatting. By nine months, the child has already learned he'll be swatted. He'll squint his eyes as his mother approaches with her hand or eyebrows raised and drop whatever he has. Swatting the child's hand is the main form of discipline.

If a child does a lot of things he shouldn't, the parents feel the child is a bad kid and needs to listen. Parents can become almost abusive, pulling the children's ears and hair, hitting them with belts, throwing shoes at them. If a child is curious and takes the radio apart, he gets a swat. Young children are reminded constantly of what they did and are told, "Don't do that again!"

Carmen Guedea, Parent Educator

Parents may have problems with their children's eating, toilet training, bathing, bedtime, and so on. Many children develop oppositional behavior. Parents' reactions tend to be spontaneous. Latino families yell and sometimes give a quick spank. There's a lot of immediate behavior on the parents' part. Parents are pretty expressive. They don't carefully think out how to guide their children so the children will learn a set of rules. A mother might say, "I keep yelling at him and telling him to eat his food, and he won't do it! We have tears every night because he won't go to bed."

Linda Espinosa, Professor of Education and
Former Director of a Parenting Program

Sometimes parents have all the toys in the closet and the kids don't have anything to play with. We have to go in and teach them that the kids need to be busy with their hands, that if you don't want them to touch this or that, you need to give them something to do. Parents think they can just say, "Don't touch it, don't touch it!" They don't move the baby away from what he shouldn't be touching and give him something else. Spanking or yelling is the way children know that parents are angry with them.

Rosa Carreno, Community Health Worker

I don't think parents really understand about natural curiosity. So many parents say, "Oh, he is being so terrible; he's not bad but he's a *pícaro* [PEE·kah·ro: a rascal]." I don't think they realize that the child is at an age where he needs to explore. More educated families do have a better understanding of this now.

It's part of our Latino culture that we get excited and scream when a child is either doing something dangerous or something that needs to be stopped. It's important to be culturally sensitive to the fact that the screaming is not abusive but just part of the culture and nature of the Latino people. Sometimes, because of all the stresses around, the mother just screams because having little children underfoot is one more thing she has to deal with. But the children just get used to it, I think, depending on the tone of voice. Even though there is a lot of screaming, the children know whether the screaming is angry or not.

When the child gets close to important papers like immigration papers, the parents get upset. They have no place else to put the papers. Also, children need to stay out of the kitchen: it's dangerous with all of the hot oils that are used for cooking.

Children also know when parents are happy with them because there is a lot of physical expression of affection. Fathers, especially with little boys, can be "rough," but it's the kind of rough that children love. Fathers roughhouse with their sons. Fathers say, "My little *machito*" [mah·CHEE·to].

Maty Brito, Mental Health Outreach Counselor

The parents believe that if they do a good job as parents, their children will be well-behaved. For example, parents encourage children to listen to the teacher when they go to school. But parents don't praise a child for what he's done well by saying something like, "What a great picture you made."

There's a lot of discipline going on ("Get off the tree; you shouldn't be on there."). They don't put it in a positive form like, "You climbed high, but you need to come down—and be very careful." And they don't explain why something should or shouldn't be done or give examples of what the child could do instead.

Many parents yell angrily, making eye contact and squinting at the child with a "You wait until we get home" look. Then there's a swat and a pinch.

Many children are very used to being yelled at, so when parents don't yell at them, when they smile at them, children don't know how to handle it. They laugh and giggle. Then the parent yells, "Shut up! Don't be silly." Children are excited to get their parents' attention, but then are told to shut up.

Carmen Guedea, Parent Educator

Discipline is usually in reaction to a crisis or in reaction to something that escalated. Maybe it's a little harsh. It's hard for families to regulate and be consistent, to develop regular responses. Their disciplining is more reactionary.

Linda Espinosa, Professor of Education and
Former Director of a Parenting Program

Latino culture believes that children are supposed to be seen but not heard, that they are supposed to respect their parents and not talk back. Kids are not listened to. Anglos encourage children to talk to them more and say how they're feeling ("If you don't feel like talking to me now, we can talk about it later."). With Latinos, it's more like "This is what you're supposed to do and, if you have a problem with that, then that's your problem; we won't discuss it."

With the hierarchical family structure, the youngest child has no say in the family. If a child is upset and has some feelings about it, the family won't listen to him. This varies with acculturation, and is especially true for recent immigrants. Parents believe in physical punishment, such as using the belt, without much explanation and without giving a child room for his own opinion and input.

Ana Morante, Outpatient (Mental Health) Case Worker

Usually parents expect the infants and toddlers to listen to the limit. The parents keep telling the child "if you do this, you'll get spanked." However, parents don't show the child another way to behave. Then they often say "I told you not to" and then may yell or spank in extreme anger when they see what happened. They view the outcome as completely the child's fault. Parents need to be reminded that very young children don't have a long memory for limits and that they as teachers of their children need to be more "proactive" than "reactive." Parents also need to learn more about follow-through.

Rosalie Prado de Ramirez, Public Health Nursing Supervisor

Parents do value having children under control and being obedient. The men especially value this. This way children don't run all over or talk disrespectfully to parents or other adults.

Linda Espinosa, Professor of Education and
Former Director of a Parenting Program

Good parents are judged by how their child behaves. This goes back to a child bringing honor or pride or shame to his family. A well-behaved child is one who is polite, quiet, and courteous in public. This child is a tribute to a parent; the parents are then seen as good.

Carmen Cortez, Associate Director, Parenting Program

If a child is afraid of you, that's considered respect. I try to teach that it's not respect and to encourage more parent/child interaction.

Carmen Guedea, Parent Educator

At home, if children value their lives, they are conditioned not to touch this or that because they'll get a good hard spanking if they do. The bigger and older the child, the more that is expected of him or her by the parents and the more they could get spanked.

Carmen Cortez, Associate Director, Parenting Program

With respect to limit setting, many Latino professionals were troubled by the idea that the child who is curious may come to see himself as a "bad" child and that punishment may be both too emotionally and physically harmful. The emphasis on good and obedient behavior is likely to interfere with some of a child's skills and future successes in this culture. The use of praise specific to a child's efforts may be too occasional. True communication, including parental interest in how the child is feeling, may also be too infrequent to allow a child to feel understood. We *can* help families *find other ways to maintain a sense of control* that does not sacrifice the child's curiosity, self-esteem, initiative, and that does not sacrifice the feeling of being understood by his family and others. Important areas of learning for the parents include understanding why children do what they do, how to talk and listen to children, and how to get cooperation without giving up their authority as parents. Approaches to getting cooperation include giving children reasons, helping them find substitute activities, praising them, giving them focused attention, and having them make amends for hurting someone's feelings or breaking someone's things, etc.

Do you feel that Mexican families view children differently than Anglo families and, if so, how?

Oh, definitely. Children in Mexico can go anywhere. You can take them to a nice restaurant and, instead of being frowned upon because they don't eat properly or because they drop something, it's considered acceptable. The parks in Mexico are made for children. Taking children anywhere is accepted. When Latino families take their children places here, the response isn't the same.

Also, the Latino attitude about parenting is different. In Mexican families you are with your child all of the time. With Anglo families, it is believed that if you take care of *yourself* you will be a better parent, that separation and distance are good for the child and will help him get used to other people. But in the traditional Mexican family, the child will stay with the family and have strong ties. There will be little contact with people other than the extended family. Part of being a good parent is taking your child everywhere with you. Also, there is the important concept, especially for women, of giving everything up so that your child will have everything. Women have been socialized to believe that children come first and they come second.

Renee Martinez, Professor of Child Development

Children are taken with the parents to visit people; you see children all over the place. Here we employ a baby-sitter and children are separated from adults in terms of socialization. They are no trouble in Mexico. Everyone is together, which makes it much easier for the child to be socialized.

Yolanda Torres, Child Care Consultant

How do the values of independence vs. interdependence affect Mexican children and families?

I work in child development and important issues in the research include those of independence and autonomy. In the U.S., you start letting the child become independent and move away from the mother at about the age of one-and-a-half to two years. That's also the age when breast feeding usually stops. With Mexicans, we are not so anxious to teach our children independence, because we have a collective community where you have family and extended family, and you have the *comadre* [ko·MAH·dreh: godmother] and the *compadre* [kohm·PAH·dreh: godfather]. Consequently, the group is more important than the individual in terms of raising a child.

By independence, I am also speaking about verbal independence. A Mexican child does not tell the parents what to do, what they themselves want to do, or their own ideas as much as the Anglo child would. Certainly, the Mexican parents take their child into account; it's not all "because I say so," but it's primarily the parents' wishes that come through rather than the child's. With Anglos in the U.S., immediate gratification takes precedence. But in the Mexican family, the child is expected to put aside immediate gratification for the good of the group. This is the basis for collectivism and group living.

Yolanda Torres, Child Care Consultant

I think tied in with the independence and autonomy is respect. We are taught respect in terms of formality in addressing adults. If you were educated in Mexico, as many of the parents were, the language is very formal. You address adults differently, the teachers differently—first because of age and then because of education. It's a very respectful kind of treatment that you give them. You don't just say "Hi" unless you are very, very well-acquainted.

Here, Latinos use nicknames, but, when push comes to shove, there is respect. In Spanish there are very formal phrases, and you know exactly how to behave with whom and when. It makes it much easier for the child.

Yolanda Torres, Child Care Consultant

Children don't learn about respect just by observation. You see, we have two words in Spanish for education or learning. One is *enseñanza* [ehn·sehn·YAHN·sah], which is learning things in school that are taught by a teacher. We have *educación* [eh·doo·kah·see·OHN], which is education and socialization at home on how to behave. When you take a child to visit, you prompt him to say, '"Hello, Mrs. So-and-so. I am very glad to meet you." He never says, "Hello, Mary." When you visit, the parents teach the children how to behave. It's the parents' responsibility to socialize the child, to not have the child embarrass them in public.

Yolanda Torres, Child Care Consultant

However, when parents are teaching the children (that is, when they are socializing them), parents may threaten with "We won't take you next time." Or they may use a form of teaching like "Remember what I told you: If you don't greet your aunt she is going to feel bad." Here in the U.S., if the aunt feels badly, well, the aunt should understand that he is a little kid. But that's not so in the Mexican culture. If a Mexican family isn't having to scramble for money and can put food on the table and the mother is at home, then she has the time to teach the child all of these values. But when they come to the U.S., if both the wife and husband have to work, which usually happens when you move to the U.S., and things are falling apart, the mother isn't home to teach values. This is where their sadness and despair comes in. You look at your child and think, "I don't have the time to do this for my child." It's very hard for the parents to see the child slipping away.

Yolanda Torres, Child Care Consultant

I would like to tell you some more about how we teach children respect in our culture. The details of respect are instilled through role modeling. Children don't see adults yelling at the grandparents. They see that one accepts and respects what their parents tell them, whether they agree with it or not;

they see that you do not discuss or argue in public. Another detail has to do with expecting children to respect the parental order or parental guidelines. Discipline is the way of setting guidelines and making sure these guidelines are carried out. In the Latino culture, you do not argue with your mother. Your mother is inherently right, whether you agree with her or not. Negotiation is almost questioning authority, and you don't question authority. So when you want to teach form of discipline other than spanking, negotiating is not an option for the Latino family because the parents feel that they will lose authority over the child. We need to teach parents and children ways that allow the parents to keep control. There are ways that the child can discuss things with parents and question them without making the parents lose respect. Teaching that is an art—an art that is developed through experience.

Josie Romero, Clinical Social Worker and
Director of a Family Institute

If the main forms of discipline are hand slapping, yelling, and spanking, how do children develop self-respect and respect for their peers?

The spanking doesn't go on forever. The children learn very quickly because, along with this hand hitting, there is an extended family and always somebody to love you or comfort you. In a nuclear family, there are not other adults around to do this. In a Mexican family, the grandmother or the aunt or the neighbor are always there. In a Mexican neighborhood, every child belongs to the neighbors, so you can be disciplined by the neighbor *and* comforted by them. I am very happy that people immigrate in families and come to live in Mexican neighborhoods because, otherwise, I don't know how they would do it. I know that people expect that the family should assimilate quickly and stop living with all those relatives, but this is a very lonely country. I think the discipline is softened by the numbers of adults around. Also, if the family is intact, all the father has to do is look at the kids and that is that.

Yolanda Torres, Child Care Consultant

The Latino culture is a different culture, a different way of raising kids, which I don't think is better or worse—it just works in other countries. It may not work here, but we should respect other ways of living and the way they want to raise their kids. They may be right about some things.

Victoria Orozco, Family Resource Specialist

The Hispanic family is not like the American family in that Americans talk to their children all of the time. In the Hispanic family, the adults are together and the children are together. To compete with the American children, verbal skills are very important. That is part of the re-educating of the parents. I also tell parents that I am not interfering in their lives or their culture. I tell them I know they want to do the best thing for their child and that following some suggestions might help. Communication between parents and children is a problem. Children are children and adults are adults and they don't communicate like American families. But the parents are willing to try what I suggest if they feel I want the best for their child—because that's what they want, too.

Flora Fortis, School Psychologist

Chapter 31

Limit Setting with Older Children

How does discipline work as the child gets older?

What happens to children's behavior as they become school age?

What is different about the way children can be treated in Mexico?

What is important for parents to learn about limit setting?

What do you do to help them learn?

Here, it is valuable to notice the impact on both children and parents when families continue to use an authoritarian style as the child grows older and experiences other limit-setting styles through his contact with teachers and other students in school. There is also a lot of discussion about parents learning about this impact through parenting classes. Note the connections between spanking, the use of physical power to make others do what you want, and violence.

Authoritarianism is a common style of discipline. When children are small, parents can be very direct, saying things like, "Get into bed" and "Do it now or else!" Because they can control children when they're small, that's not a problem. But an authoritarian style of discipline doesn't work well in this country. Too many Mexican parents who think children should be seen and not heard are still too physical in their discipline.

Using this more authoritarian and physically punitive approach with older children is difficult because children challenge their parents. Kids can get out of control and parents haven't developed any tools to change their techniques with their older children. Children, especially adolescents, often have outside influences that parents at home can't control. Outside pulls, like gangs, may be too strong. It's difficult enough for an intact family; it's harder yet for a single parent. Parents tell me that their kids run wild and the parents believe that the reason children have so many problems in the U.S. is because you can't hit your kids here. I tell parents that it's not against the law to discipline children; its against the law to physically hurt or abuse them.

Maria Reyes, Social Worker

Commands and swats are used a lot to get children not to destroy things and to be respectful. "Children need spanking." That's approved; there's no other way to do it. It is believed that children should be seen but not heard. A good child should be an obedient child. The parents want their children to be *los niños bien educados* [lohs NEEN·yohs byehn eh·doo·KAH·dohs: well-socialized children]. Children learn to obey out of fear: they want to avoid being hit. Children are frequently told that *they* are either good or bad, not that their *behavior* is good or bad. This is soaked into the child's being.

A small percentage of parents in our parenting groups disapprove of this type of child rearing as too strict, and they attempt to change how they raise their own children before coming to class. But the majority don't think about this until they come to parenting class where the others speak out. Parent educators try to teach parents to express disapproval in terms of good behavior and bad behavior, rather than good children or bad children. This is a hard concept for parents to learn. It's related to religion: if you're good you go to heaven; if you're bad you go to hell. This concept is very strong and is reflected in what they reward and punish their children for.

In some families, small children are seen as entertaining, so a toddler will be allowed to get away with murder. But when it's not "cute" anymore, the parents will hit the child. Children are usually taught to be well-behaved by age five or six, but things change when they get into school. They have been trained to be obedient at home with an authoritarian person in charge—the father or the father and mother. They go to school and the teachers have different styles and expectations than the parents. Parents have used fear to instill obedience in children. Children become confused; the other children at school may not be obedient. Mexican children notice that the others run around and get away with murder. They wonder, "Why can't I?" By middle school, peer pressure is strong and may prevail unless the family is *very* strong. There is a lot of conflict between parents and kids, beginning when the child enters kindergarten. Parents start to become uncertain and may try to control with stronger limits and stronger punishment or give up on setting limits and trying to control their children.

Dolores Ramirez, Multicultural Director

As children start to go to school and see the style of the more American kids, they get in touch with a more modern style of communication. In first grade, Mexican children are often inhibited. They're not talking much because of their home influence. But as soon as they have more experience with the other kids, Mexican children might become more direct in the way they talk with their parents and friends. Later, the children may want to express their opinion, which is not well-taken by traditional Mexican parents. The more educated and acculturated parents might be accepting of this. In traditional families, the parents and children become increasingly unhappy and angry with each other's behavior. Children may withdraw from their parents.

A lot of 8- or 9-year-olds threaten to "call the cops" if their parents hit them again. Kids learn from each other about this option. Many parents can be frightened by this threat. Only a few parents say, "You can call whoever you want; I'll still do what I think is best"—especially those parents who know they didn't do anything wrong. Other parents, who may be less informed, may feel there is nothing they can do to control their kids. They believe kids only obey out of fear. I try to help them learn about and choose alternatives to physical punishment.[9] I encourage parents to listen to their kids and find out what their kids like and don't like. These likes and dislikes can then be used as consequences for bad behavior. However, I suggest they make sure their children know that, even though the parents are listening to them, they won't necessarily agree with them and the parents are not giving up their authority.

Ana Morante, Outpatient (Mental Health) Case Worker

---

[9]She is referring to the same approaches to limit setting that are taught to any parents. These include parents explaining the reasons behind their rules, hearing their children's thoughts and feelings about issues, providing supervision for the children, motivating a child to want to accept the rules, praising children, using consequences, etc.

If a family is traditionally authoritarian, whatever the husband wants is what is done. The husband is not used to explaining his reasons. Wives have to succumb to their husbands' decisions, even if the reasons are vague and they don't understand them. For example, he might like it to be quiet in the evening; he might be permissive about bedtime; he might be a "good guy" and not correct a child about roughhousing. The wife can't really confront her husband, though she might be feeling very angry. Eruptions can result from this built-up anger. The mother takes it out on the kids. She feels helpless; she can't change the situation with her husband. There is more built-up anger in the wife toward the husband than vice versa. It comes from poor communication skills and a lack of expression of personal feelings.

Dolores Ramirez, Multicultural Director

A mother who takes some parenting skills training may disagree with the father about hitting the children, but in most things she goes along with him. Women often try to avoid conflict with their husbands. It's expected that women will be less powerful than the men.[10]

Maty Brito, Mental Health Outreach Counselor

A mother may like the new ideas she learns about parenting and want to try them, but if she has a husband who is not cooperative, it's hard to try them out. If the Latino male is too set in his ways, it's very difficult. Lots of the moms come to the meetings and seem more open to making changes in their ways of raising their children. Yet they say, "My husband won't approve; my husband isn't interested."

Spanking has immediate results. Parents are being taught to replace spanking with something else. Parents most readily use what they learned as children: spanking, reprimanding by yelling or taking something away. They say things like "be still; be quiet; wait till your dad gets home; I'll talk to you later." They don't tend to think about other ways. They don't have knowledge about other ways of limit setting. Once they learn about different ways, they may also be impatient because the new methods don't have the immedi-

---

[10]For further information on the roles of mothers and fathers, see Chapter 22 (p.97) and 23 (p. 101).

ate results that they're used to. When we teach them new methods, we also have to teach them that the new different methods will take a while to show results.

Beatriz Cerrillo, Family Resource Specialist

In the parenting classes I teach, I deal a lot with self-esteem and punishment because our laws here are different from Mexico's. If you spank a child in Mexico, it is no big deal. Over here, if you spank a child and you leave bruises, we call Children's Protective Services. So we have to re-educate the parents. Discipline is a big thing in our work with parents. We cover issues like how to discipline your child, how to value your child, and how to begin to pay more attention to your child. We don't have a written program available. The few programs available on these topics are mostly for the middle-class parent.[11] Things are different for those Mexicans who may have been working in the fields all day. They come home and the last thing they want is to sit down and read a book to their child. So our program has to be molded to their needs. The three things that we focus on are self-esteem, discipline, and how to communicate better with your child.

Flora Fortis, School Psychologist

Latino children from traditional families are not talked to about what they think and what they feel. We try to teach parents how important it is to encourage a child to express his feelings and have his parents be interested. I try to get parents to take their child out for a walk or just outside where there is some privacy and get him to talk about and focus on his feelings—what made him happy or sad. There are many things that might have hurt him and he doesn't know how he feels or why he is upset or angry. Talking about feelings helps release tension. I try to help parents understand why the child may feel certain ways. I'm 30 and I was never allowed to talk about my feelings. Latinos have to go to a therapist to talk about feelings. First our parents drive us crazy and then they drive us to therapy.

Carmen Guedea, Parent Educator

[11]See Appendix E: Resources for a list and description of useful parenting education programs designed for low-income, limited education Latino families.

When I talk to parents about their children's behavior, I begin with saying that we want the best for their children, that I am not imposing my style on them, that these are just suggestions, and that I am trying to help them help their children succeed. My theme is that parents are the mirror of their children, so how they treat and value their children is important. I tell them that this is the U.S. and they have to follow the rules. I also tell them that middle-school children need to feel proud of who they are because living in two cultures can be very confusing and hard. We also get a lot of questions from the parents. They are very situational questions: "My 15-year-old won't obey me. How do I get him to mind me?" Again, most of the parenting books are written for the middle class and say things like, "If your child doesn't behave, send him to his room." What if he doesn't have a room? We have to help parents make the best of what they have, so we tell them to find a quiet corner for the child to go to. I also encourage the parents in the group to help each other. That way they get advice from their peers; it's not always me telling them what to do. When they go home, they think, "Oh, yes, Mrs. Rodrigues had the same problem and she handled it this way." They can relate to that.

Flora Fortis, School Psychologist

Parents need to learn to take time to explain their rules to their kids, for example: why they shouldn't hit other kids, not just that they shouldn't. Some people (including kids) like to break rules, so it's important that they know why they shouldn't. Parents aren't used to teaching this or explaining these kinds of things to their children. Kids are given rules without being given the reasons behind the rules. It's not enough.

Victoria Orozco, Family Resource Specialist

Home educators help families learn how to discipline their children to help the children fit in at the beginning of kindergarten—to be able to listen without being yelled at, to be cooperative, to know about time-out, to be ready to accept kindergarten practices. A child who is disciplined aggressively at home will expect aggressive discipline from a teacher. If a parent can incorporate some of the school's approaches to discipline, the child will be able to make an easier and smoother transition to school.

Each child in a family responds to something different. Parents need to have the tools and knowledge to try different approaches and make the appropriate changes. When parents don't know about other methods of discipline, they are stuck in the one way they are used to. That's a problem for parents of school-age children. Sometimes, parents may need to spank—and that's OK as long as parents have other methods to choose from and are not just doing what their parents did.

Beatriz Cerrillo, Family Resource Specialist

Adapting to the need for new methods of discipline is very upsetting for parents, especially when they don't have any new methods to use. When we talk about children and school, I try to teach parents to have more of a partnership with their children's teachers about methods of discipline and expectations about listening, raising hands, and giving answers. I suggest that they ask for time off of work to go to the schools' open-houses. (Many parents don't realize that employers might give them time off). I advise parents that what worked in Mexico was great there because that's where the children lived, but now that they live in the U.S. they have to change their methods in order to prepare their children for life here. We try not to put any culture down. We don't say that what they did was wrong or that everything we do in the U.S. is the best.

Dolores Ramirez, Multicultural Director

In parenting, you really need to convince parents that knowing what their child is doing and why he's doing it is important. There is a misuse of time-outs that is very authoritarian. You have to convince parents that changing the way they discipline is for the child's betterment. A lot of Mexican families use "tough love" with teens—it's very authoritarian and thus familiar. We need to go back to the issue of control and help them see that the important thing is to help the child control himself.

Renee Martinez, Professor of Child Development

A central theme is that the authoritarian, more punitive style doesn't work for the child as he grows up in the U.S. culture. Many approaches to "reaching" Mexican parents and helping them understand their children's behavior are discussed. There's an emphasis on parents learning to explain the reasons behind their rules, on increasing the respect the father shows toward the mother, on listening to a child's views and feelings, on giving praise, and on using more relevant consequences as discipline to help a child learn. Many professionals have had success with using parenting groups to teach new disciplinary approaches.

Many families don't think there is a better way to discipline children, so I try to be very patient and teach them to discipline in a different way, but this takes time. Punishing is still the main way they choose to try to change their children's behavior. I think this form of discipline is an important thing to change, and this is one of the hardest things for parent educators to help parents do. We need to teach them different ways of disciplining their kids so they'll have some options. Parents always ask me why they shouldn't spank their children. I tell them that we want to provide positive discipline so that the kids will learn how they should behave. There's no guarantee that spanking will keep the child from doing the same thing again. The child doesn't connect the spanking with the misbehavior. If we hit children, we are teaching them that punishment, spanking, and hitting are good ways to make other people do what we want them to do. This teaches children to be violent. This is probably one of the main concerns about punishment. But we don't tell parents just to stop doing it. We advise them to look for a different way to teach their kids discipline, to try to avoid using physical punishment.

There's a small difference between physical abuse and punishment, and people might not be able to tell the difference. It's important for parents to understand this. Physical punishment of children is not illegal in Mexico.

There are lots of problems with regard to the physical abuse of children—not only in Mexico but in other Latin American countries as well. In Mexico, there are no laws to protect a child. It's the same with the abuse of women. Men feel that they have the right to physically beat or abuse their women and nobody can do anything about it. "My wife is my possession and I can do anything I want with her." This is the traditional way; now things are changing. Now there is more concern in Mexico about the rights of women and children. It's a good step. But it's hard work to change the adult's perception of this.

People from small towns are very different from those from large cities due to their lack of access to education. It is very important to know what services Mexicans were used to before coming here (social services, medical services, etc.). This can help us provide services in a better way. People from big cities have access to new advice, new education, and parenting classes. For example, there might be a program on the radio on how to raise children. This could make a difference in how parents raise their children. People from big cities also have more access to schools. Education will probably help change the way they raise their kids.

When parents come here, especially from the small towns, it's hard for them to understand that the laws on child abuse exist to protect the kids. "They are my kids; I have the right to do with my kids whatever I want to do. And nobody has the right to stop me." When the values that have been normal throughout your life are challenged, you protest. "My parents and my parents' parents had the right to hit their kids. Why do I lose that right when I move to the U.S.?" We are trying to work with the parents so they can see what their rights are.

When I first came to the U.S., I volunteered for an agency and learned for the first time about the concept of domestic violence. I was surprised. I worked with women who were victims. I saw how this related to abuse between men and women in their relationships. It was mostly men using violence against women. Our children are seeing this violence and feeling this violence; they are victims of this violence. They see it with other families, friends, on the streets, on the television, in school—everywhere. Kids learn that power is the way to resolve differences and they try to force other people to do what they want them to do.

Raul Rojas, Parent Educator and Community Outreach Coordinator

Although there are some things that need to be changed, we have a lot of good things going for us. We have to recognize the strengths and get rid of those aspects of the culture that don't work. Parents need to learn how they can discipline without hitting. We need to teach them the difference between discipline and punishment, teach parents that they don't need to be physical to teach children about consequences. I try to teach other ways to discipline and also ways to reward and give recognition for good behavior. The parents' ability to learn depends both on their abilities and their problems.

Maria Reyes, Social Worker

When we ask parents about their childhood memories of spanking, some remember how they felt and feel it didn't always work; some feel it made them into the good people they are today. We give parents spanking guidelines and child-abuse laws. Sometimes Mexican parents think American parents are too permissive and that American-reared children show disrespect for authority. It's important for parents not to feel that they would have been doing fine if the American laws hadn't gotten in their way. It's also important for their kids not to blame the schools for their failures ("They didn't teach me English; they didn't pay attention to me because I was Mexican.")

Dolores Ramirez, Multicultural Director

Every child needs a different form of discipline. Some kids need a light spanking because it is all they respond to. Some families spank too much. I don't believe in keeping children in their rooms for long periods, but I do believe in giving them a half-hour lecture, which they hate, and having them write things over and over—it's very boring.

Victoria Orozco, Family Resource Specialist

When children do things we think are wrong, we should be careful not to take the authority away from the parents. A child shouldn't suddenly sense that their parents' authority is gone. If the parents don't keep their authority in the child's eyes, respect disappears. If a child loses respect for his parents, he loses respect for everything.

Victoria Orozco, Family Resource Specialist

Chapter 32

Girls' and Boys' Roles

What responsibilities do children typically have at home and at what ages do they start?
What differences, if any, are there in what is expected of boys and girls?
What are the ways in which they are treated differently?

In this chapter, we explore the beginnings of gender and role learning. Some of the Latino professionals would like to educate families about modifying the strong role divisions.[12]

A mother will give more responsibility to the girl. Usually boys don't go to the kitchen; they don't do "girl" jobs. Even if the girl is ten years old and the boy is twelve, she will fix his lunch because boys are not in the kitchen. This is how girls begin serving men. The mother will teach the daughter at a very early age how to do chores in the house. The boys will go shopping for dinner or something like that, but only because parents think it would be dangerous for the girls. The mother will do more things for the boys—give them presents, do things he likes, make him food. A boy takes the role of protecting his sisters. At an older age, he takes the role of the father. If the father doesn't have a job, the son is expected to take care of and help the family.

Rosa Carreno, Community Health Worker

---

[12]See Chapter 23 (p.101) for a detailed discussion of mothers' and fathers' roles.

Boys are expected to play more roughly with each other than girls. They say, "Oh, it's the boys, it's normal. Let them play." When boys fall down, they are not supposed to cry. They need to be macho men. When they cry, mom may say, "You're not supposed to cry; you're not a baby girl." They emphasize the word *girl*. If a girl gets mildly hurt and makes a big deal of it, it's considered OK for her to cry, even if she's eleven or twelve. But a boy needs to be tough—a little *hombre* [OHM·breh: man]. Children are given these messages at an early age. When the girls are eight or nine years old, they start to help their mothers. A mother will teach the girls home skills, mothering skills. Boys are not expected to do home chores. When a boy gets older, the father may take him to work with him. But he won't take the girls.

Maty Brito, Mental Health Outreach Counselor

Girls are taught that they're not supposed to play outdoors as much; boys are sent outside more. Girls of school age are expected to wash dishes, sweep the floor, pick up after themselves and their brothers, cook, clean house, crochet, and embroider. Boys don't do any of that; they're told to go do whatever they want to do outdoors. Boys are not responsible for housework, and males become very dependent on the women. When they're old enough, a boy will help his father with cleaning up the yard if they live in a house. If they live in an apartment, boys don't do much. They become more street smart and learn how to fight and protect themselves. Fathers want their children to do well—especially the boys. Mothers don't expect their daughters to have a different life. Girls are taught that they have to listen to what men say. They can go to grammar school, but, here in Salinas, they often have to stop going to school to help in the fields. A girl can find a boyfriend in the fields, not just in school. I believe that sons need to learn to take care of themselves as well as daughters do. Boys and girls should both be taught indoor and outdoor jobs. There shouldn't always have to be a woman around to do things for them.

Carmen Guedea, Parent Educator

Boys are expected to have responsibilities when they become men and get jobs. Until then, they are often not expected to anything but play. In some families, the father will have the boy get a job when he's 11 or 12 years old (like a newspaper route or shining shoes). At an early age, girls start helping with chores, with siblings, doing dishes and laundry, and sweeping. Girls often learn to be manipulative to get what they want from their fathers. They learn to be pretty and coquettish, but not too coquettish (or they're considered a whore). They learn to be nice and sweet and passive (but with an agenda). Boys are spoiled by their mothers; they get anything they want from her. Sons manipulate their mothers. Once they reach their teens, boys are not obedient to their mothers and it's hard for mothers to control them. A lot of responsibility may be placed on the eldest son—especially when the father isn't there anymore. But that only works if the boy has been trained in responsible directions.

In our parenting classes, we are trying to lessen some of this gender stereotyping. I have parents do a chores chart that includes all the children, regardless of gender. The chores include vacuuming and washing dishes, and the kids trade jobs each day. I tell parents to let the baby observe and one day he'll be on list, too. Our parenting class tries to encourage the idea that girls should have a chance to explore their interests and be able to choose who they marry. Parents tend to feel that a girl doesn't need school or further education.

Dolores Ramirez, Multicultural Director

Males are encouraged to get away with more and females are taught the basic survival skills. If there are only male children, males might take over some of the traditional female household jobs; but if there were, for example, three brothers and one sister, then the sister would do them all.

Renee Martinez, Professor of Child Development

The strong distinctions between boys' and girls' roles are slowly fading away—but that's only recently started to happen. The girls are still more protected as far as going out. The boys are allowed to venture into the community more than the girls. The girls are also indoctrinated into doing housework. The boys don't do the "female" work. If the boy is the oldest, he in a sense becomes the father of the other kids; he can boss the other children around, but he is also responsible for them. I also think that if push comes to shove as far as higher education goes, it will be the son who is helped by the mother to get to college because he is going to be the head of a household someday. This is assuming the family has a little money.

Yolanda Torres, Child Care Consultant

Chapter 33

Family Days/Family Time

What do families do on their days off?
Do parents feel the need to go places without
their children?
If so, who will take care of the children?

Saturdays, parents stay home if they don't need to be at work. They do the wash and the yard work. On Sunday, they go to church in the morning, then the whole family goes shopping to buy groceries, etc. Everyone comes along on errands, partly out of necessity but also because families do things together. Children are not protected from adult conversations (again, maybe because there is no place for adults to go to be alone). In the evening, the family might barbecue outside or maybe relatives will come over.

Carmen Guedea, Parent Educator

Families like to go to church on Sunday. They like to get together with friends. It's a day that the father drinks. Men start out drinking socially, but it sometimes goes further. There is less drinking here than in Mexico. Sunday is the father's day off from work and he takes the whole family out.

Rosa Carreno, Community Health Worker

Recreation is a family affair. The father, but not the mother, may have some recreation without the family.

Dolores Ramirez, Multicultural Director

They like to spend free time cooking-out, maybe in a public park; they enjoy spending their time with other relatives and friends (*compadres* [kohm·PAH·drehs]). Kids play outside. Women talk and cook. Men play cards. Families don't usually make plans to go places without the kids. They often take their young kids with them. They might leave the younger children with older siblings for some periods—but not for long. Parents might even pull older kids out from school to take care of their younger siblings. The older child might be a 10- or 11-year-old and the younger child a preschooler. Our parenting program doesn't consider this safe.

Carmen Cortez, Associate Director, Parenting Program

On Sundays, first the families go to church, then they may go to the park. Sundays are like the magic days; they're the days that the parents don't have to work. Sometimes families get together and the men play dominoes and the women talk. Going to the park is a way that parents show their love to their family. Because they have little money, going to the park is an inexpensive way to have some pleasure. Parents hardly ever leave the children but, when they do, it's always with someone they know well—maybe a relative. They want these people to treat the child like they do—with a lot of love and care.

Maty Brito, Mental Health Outreach Counselor

They rarely go out without the kids. Maybe they'll go to the doctor's without them. But, when they do, the children usually stay with another family that has kids. If it's a single parent, she will leave the children with a friend. The parents want the baby-sitter to feed and protect the children while they are away.

Rosa Carreno, Community Health Worker

Most children go to church with their relatives. Mexican parents don't use sitters much. If the parents have to go somewhere without their children, a relative or an older child takes care of them.

Linda Espinosa, Professor of Education and
Former Director of a Parenting Program

If the family is Catholic, they usually go to church. Then having a picnic in the park is popular; sports are popular—especially soccer. Music is very important—*mariachis* [mah·ree·AH·chees] or *conjuntos* [kohn·HOON·tohs: small groups of musicians] may play. Dances and bars are popular with men (they drink beer). Families spend time visiting with friends, seeing *compadres*. Of course, it depends on the number of friends they have here in the U.S. They don't typically join clubs. There are very few Latino clubs. Latinos have lots of fun in the park. They love music and laughter. There are jokes, joyousness, spontaneity, and emotional release. Latinos are warm, loud, hugging-and-touching people.

Dolores Ramirez, Multicultural Director

PART IV

THE SCHOOL
EXPERIENCE

Chapter 34

The School System in Rural Mexico

What is the school system like in rural/
*   semi-rural Mexico?*
Do most children go to school?
What are the teaching methods like?
What are the differences between schools in
*   Mexico and those in the U.S.?*

This chapter helps us better understand what expectations parents and children have of schools, based on their experiences in Mexico. This is an important starting point in understanding why their school experience in the U.S. is so very different for them.

You need to remember that Mexico is not like the U.S. Things in the small towns are very primitive, even in towns that have a lot of people. The school system in Mexico is not like the system here. In the small towns in Mexico there are schools, but for people who come from the *ranchitos* [rahn·CHEE·tohs: small farms], the schooling is very minimal. A lot of the children work in fields, even in the small towns, so they don't go to school as consistently as they would here. Many of the children who come here have never been to school. In Mexico, as in other Latin American countries, there are social classes, and if you are part of the middle or upper class, you typically go to private school (which is Catholic school). And if you are part of the lower class, you go to public school or no school.

Flora Fortis, School Psychologist

There are schools like one-room school houses in some of the small towns, but the towns need to have a certain number of people before there will be a school. The schools teach only reading and writing—enough so that the children can read elementary books (up to the third grade level) and write enough to be able to sign documents. There is an emphasis on calligraphy in the schools because they want to make sure that people will be able to sign their names clearly. There is a lot of drill and practice on letter formation. Because many adults in rural Mexico cannot make the letters of their name, they use lines or symbols to sign things. The government wants everyone to be able to sign (handwriting, not printing) their names on legal documents. There is an emphasis on neatness in school because of this. On the *ranchos* [RAHN·choes: ranches] or *ranchitos*, children may have to walk two or three miles to get to a school, or there may be no school for them at all. It is also difficult to get teachers to go into these small rural towns because the pay is very low and the living conditions are quite primitive. Many teachers feel that after all the years of their own education, they want to work in a bigger, more urban town or city. At all levels, children need to buy and bring to school their own books, pencils, and paper.

It has only been in the last 10 to 12 years that many of these schools in rural towns have been established. So the parents in rural areas may never have been to school themselves and do not see or know the value in education. What's valuable for them is having their children learn to work in the fields. Teachers are respected and looked up to, but for some families it is difficult for the parents to understand the value of school for their children because they can't see the children being in any setting other than living on the ranch and working in the fields. There is no law in Mexico that requires children to go to school, but school is encouraged now by the government. The public schools go from kindergarten to sixth grade, but the level of teaching is very basic—enough so that the children will not be illiterate. After sixth grade, most of the rural children do not go to school. Many do not even stay in school through the sixth grade because they need to work. There is something called Sunday school in many of the rural areas. This is more for the children who live on the *ranchos* and *ranchitos*. Volunteers from different churches (Protestant, Jehovah's Witness, Seventh Day Adventist, etc.) go from small rural town to small rural town or *rancho* to *rancho* to teach the children primarily religion and secondarily reading and writing. But, again, it is on a very elementary level.

If children go onto *preparatoria*[13] [preh·pah·rah·TOH·ryah], they must go to a larger town and leave home. This is very rarely done. Also, there is an enormous amount of paperwork and red tape that they need to go through. After sixth grade, education must be paid for. There are some private foundations that may help rural children go further in their education, but very few.

Rita Rossi, Librarian and Resource Center Staff

The rural Mexican educational system is based on a traditional, conservative model. The emphasis is on learning by memorization, recitation, and copying, and there is a lot of value placed on neatness and organization. Critical thinking is not emphasized. The educational system does not use a hands-on discovery approach. In more urban settings and larger cities, though, the educational innovations and approaches are more similar to those in the U.S.

In Latin America, there's a big difference between private and public schools and between education in rural and urban areas. Private school is very popular because it's inexpensive for the middle class. Public schooling may be deficient because they lack resources and materials. There are too many children. A private school has more control of its setting and resources. In Mexico, going to private school is not the snobbish issue that it may be here. In Mexico, parents don't have the input into public school that they have in the U.S., and private school can be a good recourse.

In small towns there is often a school building, but the teachers are itinerant—appointed by the government. Once appointed, they are delegated to the area. They can't find housing, so they don't come to teach regularly and education is not consistent. Some schools have no supplies, so supplies have to come from home. The schoolhouse has benches, but the children have to bring everything else they need. Depending on the teacher, the teaching could be excellent or extremely poor. I've heard of children being beaten in school and being terrified of their teacher. That's not institutional; it's individual. Mexico is large and some rural areas are so inaccessible that there's very little supervision of teachers. Teachers may not feel comfortable in rural areas. Rural areas are culturally different from urban areas. There's a lot of tension and conflict for these teachers, many of whom are young. A lot of families look up to them because they are teachers. They look up to them as advisors and guides, and that's a heavy load.

Alice del Pinal, School Psychologist

---

[13]Beyond the basic six years of elementary schooling (usually between the ages of approximately 6 and 14, there is a basic high school education, sometimes referred to as secundaria [seh·koon·DAH·ryah], which requires three years to complete. There is a more advanced level, preparatoria [preh·pah·rah·TOH·ryah], which requires an additional two to three years to complete. At preparatoria, students usually focus on the subject they will major in when they go to the university.

Chapter 35

School in the U.S.:
The Experience for Children and Their Parents

What is going to school in the U.S. like for Mexican children from rural backgrounds?

How do the children and parents view the school, the teachers, and the family's role in the school?

What works well and what is problematic for the children and the families with regard to school?

In this more extensive chapter, there is a lot of emphasis on the adjustments children have to make. Teaching parents why we socialize and educate children the way we do in the U.S. is also emphasized. This is seen as a necessary step toward having the parents understand why their children seem to be changing in ways parents often see as problematic at home. It also helps them begin to make some changes in the ways they relate to their children. The important but often mismatched relationship between the parents and the school is also discussed—with an eye toward both parents and the school modifying their expectations of each other.

What is going to school in the U.S. like for Mexican children?

First, in this population, most parents came from poor areas and didn't have the opportunity to go to school. They don't know how to read or write and school is not their first priority in life. The first priority is to make money to live, because without it they can't survive. When the children start school, they often start without much encouragement or incentive from home, without, for example, parents helping them to read. Because parents may not be able to read or write, they can't help the child with his homework. Also, many of the parents only speak Spanish. English is also a new language for many of the children, and, because they think mostly in Spanish, they're often confused when they first go to school. The teachers need to take all of this into account.

It is different when a child comes from an environment that is free of major stresses, where they have a good breakfast and their mother is with them. Many of the Mexican children here face a great deal of stress in their home life. They may not have enough food or money; they may live with a lot of people in a tiny apartment. Many of the children lived their early childhood in Mexico, moved to a new country with a new language, and don't understand why. Their mothers and fathers are both working. It's hard, at first, for the children to be free of stress and concentrate in the classrooms.

Maty Brito, Mental Health Outreach Counselor

Young children love school; they get to dress up. It's an important part of their lives. They have no real trouble adjusting to school, especially after the first few weeks. They fall in love with their teacher. Language is a problem, though.

Linda Espinosa, Professor of Education and
Former Director of a Parenting Program

Parents usually prefer to start their children in school when they're a little older—when they are around six years old. But more families are starting to put their kids in pre-kindergarten. We tell them that the kids won't be studying a lot in pre-kindergarten and that the school will also let them have time to play.

Rosa Carreno, Community Health Worker

Parents want their children to start school as late as possible with regard to age. They feel it's a mother's role to be with her children and teach them to be well-behaved. Many families have to send their children to pre-kindergarten or preschool because both parents work. They do it because they have to, not because they want to.

Maty Brito, Mental Health Outreach Counselor

In our experience, parents have no problem with their children attending a formal preschool by the time they're three years old.

Linda Espinosa, Professor of Education and
Former Director of a Parenting Program

Children are often very social and outgoing at school. They like to sit on the floor, hug, and hold hands. They like singing, dancing, and cooking. They're very food-oriented and they love art and hands-on experiences. They are very sensuous, outgoing children; they have to taste and smell.

Graciela Ybarra, Resource Teacher

Children start school at kindergarten, or sometimes as preschoolers at age 3-1/2 or 4. We really encourage parents to let their children go to preschool because children learn there. Children love their teachers, and whatever the teacher says, the parent believes. Parents praise the teacher almost like a god. Throughout school, parents revere teachers. Their children learn a lot from teachers and the parents love the school. They're proud of it, and they take newcomers to see the school.

However, children are nervous about going to school; they cry a lot during the first two weeks. It's overwhelming; they've never been separated from home; it's a new setting for them. Even though children are not talked to a lot by parents, they're still used to being at home with their mother. Their teacher may not speak Spanish. It's hard to get kids to follow rules, especially around circle time when they're in kindergarten. Children are not used to a routine. They have problems adjusting to school. They might go to play with blocks during story time. They learn fairly well. As soon as they understand the routines of kindergarten, they have the routines of the next grade to get used to. Children, though, catch on fairly well by the second grade.

Carmen Guedea, Parent Educator

How do you help the parents feel more comfortable with leaving their children at the center because they have to go to work?

Separation is hard in any culture. I've worked at some child care centers where they rush the parents away and don't let the parent or child grieve enough. It's hard to leave a crying child day after day, and grief has to be acknowledged. If the parent can see that the child is being held, that it will be OK, and that the people at the center understand the parent's grief, the parent can feel that the center is a good place—that it really does understand the child and understands what the parent is feeling: "I am separating and it hurts and my child is separating and it hurts." We have to have this empathy. Once we do, we can begin to look at the cultural issues and be able to explain to the parents that everything will be all right.

Yolanda Torres, Child Care Consultant

If in the Anglo culture you can tell the parent that their child is learning to be more independent, what can you say to the Mexican parents who don't value independence so highly?

I think we can talk to the Mexican families about what the child is learning through the experiences of painting, block playing, etc. You can emphasize to the parents all that the child is learning, not in terms of the independence but in terms of being educated.

Yolanda Torres, Child Care Consultant

How do you talk to Mexican families about the value of independence in the U.S. culture?

That's why it's important to have bilingual and bicultural people teaching a cultural group: the teacher needs to understand the particular culture's philosophy of raising a child and understand that this child has to bridge two cultures. If you explain to the parents about independence and autonomy and how it helps the child here in the U.S., it doesn't mean that the parents are going to give up their culture to have their child be that independent. But it's important for the parents to understand the reasons for their children's behavior in terms of the culture here in the U.S.—to understand why their children are speaking out and questioning the parents as they see their friends doing. This is why it's so important to have bilingual and bicultural staff who can explain these things to the parents and who can understand the parent's conflict about them. If a young child goes home and begins to speak out, he can really be put down by his family. This really confuses a very young child. In a sense, the U.S. culture is saying, "We know better than your parents," or "Your parent is not a very good parent." That puts both the parent and the child in a bind.

Yolanda Torres, Child Care Consultant

Traditionally, families have thought of the schools as sacred ground that they are not to enter into. Whatever the school says, goes. The school is expected to teach the child to read and write. Parents and children look forward with excitement to going to school; it's a big milestone. Unfortunately, when they get to school, it's not such a happy experience for many of them. Many parents don't feel comfortable questioning the school or trying to find out what's happening there. They are not aware of legal problems surrounding excused and unexcused absences. Our parenting program tries to teach parents how to talk to the school and to the teachers, how to avoid giving control of a child's life to the school. There are lots of special remedial services available for the children that parents are not aware of. A lot of parents are not aware of what the services are or what their impact would be on the child.

Parents are not used to being active or involved in the schools. There are tremendous benefits when parents and teachers work together. It helps build a mutual respect. However, when their children are not doing well in school, parents feel even less comfortable about going to the school. A lot of these parents have had negative experiences in school themselves. Perhaps they, like their children, got behind and got bad grades. There is no incentive from home or school for a child to keep going to school if he's getting bad grades, especially if he's not getting extra help.

Carmen Cortez, Associate Director, Parenting Program

A child may be quiet in school because he is shy, or because he doesn't want to interrupt, or because he is being respectful. You have to be in tune with where the children are coming from. As children become more acculturated, this can change. A child needs help in school to make choices and express himself. To reach a child you have to build trust, build a relationship. You can reach families through the child if the child will open up. With very quiet children, we might talk to the parents. If his older brothers and sisters are talkative, the younger one will sometimes change.

Rafael Ramirez, Elementary School Principal

Mexican parents don't see themselves as teachers. They see themselves as controlling their child's behavior. Education and whatever a child learns beyond behavior is the responsibility of the school. Parents' views on this can change as they become more informed.

Dolores Ramirez, Multicultural Director

These parents come from a country where teachers are dictators and have a right to beat the child. The parent has to make a child submit to that teacher. The teacher is the expert and neither the parent nor the child should argue with the teacher. The parent comes here and expects the same thing. So if a child isn't behaving himself, the parents expect to be informed by the teacher so they can make their child behave.

Teachers here see teaching as a partnership with the parents and want the parents to help the child with his homework and be involved with the school. This is an example of different expectations and one of the cultural conflicts between Mexico and the U.S.

In a U.S. classroom, teachers don't control by threatening to spank a child. Mexican children in the U.S. have more independence and choices than they're used to. They don't know what's expected; they may feel confused and ignored and start to do their own thing. They have language problems. Their Spanish deteriorates in school. Young children from Mexico often have poor listening skills—even in Spanish. In school they have behavior problems; they wander around and talk out of turn. The children may be shy or they may be hellions. At home, parents don't invite children into adult conversation because of the belief that children should be seen and not heard. In school, children are asked to have opinions and ideas. They're not used to this and it takes time for kids to learn these skills.

When Mexican children are quiet, a teacher might interpret it as a lack of intelligence when it's actually a lack of experience in responding to questions, etc. Children may need one-on-one assistance to learn. Mexican children can start falling through the cracks even in the early grades. A child might feel incompetent and inadequate and may be unable to catch up with the rest of his class, especially when the child can't understand what the teacher is saying. The first years of school are crucial because these feelings of inadequacies may persist.

As children learn English, there's more conflict. Parents expect children to be interpreters. They pull them out of school to go to the doctor's office. It would be good if parents were learning English along with their kids, even though parents won't pick it up as fast. Parents should take classes in English; learning never stops. Parents need to be able to help their children learn at home.

Parents should continue to speak Spanish to children; it gives them roots and heritage and makes them bilingual and bicultural. It takes four or five years (kindergarten through fourth grade) for a child to be truly bilingual. Kids learn a lot of their English in school from their peers.

Dolores Ramirez, Multicultural Director

When you come from an authoritarian way of teaching and are put into the American preschools, you are probably either lost because you are asked to make choices or you act out because you don't have the strict rules of an authoritarian classroom. These children have to learn to make choices, and they have to overcome the language barrier.

Renee Martinez, Professor of Child Development

In the Latino culture, the children have no decision-making role. Parents make all the decisions and see the children as needing protection and needing to have everything done for them. They don't give children the opportunity to make even small decisions for themselves. A child may not have a chance to make a decision for himself until he is 15 or 16. It's easier and comes sooner for boys than for girls. The girls have a real hard time making any decisions at all.

Maty Brito, Mental Health Outreach Counselor

Latino children are not used to making choices for themselves. The children will probably have difficulty if they are asked to make a choice or tell the teacher something directly. They are not taught these things at home.

Ana Morante, Outpatient (Mental Health) Case Worker

Parents often ignore kid's questions—especially about sexual relations (such questions could earn the child a swat and being sent to another room). On other questions, they are often given answers that are inaccurate or incomplete (for example, "Why is there no moon out?" might be answered with, "Because there was no moon today"; "Why can't I touch the sun?" might be responded to with, "Don't be stupid; the sun is not to touch.") When children learn the true answers at school and find out their mothers and fathers have been lying to them or making fun of them all this time, they just stop asking questions. Sometimes, they also feel they can't trust others.

Carmen Guedea, Parent Educator

Parents don't understand what is happening at school. Children often get no help at home. Parents have to become more Americanized and become more involved in their children's education. They need to talk to their children starting when they're young. We need to teach parents that they don't have to the dominate conversation, that they should have a time when they are talking to their children on their children's level, asking them their opinions—not just talking at them. Parents need to listen when their kids talk to them. Parents try ideas like this that they get in parenting classes. They are definitely interested in the well-being and education of their children. They learn that they have to change what they do at home to help their child develop.

Dolores Ramirez, Multicultural Director

Mexican families are close emotionally, but parents and children have little dialogue. Children are used to playing at home with each other. The parents are generally uneducated and have weak language skills. Most Mexicans that we see have farming backgrounds. The hardest part of going to school is being separated from the family. Children are very dependent. The child clings to the teacher. And they haven't been prepared for critical thinking, working with manipulatives, and initiating (they don't play on their own). Mexican children expect commands and permission. At our school, we want the child to be a thinker, an initiator. We use a whole language approach and our teaching is all hands-on; it's creative, with no texts. Children have trouble understanding the kinds of directions we give them because the directions contain choices.

Latino children feel differently about their families than Anglo children do. If a Latino parent didn't turn in a school form for the child's free lunch, and the school tells the child he can't have the free lunch, it hurts the child's feelings. Latino children take things like this personally; they feel ashamed and feel their mother was insulted. An Anglo child would protect himself in a similar situation by blaming his mother. The Latino child feels vulnerable and doesn't protect himself. He may start to isolate himself because he doesn't trust his family. As these experiences continue into the child's teens, the child might join a gang or get pregnant.

Schools in Mexico teach only facts, so Latinos expect values to be taught at home. In the U.S., schools teach values, such as independence and civil rights—and Mexican and U.S. values contradict each other. At U.S. schools, they discuss gender equality, but it does not match what Latinos see at home. Latino boys have control over their mothers; brothers can hurt their sisters, but their sisters cannot hurt them. So children are confused about what to believe. These different values create a chasm between children and parents. Teachers notice that Latino girls take care of everyone's needs but their own as early as age five. We have to teach girls that it's OK to take care of others' needs as long as you take care of your own needs, too.

Graciela Ybarra, Resource Teacher

Certain themes emerge over and over in this chapter about the discouraging experiences of Mexican children beginning school in the U.S. Children are not used to asking questions and expressing opinions to adults; children are used to stronger methods of control from the parents than are considered acceptable or legal for schools to use; parents have not learned enough English to relate to the school and to the children's school work; and parents aren't participating at school.

What are some of the other issues you see in the school setting?

There are marked differences in the ways teachers treat boys and girls—even in the '90s. Girls are socialized into very limited roles. I was a substitute teacher for fifth grade; the girls didn't say anything; the boys clowned around, talked to me, put their hands up to answer questions and get attention. Boys set the tone for what the kids would laugh at. The girls were nearly invisible; they lacked self-confidence; there was a self-consciousness about them. They didn't want people to look at them. (They were also going into puberty.)

Overall, the kids were eager to please, good-natured, and highly amiable; there was a low level of hostility, and the kids were eager to do what you wanted. The boys' papers weren't very good, but the boys were good at trying to get the teacher to do it for them. Girls did much better work on paper—they were precise and creative. But they lacked the confidence to have any kind of leadership role in the classroom. Girls were fading into the background. I felt that within a few years, school would become less relevant for the girls, that their success in life had nothing to do with whether they could write a composition.

Linda Espinosa, Professor of Education and
Former Director of a Parenting Program

Overall, the schools are not doing enough to educate our children. They're not strong enough at teaching what is important. Kids get exposed to a lot of other kids and that becomes more important to them than what they get from teachers. The curriculum should be better—more challenging. It seems that Latinos are being underestimated by the schools. This happens so much, especially for young Latino men. I don't think Latino girls feel as much discrimination and prejudice in the school setting as boys—especially if the girls are quiet. Boys may get picked on, need to protect themselves more, and act aggressively. Or they might get threatened by others and end up fighting. Teachers set expectations too low. If expectations are too low, children are not challenged, they lose interest, and they drop out. Children start school enthusiastically, wanting to learn. Latinos score high in first, second, and third grade; by fourth grade, their scores start to go down and never go up again. I put my daughter in a private school and her attitude about school and about how and what she is learning is much better than our son's was; he went to public school.

Children are influenced by what goes on at home. It's important for children not to miss school; it's important for the family to be organized about getting kids off to school. Some children leave their mothers more easily to go to school; others cling to her. This is related to the parents' willingness to expose kids to things and opportunities and to the encouragement the kids get.

Maria Reyes, Social Worker

Mexicans believe people in the U.S. are prejudiced against them; they believe that they won't get any help because of racism. One child had bangs growing over her eyes and her teacher cut them. The child went home crying. The mother was angry, but she felt helpless to do anything about it. We need to treat Latinos with respect and treat them as equals, with feelings, etc. Parenting classes help parents learn to speak out. Latino children at school are also very silent; it's a mark of respect. And they often don't look you in the eye. The belief is that if you look someone in the eye, you look into their soul. This doesn't work in the U.S. Here, Latinos have to learn to look at others directly. When Latinos look down, it implies to Americans that they are not sure of themselves. Latinos have to take the responsibility for learning some things themselves, and professionals have to treat them with respect and be clear about expectations.

Dolores Ramirez, Multicultural Director

Do parents feel they have a role in their child's school or education?

Parents think their child will learn how to read and write in school. School is a place that parents send their children; they are not involved. Often the children who are new here from Mexico feel lost. They don't know the language or the ways to act. Sometimes children come home with stomach aches because they don't understand the class. And if children have a stomach ache, the mother won't send them to school. Even if it happens every day, she won't find out why. Mothers really don't make much of an effort to send their children to school if the child complains of even a minor discomfort.

Rosa Carreno, Community Health Worker

There are a lot of absences due to chronic lice, especially when lots of people are living in the same house. This is a problem. They get behind in school.

Carmen Guedea, Parent Educator

Parents really respect the school. But it's difficult for the families to understand that the school is not only for the children. In Mexico, parents just go to the school for special events. When they come to the United States, they have a hard time understanding the need to be involved in the school. They believe that school is supposed to be there for the children.

Maty Brito, Mental Health Outreach Counselor

Involvement is pretty much a social class issue. You see more involvement in the schools with higher income and educational levels. In the lower income and educational levels, mothers will help out in the classrooms, but they don't have a feeling of power. Helping out in the classroom sometimes helps the mothers feel that they can go beyond their traditional roles.

Renee Martinez, Professor of Child Development

The Latino family supports schools in many ways, if they feel comfortable with the school. When a family first comes to a school, they can feel how the school feels about them. For example, if the secretary can't understand their language, that alone can be a big problem.

Rafael Ramirez, Elementary School Principal

Parents can benefit from having school calendars that show the important dates at school such as celebrations, school holidays, shortened days, field trips, etc. It's helpful to teach the families about the importance of these calendars and suggest that they hang them very visibly. This helps the families keep track of days that will be different from the usual for their children.

Rita Rossi, Librarian and Resource Center Staff

There can be a lot of mother/father conflict when the mother is learning new ways. If the mother can be persistent and she has support from school, little by little, she can have the husband come around. But this takes a long time. Sometimes he'll say, "You just do it." But the mother needs support to feel that what she is trying to do is good for the children and herself. Both parents can be anxious about coming to the school and talking to the teachers. If she can bring her husband to the school and let him see other fathers, it becomes more acceptable to him. A father might cooperate enough to allow the mother to come to school for a meeting after dinner; perhaps he will watch the kids. She needs his support for this whether she's working outside of the home or not.

Parenting skills classes are catching on in our school district. It's very difficult for parents to make changes. I think all parents want their children to be successful in school, but they don't know how to make sure that they will be. The earlier they start helping their children, the more likely their children will be successful in high school. Information that parents learn at schools about parenting their older children ("I should be doing this with him" or "I should shut off the TV") can help them parent the younger siblings.

Beatriz Cerrillo, Family Resource Specialist

Mexican parents don't feel they have any power in the schools. There are two reasons for that. One is that there are very few administrators or teachers that are bilingual and bicultural and it is very difficult for parents to see themselves as a part of the institution. We have to realize that perception has a lot to do with power, with feeling that you are empowered. If you don't see people like yourself being doctors, lawyers, teachers, whatever, you don't feel that you can do it. The experience of minorities in the U.S. has been very much one of "You can't do it"—because of the barriers and obstacles that they encounter. There are very few people like myself and others who were insistent enough and tolerated the injustices enough to get through the system in order to achieve our goals. So, if you don't perceive yourself as part of an institution by seeing people like yourself, you are not going to feel empowered, no matter how many invitations you get. If you don't have professionals that look like you, talk like you, that understand what you go through to raise your bicultural children, you don't feel that the institution is yours. It takes more than an invitation and a bilingual aide, and more than just an out-reach worker; it takes a whole flavor of an institution, one with policies that reflect inclusion and practice it.

Josie Romero, Clinical Social Worker and
Director of a Family Institute

Given that schools are the way they are, what are some of the things that teachers can do to help parents feel more empowered?

I think that indigent parents don't feel that the teachers work for them. I think first and foremost, the teachers need to take the time to establish a personal relationship with each parent, to make that personal connection. If I'm a teacher and I have a Hispanic family, I should know that engaging parents about their children's education is going to be harder when the parents don't speak a little English and I don't speak any Spanish. I'm going to be humble to that communication problem. I have to remember that there are a lot of ways to communicate—by attitude, by facial expressions, and that these forms of communication come across to parents as well as the words. Through the students, teachers can communicate to the parents that their children are special to them and that the parents are an integral part of the program as well. You can send written materials home in the parents' language, again with humble apologies that, as a teacher, you don't speak the parents' language. I think that teachers can transmit their caring spirit and their respect through their smiles and their attitudes. Never stop communicating with the parents. When you establish a relationship in our Latino culture, you go beyond the formality and you establish a friendship. In the Latino culture, friendship comes with responsibility and accountability. Trust and respect are two criteria of a friendship. What this means is that if you were to need something or if you were to ask me for something, I would be more committed to respond in your favor. It is that commitment to friendship that is going to get a parent into the classroom—because you took the time to call her or you sent her enough notes praising her efforts as a parent and telling her about how her child is doing and what he's learning. It is those kinds of engaging ways that are important.

Josie Romero, Clinical Social Worker and
Director of a Family Institute

Well, I think that one of the important things to remember is that parents get involved with the schools because they were developed by and for parents. Schools in Mexico traditionally have used a different model. So Mexican parents have less trust in this model. Most of the people who come to the U.S. from Mexico are not from the middle class (those from the middle class have no reason to come) and they have little experience with institutions in general. So they tend to stay away, unless they see that the school understands what their needs are. Rather than trying to fit the families into the institutions, the institutions need to change to fit the needs of the families. They need to find ways to incorporate the Latino expertise of their staff. They need to use these people on a broader basis and get their input about how the institution is doing in serving the Latino community, about why some programs are working and others are not.

Most institutions are still operating with the idealistic and false notion of the melting pot, so they want people to fit into the mold. Experience has shown that the melting pot is not real. There is a mind set about what Mexicans need to do to be successful. Some people believe they have to become like Anglos. But most of the minority populations cannot do this.

There's a combination of things that schools could do to work more successfully with Latino families. Some of them are structural; some of them deal with training; some of them deal with staffing patterns. Part of the problem that Latinos face vis-a-vis institutions is that only some of the institutions can relate to the Latino people. Most cannot because the institutions and the people working in them are not culturally knowledgeable. The institutions need Latinos on the staff at all levels. As a clinical social worker, I would not do therapy through a translator. Research shows that the more a service provider is like the client, the greater the chance of a successful outcome for the client. Even the surroundings of the center, depending on the acculturation level of the client, make a difference. The pictures on the wall and how people are greeted are important.

Jorge Gonzalez, Psychiatric Social Worker

If you were working with a family that had just immigrated, as opposed to a family whose parents had immigrated, how would you work with them differently?

It's a hard question to answer. I would have to learn more about the person. Is that person from Mexico City? Is that person from a village in the hills? There are subtle cues that one picks up after working with any population. Generally, the Mexican population is more formal, so I would shake hands. But then again, if they were from some of the Indian tribes, you don't shake hands at all. The Mexican population is very heterogeneous. I think you could say that you need to be businesslike, but warm and friendly. In dealing with parents, you always need to let them know that you are working toward giving them control of the situation. We don't have a good history of having our U.S. institutions serve Mexican people well. Even people who come from Mexico who have no experience with the U.S. institutions feel you can be friends with Americans, you can open your house to Americans. But it's something else to trust that Americans understand what you've been through or where you're coming from. Politically, the U.S. has been looked upon as an enemy of Mexico—an enemy with a history of taking your land away. Mexico feels the presence of their northern neighbor and feels they really have to assert their identity. So people who have gone through the educational system in Mexico have gone through a very nationalistic system.

A friend of mine who works for one of the schools here in town has been very successful in attracting "working poor" Mexican parents to participate. She really understood the immigrant population and realized that their problems were not just the problems of kids coming to school. They also have problems of clothing, jobs, etc. My friend had a clothes closet in the classroom where parents could get clothing; she had a list of referral services for the parents and she spoke the language so she could communicate. She looked at the whole family and their needs. In the Mexican culture, especially in the traditional families (the families closer to the Indian traditions), they emphasize interdependence a lot more than independence. So sometimes the problems of a child have to be put in the context of how it affects the family.

Jorge Gonzalez, Psychiatric Social Worker

The Head Start Transition Program is an example of a successful program because the school is working with the parents teaching them to be part of designing the curriculum, making decisions about the school, attending meetings and being part of the school board. Offering ESL, math classes and community resources in their own language and at their child's own school and with role models is very valuable.

Rosalie Prado de Ramirez, Public Health Nursing Supervisor

How can schools and their teaching staff seem less like revered authorities and more like partners to Mexican families?

In our Latino culture, teachers and the educational system have the highest status—higher than doctors. In the Latin American countries, teachers are closer to sainthood than anyone else. Therefore, when you get to be a teacher you have earned a status and a position of respect and authority and the parents are not going to role model questioning that authority to their children. So if they question teachers at all, they will do it after the school has fouled things up so much that someone else has to intervene for that family. What they will usually do instead is withdraw, thinking that the school might be right and questioning what they know is right for their child. Schools have to refrain from saying, "Come in and demand your rights or what is right for your child." Instead, they might say, "We need your consultation to make sure that what we are doing fits the needs of your child." When you ask for the parents' consultation, you have given parents permission to give their viewpoints without demeaning the school or insulting it or questioning the school's authority.

Josie Romero, Clinical Social Worker and
Director of a Family Institute

What would you tell the teachers who are working with Mexican children?

I would tell teachers to educate themselves. I would tell them to expect things of the children, to stop teaching by the child's color. The children will live up to your expectations. There is a book called, *The Vulnerable Children*. It is about ethnic people from the ghettos that "made it." And the one variable throughout was that there was one person in the schools that cared about them. Somebody gave them a little push and cared about them. And whether you speak the language or not, there is a message that you give to parents and children and if it is negative or condescending, they know it. It is a very difficult job.

Flora Fortis, School Psychologist

What do you tell parents about how they can help their children?

I give parenting classes in Spanish, and when I do IEPs [individual education plans] I encourage the parents to talk more to their child, to listen to their child even if they don't understand what the child is reading. By talking and listening they can give their child the message that they care. I tell them to tell their children stories about when they were growing up and to ask questions of the child. And I tell them to talk to their children when they go to the supermarket. They can say, "This is a fruit, this is a vegetable." I suggest that they have a continuous dialogue with their children so they will increase their vocabulary. In our system, we have bilingual education, and the theory of bilingual education is whatever you have in your primary language you transfer to your secondary language. So if your primary language is enriched, then you have enough to transfer to your secondary language. Mainly, the message that I give them is that the children need to know that they are cared for, and that, whether what the child is learning in English or Spanish, the parent needs to be interested. Most of them care and want their children to have an education.

Flora Fortis, School Psychologist

I try to get parents involved in their children's education. The majority of the parents whose children attend this school don't have higher education. So we felt educating the parents would help them become educational role models for their children and, in turn, the children would be motivated to learn and their test scores would, hopefully, show improvement. We are educating the parents in basically everything. We have classes from literacy skills in their own language, English-language classes, parenting classes, and limit setting classes to computer classes, art classes, and exercise classes. We sent out a survey and asked them what they wanted. This is the first year and we have about 50 parents participating. That's a good start. Our grant is called, "Parents as Learners, Teachers, and Partners," so our first goal is to make them learners. Our second goal is to make them teachers so they will teach their children. Then we will use these parents to teach other parents.

Graciela Ybarra, Resource Teacher

I helped an elementary school out on the coast implement an immersion program that I am really proud of because it worked. The population was half Mexican and half Anglo and represented two extremes in economic levels. The Mexicans were mostly below the poverty line and the Anglos were middle to upper-middle class. So the program had to be designed to benefit both groups. It was an immersion program in that in kindergarten all children spoke only Spanish. Then, as the years progressed, they added more English, and by fifth grade they were speaking half English and half Spanish. By the time they were in junior high, they were bilingual. The reason that it worked was that the parents were very supportive and were positive role models for these students. The fact that the Anglo parents were professionals provided a positive role model that their children modeled. In turn, the Mexican children modeled after the Anglo children. While the Mexican children didn't have the motivation from home, they had it from school. And because there was not a language barrier, the Mexican children were even more motivated. The Anglo children saw the Spanish language as a challenge.

Graciela Ybarra, Resource Teacher

Why doesn't our traditional way of immersing the Mexican children in English with a little Spanish work?

First of all, not only do the Mexican children not get support at home but they also don't have the role models and the motivation to be challenged in this new language. It is a challenge they are not prepared for. The only parents who get involved are those who are motivated. And what I found motivates them is personal involvement in their lives. They have a lot more problems. We have to take care of their basic needs before they can get involved in their children's school. We have to try to get these parents functional.

Graciela Ybarra, Resource Teacher

What could schools do to help families and children fit in, feel more accepted, and get the most out of the institution—while staying part of their Latino culture?

You have to respect the people and what they bring with them. The institutions also have to acknowledge that people are dealing with grief and that they need time to get through it before they can jump into the activities of the schools. They also need to let parents know that they recognize how difficult it is for them to adopt the American ways, but that their children will need to know those ways to live in the U.S. Schools also have to acknowledge that American ways are not better than Mexican ways—just different. It is also important for teachers to keep the children bicultural and help the children feel proud of their heritage and their customs. Teachers also need to understand why Mexicans want to keep their culture. American teachers have to find a way to articulate what American culture is so that parents will have some understanding of what their children will be gaining rather than just what they will be losing. Why would any parent want their child to adopt aspects of another culture when those aspects and values are not articulated clearly? Teachers need to celebrate the children's cultures as well.

Yolanda Torres, Child Care Consultant

What about the contrast between the values of the U.S. schools and the values of the Mexican culture?

I think we need to understand that schools in the United States are part of the mainstream culture. The things that are valued and stressed, the kinds of things that are rewarded or punished, reflect a certain vision of the world. This is what we call culture. So, there is a culture of the school. For example, the values of individuality, the values of assertiveness and independence, would be seen differently by schools in other parts of the world. Schools socialize children into the mainstream culture. People from the Mexican culture value different things: dependence rather than independence; silent compliance rather than assertiveness; children interacting with other children rather than with adults. Some of their values are diametrically opposed to the values of the mainstream U.S. culture.

The Mexicans' different values, along with the different ways they speak and move, create a certain tension between the socialization practices of Mexican parents and the practices of the U.S. schools. For example, a parent may come into the school and say, "If my child doesn't behave, just hit him." The U.S. teacher thinks, "My God, these parents are child abusers." But that isn't it. It's a question of context. Another example is that young Mexican children are taught not to look adults in the eye because looking into someone's eyes is a sign of power. Many U.S. teachers go up to Mexican children and say, "Look at me, look at me!" The teachers see this as a sign of not caring, but the child is actually following a cultural pattern and showing respect by not looking.

Remember, too, that their own Mexican school system was very authoritarian. Parents think that what they need to do is make sure they teach their child how to behave so they can be receptacles for all the information the "experts" are going to give them. So a lot of parents respond to teachers' complaints about their children by giving children more discipline. When that doesn't work, the parents are put to shame. That shame is on top of their poverty and minority status, and the stresses of being an immigrant and not white, and being poor in this country. We need to understand that the things that we value—school success, independent achievement, assertive questioning—is only one way of being in the world. These things are only our cultural construction of how kids should function. It has its advantages, but it also has its disadvantages. We have a lot of unhappy people in this country who are lonely and live in a rat race. We need to see that there are advantages to other cultural constructs like peer connectedness and dependence. We need to learn from the different cultures. There's value in a bicultural person who may be able to see beyond their native culture to other constructs.

The U.S. culture values developmentally-appropriate practices, children taking a regulatory role, answering questions, and asking questions of adults. These things are not really valued in Mexican culture. Children in the Mexican culture are expected to learn by observation and silence rather than active participation. This came about because children were included in the work of the parents and learned by observation in the fields, the kitchens, and the sowing places from a very early age. We do not bring our children to work in the American society. American children are actually removed from the world of work. Our schools are supposed to prepare them for that world. Americans don't teach children through observation.

A Mexican preschool child who has been socialized for compliance and silent observation gets very lost when put into a preschool influenced by Piaget and Montessori where there is lots of active participation and children go from one activity to another. Even worse is that the teacher blames the child's parents for being too controlling and not caring. Teachers treat a child's training in compliance and observation as a deficit. In a sense, teachers are correct in their belief that the child has difficulty talking and doing things the other children do. But this is because they were not socialized to do it. It is not a deficit. It is a behavior that has meaning within their social culture. I am all for having these children develop the skills of assertiveness and active participation, but that has to be done very sensitively, outside of the deficit model. I think that Latino parents can be brought gradually to understand.

There is a lot of blaming Latino parents because they don't come to school or participate. People don't realize that Latino parents feel very ashamed in schools because they do get blamed for a lot of things (for example, "You are not teaching your kids how to read."). Latino parents were not socialized to understand that you can sit down and read something to your child. Literacy was taught in the schools, not in the homes. These parents really want their children to do their best in education and feel they should be taught by the best, the experts—the school, the teacher. The parents don't feel qualified to teach their children ("I am not the best"). These parents are continuously put to shame.

In a project I did with Mexican mothers teaching their children, I wanted to help them learn to teach their children by integrating more active participation and more developmentally-appropriate teaching methods—like teaching with questions rather than with commands. Mexican parents can do this. If you want to teach parents to be collaborators with their own kids, schools need to be collaborators with the parents instead of being controlling with them. It's funny that while trying to help parents be more collaborative, we tend to become very controlling. If you want a child to actively participate, you reward a lot, you focus on the positive things. You tell that child that he has done really well. You find the one thing in the work that he has done that is good, even if the rest of it is not right, and praise him for that. That will encourage him to participate more in his work. We need to do the same thing with Latino parents. We need to see what they are doing that is very right.

Rafael Diaz, Professor of Education

Are the schools responsive to the needs of bicultural families?

The schools are about 100 years away from understanding the dynamics of teaching bicultural children because they teach bicultural children from a deficit perspective. Teachers assume the child is slow because it takes him time to process; they never value the fact that the child is processing things in two different languages, two cultures, and two contexts. In any other country, that is brilliance; in this country, it's retardation.

In my opinion, the weakness of the bilingual programs we have in the U.S. is their lack of integration with the whole. This country is afraid of different cultures. The schools don't integrate the culture into the bilingual programs or take into consideration the cultural differences of doing things, or looking at things, or understanding and interpreting things.

Josie Romero, Clinical Social Worker and Director of a Family Institute

How would you help teachers make the necessary changes to help Mexican children and parents take advantage of education and feel more respected in the schools?

Respect is important; respect for styles. I think teaching and learning is ultimately about finding new ways of being in the world, finding new styles and seeing new things. There's a healthy tension when you stretch a person's style to have them see new things and other ways of being in the world. So I think that any program for Latinos, while it should have a lot of sensitivity to their cultural ways of seeing things, should challenge *machismo* [mah·CHEES·mo], the double standard, the tendency to comply and obey commands. I think education programs need to challenge styles. It is one thing to say you have a deficit, that you are doing it wrong; it is another to challenge ideas and expand possibilities. There are times to be controlling with children and times for letting them speak. We need to have the full repertoire of possibilities. So I would advocate for a program that would expand the possibilities and really get to know who these kids are. In order to do this well, you have to have a clear understanding of the meaning of behaviors. Respecting their culture does not mean that you are necessarily going to let them do it in the way they are most comfortable. You can respect a culture and still expand their possibilities. You have to collaborate with a child so the child can develop to a higher level of ability, a higher level of competence. And as the child reaches these levels of competence, you can withdraw your scaffolding.

Parents should be involved in constructing the goals of their child's education. Ask, "What would you like your children to be learning?" Then the parents are truly involved in the educational process and they feel respected. This requires teachers who respect the diversity and make Latino parents feel respected, not wrong or ashamed. They could invite the parents to come into school and watch a play or participate in a party. This is a way to make a connection with the parents that is not based on their performance as parents or on their child's performance in school. It is a way to make a connection and allow parents who are not used to actively participating in the schools to come and be observers. That's a role that is familiar to them in a school setting.

Rafael Diaz, Professor of Education

Many of the Latino professionals we interviewed feel that families can be encouraged to participate in the schools. This can be done partly through offering many kinds of services—almost like a community center—including English classes, GED classes, and community resources and information on such issues as naturalization, tax preparation, etc. Schools with at least some bilingual and bicultural staff seem necessary. It's been found helpful to have parent involvement through parent evenings and parenting classes that help explain what is expected of children and some of the reasons U.S. schools work with children and parents the way they do. It is important to use warm, welcoming approaches with Latino parents that enable them to share their culture through music, food, dance, soccer, etc. It's important to help them realize that the school respects and values the parents' views. This might lead to getting the parent's support for what the teachers and schools are trying to do.

Chapter 36

Using Special Education Services

What are the issues in evaluating special needs of children from rural Mexico?

What are parents' and children's views of special needs?

How can you communicate with Mexican parents about their children's special educational needs?

How can you involve parents in carrying out recommendations and in helping their children?

How do Latino parents view mental health services?

Of particular interest in this chapter is the way special education is viewed in Mexico and suggestions on ways to learn what the Mexican parents' observations are about their children's special needs. Both are necessary if we are to learn how to talk to parents about our findings and recommendations and to gain their cooperation in carrying out these recommendations. These issues are all included here. In addition, there is a description of how Latinos view mental health services. While some Latinos are beginning to use counseling services, there are long-standing beliefs and other priorities that make this difficult.

How do children get classified for special education?

Our American curriculum is very sophisticated, and it's not geared for children who come from Mexico. It is geared toward American children. Mexican children are watchers and the American curriculum is for "do-ers." In our school district, we have bilingual education. All children, when they begin school, take a test to see what their dominant language is. If their dominant language is Spanish, they go to bilingual classes and are taught in their primary language until the third grade. Then they make the transition and learn to read and write in English. At the elementary level, we have "dropout" counselors that work with the children to help keep them in school. We try to get as many bilingual people as we can. All of the teachers are being educated in second language acquisition and special education. So the children that I see are not making it in the regular classroom and may have already been through a lot of special programs in the classroom. That is when I come in and try to find out if he or she has a learning disability or if it's some other problem. We do the testing in Spanish and in English.

In order to be classified for special education, there must be a difference between your ability and your achievement. You also must have a learning disability. We don't place children just because of a language problem. The Latino children who need special education have the same types of learning problems that other special education children have. But they have the language discrepancy, the process of acculturation (if they are first generation), and poverty on top of the learning problems.

Flora Fortis, School Psychologist

How do you know whether a problem is due to a lack of experience or to a learning disability?

That's very difficult because these are children who may have been born here and schooled continuously for a couple of years. Yet their way of dealing with situations and their command of language is closer to that of children who grew up in Mexico. Because of this sort of cultural isolation phenomenon in the U.S., we have these U.S.-born children arriving in kindergarten feeling and looking like they just came from another country. It's difficult to sort out what's what. Another problem is children who come from abroad in the fourth, fifth, or sixth grade whose lack of school experience often looks like a learning disability. So in a lot of our decisions we also have to use our experience and our intuition.

Alice del Pinal, School Psychologist

What kinds of problems and special-needs children do you work with at school?

Most of the problems I see are learning problems. The children are unsuccessful in the classroom and this is usually related to a learning disability. I do an assessment and make recommendations. With a younger child, a learning problem is usually due to a learning disability. But many times there's a behavioral/emotional component. Often, another factor is the child's lack of educational experience, especially for fairly recent arrivals in the U.S. Also, it's a growing phenomenon for parents to bring adolescent children to the U.S. because they know we have a lot of services to offer, where in Mexico there may be none. In some very rural areas in Mexico, there may not even be a school. Children who need special services in rural Mexico may stay in the same class for five years until they drop out of school—getting further and further behind because they haven't had any special education. So a child arriving here may look much more disabled than he really turns out to be when he's given an opportunity. It's hard to justify that he's not as delayed as tests suggest.

Alice del Pinal, School Psychologist

Are there any special education programs in Mexico?

There is special education, but it's for retardation. When you refer to special education in Mexico, people think you are talking about retarded children.

Alice del Pinal, School Psychologist

Yes, there are, but they are only in the big cities. These services are not available in the rural schools. In the rural areas, they just keep you home if you have trouble learning.

Flora Fortis, School Psychologist

Special education is nonexistent in the public schools in Mexico. If you have a child who needs special help, you keep him home unless you can pay to send him to a private school, which are usually in the larger towns or cities. When a child is labeled as needing special education, it is thought that he is retarded. They do not have the concept of learning disabilities. There is more of an understanding in Mexico City and other big cities, but not in the small towns.

Rita Rossi, Librarian and Resource Center Staff

How do the families feel about having a child who needs special education?

In some of the Latin American countries, including Mexico, children with disabilities are hidden. They see it as a punishment from God. They don't have the resources over there for training and education. It's in the culture to feel ashamed. The Latino families need to know that there are other families who have children with these disabilities. I know the parents feel alone and ashamed even if it doesn't come up. I encourage them to get some support. Organizations such as Parents Helping Parents that have a group of Spanish-speaking parents can be helpful.

Flora Fortis, School Psychologist

Parents usually keep a child home if they are told their child needs special help. They are ashamed. They blame themselves. And they blame their child for being lazy and stupid. They never think it could be poor eyesight or poor hearing, etc.

When a family comes here and their child needs special education, it is *so* important for them to have a bilingual psychologist who can help them understand *why* the child needs that help, that it is not their fault, and that the child is not retarded or lazy or stupid. Many parents need a lot of encouragement and support to allow their child to be in a special education class. We also find more child abuse in families that feel ashamed. They are angry at their child for bringing that shame on the family.

Rita Rossi, Librarian and Resource Center Staff

Any major difference in physical appearance is often viewed with a certain amount of superstition. Some disabilities, like cleft palate, harelip, and retardation, are viewed as either God's punishment for something the parents may have done or due to the phases of the moon. A lot of them believe in supernatural causes. There is a certain degree of shame connected to it: "It's my fault. Perhaps if I hadn't done that my child would be normal." This may be changing.

Alice del Pinal, School Psychologist

What are helpful ways of talking to parents about special needs?

When a problem is not physically obvious, there is not the same sense of shame. Still, the parents are generally very aware that something is different about their child. When asked, their answers usually show a good, clear grasp of it. "Well, she never remembers what people tell her, and she can't go to the store and buy a few little things because she forgets what I asked her to buy." Or they might notice that this child is a little slower or just didn't learn as quickly or didn't talk as soon as their other children. So, they are aware that there's a problem. What parents lack (and, maybe, it's for the best) is a label for it. So they don't say, "My child has a *learning disability*" or "an *emotional disturbance*." They just have a naturalistic observation of the child's behavior, but they're very accurate. So, in the classroom, when we mention behaviors that parents recognize in their child, they acknowledge it. A lot of times the parents might say, "I wonder if that's because my daughter or son is *tontito* [tohn·TEE·toh: a little dumb, as in dull]."

Parents will speculate about causes, but they have very little understanding about learning disabilities. They get confused and believe that a child who can't learn to read must have inferior intelligence. (Of course, this is hard in the Anglo culture, too.) Parents are usually very descriptive about emotional problems as well. They may say, "My child throws tantrums and is very isolated." They are often aware that one of their children is different in that way. With a quick question such as, "Is this child like anyone else in your family?" I generally get that the child is exactly like other family members. There is a willingness and acceptance of what is.

Educators should speak in terms of specific behaviors and not use categories or labels like "learning disability." They need to help the parents understand that we refer to certain behaviors as learning disabilities, but that we don't mean the child is not intelligent. They often wonder whether the child is just being lazy or contrary. Getting the parents to understand that he's not is a big chore. It's important that they know that no matter how hard the child tries to do a particular thing, he can't do it. We do not want parents to be punitive toward the child. Parents are often eager to catch on. (When talking to parents, I don't get into some of their thinking about the supernatural causes of problems that their children have. I focus more on what the parents see as happening NOW.)

Parents are generally willing to follow any recommendations, even at the high school level. Parents are usually very grateful that some attention is being paid and are willing to spend time to help their child. Latino parents, however, may be disappointed with what happens in the long run. That's another issue and very individual. In rural areas, especially in the past, parents had an inclination to passively accept what comes and not try to do anything. They would just let the child with a disability be at home, as though he were another pet, or sit in a classroom even though he wasn't learning anything.

When I think about talking to parents about their children's special needs, I try to remember that the families are here in the U.S. for many reasons. Some want change; they're willing to depart from their traditions and try new things. You'd have to do that to come to a new country. So some of these parents are in a better position to get help and try to do something for their children. A lot have no education, but they are bright people. So if they can't directly help their children because of their own lack of education, they'll listen to suggestions like, "Let your children read to you. You listen."

They may not be able to do any formal education with their children at home, but they'll entrust the school with beginning the process. They'll be whole-heartedly behind the school's efforts and very glad that someone is helping. It's most important that they be solidly behind the school. With newly arrived Mexican parents, there's a great deal of respect for education and for educators. "If a teacher says it, it must be right." They don't critically evaluate education. "If that's what your teacher says, then you do it." Parents are willing to take some steps as long as someone else will try to help. In Mexico, they've had less educational benefits. The education they find in the U.S. might seem like paradise. Their children get paper, pencils, and books here. Back home, parents have to save their money to buy all the supplies. Lots of parents come from limited resources and are overjoyed with the schools. Many realize their own lack of education is a hindrance, so they are very motivated to see that their children get educated. Sometimes this changes by high school due to the family's need for their child to work, etc.

Alice del Pinal, School Psychologist

How does a child view his own special needs?

Younger children realize that there is something different about themselves, but they may not know what it is. With an older child, we need to be as clear with the child as we are with a parent. With both younger and older children, we need to help them understand why they can't remember, etc. At the high school level, we do some counseling and education with the student about what it means to have this disability so the student can be an active participant in the decision-making process.

Alice del Pinal, School Psychologist

Who tells the child about the special education placement?

We have a process in our district. Before the child is even tested, we have what is called the Child Study Team. We have a meeting to talk about the child and what is needed. The teacher or the mother is the one to talk to the child. By the time the child comes for testing, he knows that there is a problem.

Flora Fortis, School Psychologist

Does a Latino child with special needs feel differently than any other child with special needs?

The stigma of being labeled seems like less of a big deal with Latinos than with children of other cultures. There's more acceptance. In fact, other kids may feel envious that this child gets all the special attention. However, sometimes by the time they get to high school, the children with special needs may feel bitter that they haven't learned what others have and that they've been labeled. They are in a program called Resource Specialist Program. They are referred to as RSPs. Fellow high school students tell the kids that RSP means "Really Stupid People." The Latino community is not as vicious as Anglos about labels. We need to better explain to children what program they're in and what it means.

Alice del Pinal, School Psychologist

How do Latinos feel when their children are having problems in special education and mental health areas?

Latinos tend toward a closed system—they solve problems inside of the family instead of outside; they try to handle problems through folk methods first rather than going to professionals. With speech therapy or learning disabilities, there's not much they can do about it through more traditional methods. If parents are not educated, it's not something they would see as very, very bad. Once they see there is a need and that there's help available, they're open to taking the help—especially once trust has been established. Then they'll be more open and honest with you.

Ana Morante, Outpatient (Mental Health) Case Worker

Is it reasonable to ask families to help their children practice such things as fine-motor skills at home, despite the enormous stresses there?

The less educated they are, the less value they may find in practice. "I went through life without going through this." So they may not do what you ask them to do. It's important to establish a rapport, to show them a lot of respect, and show that you value their opinion—especially the father's. If we help them see how important they are and that what they do will be very good for their child, there's a greater chance that the parents will follow through. If the child has too many problems, some parents may not invest much time with him. Help parents understand that with their help things can become easier for their child. Stress the importance of the parents' role in their child's life.

Ana Morante, Outpatient (Mental Health) Case Worker

Who should you talk to in a family for permission to evaluate a child and discuss findings and recommendations?

I do a lot of this by phone. But, first, I try to ask the child, "Who's the best person to tell me about you or to ask permission to work with you?" If the child can't tell me, I'll just call and ask for the mother or the father. I say why I'm calling and ask, "Are you the person I should talk to about this?" If the person I talk to suggests another family member, I support that. I let the family tell me who should be consulted about this. I don't pressure them to do it differently. The father has the status and prestige of head of the family; he's in charge of discipline. The mother is in charge of education. And because the mother is the heartbeat and control center of the family, I usually talk to her. Sometimes, the person to talk to is an older sister or brother. Families may have an unusual composition.

If I'm talking to the mother, I say, "We'd like to include you and your husband." It's not much of a problem with educational matters. Educational services that families don't pay for are the easiest for parents to accept. If issues come up that involve any costs or fees, we need the whole family's involvement. They can't sacrifice new shoes for ten sessions of speech therapy. There may be more resistance with psychotherapy, which is an emotionally loaded topic.

Alice del Pinal, School Psychologist

It helps a lot for families to understand what is going on. It's important to explain what this is all about, what will happen, who will be there, and why the school is doing things this way.

Maria Reyes, Social Worker

How do you find out if they understand and accept what you tell them?

Parents come in to hear what you have to say. They will be respectful. They're not likely to object at that time to what's said; they'll listen politely and, if you ask if they have questions, they often will politely say no. They will leave without telling you what they think. Maybe they haven't formed an opinion. They'll do that later. So call them later and ask, "Now that you've had a chance to think about it, what is your opinion?" or "Do you have any questions now? If any questions come up, write them down," or "Are there any other family members who might have questions or that you'd like to have talk to us to find out what we're talking about?"

The husbands often stay out of these conferences and discussions. Husbands can be very influential and they need to be supportive. If the husband doesn't understand what's happening, he might discourage his wife from coming for help.

Maria Reyes, Social Worker

How do you talk to the Latino family about the results of an evaluation and help them through an IEP (Individual Education Program) meeting?

At the IEP meeting, parents get overwhelmed by all the various school personnel that are there. They may also have an interpreter who doesn't do a good job and the parents can't get their questions answered. And the IEP staff will use initials that parents don't understand, such as IEP. The parent signs a paper and leaves without a good idea about what is happening, what a learning disability is, what's going on with their child; how they could help their child; what techniques or materials will be used with their child. To help the family, the IEP meeting has to go more slowly, taking time to translate, and the staff has to develop rapport with the parents. It would also help to give the parents more preparation and have more follow-through with them.

It's important that parents understand the information from the meeting. They might have missed something or misunderstood something—even if the information was given in Spanish. Some interpreters are terrible. So now I don't take chances; I go to the meetings with my clients and, afterwards, ask them to tell me what they understood. I will say, "It's really important that there's a good understanding between us on this issue, so could you tell me what you understand of what I've just explained?"

Maria Reyes, Social Worker

Mexican parents are usually less educated than Anglo parents. It's my job to explain to the family that their child has a learning disability and is not retarded. That is usually accepted and understood. We have all of the information written in Spanish, including the IEP forms, and we make sure the parents understand. The parents have a choice about putting their child in special education. Because we try to educate the parents as much as we can, putting a Mexican child in special education is no more of a problem for the Mexican parents than for the Anglo parents. There might be fewer questions from the

Mexican parents, but we try to explain so thoroughly that we answer most everything.

Flora Fortis, School Psychologist

Which family members should be invited to the IEP meeting?

Most of the time, it's the mother who comes. The father is either at work or not around; he may have gone back to Mexico because he couldn't make it over here. So we have a lot of single-parent homes where the woman is the head of the household. Sometimes the mothers bring in all of the adults that are living in the house—grandma, uncles, aunts. They are close-knit. Remember, too, that second generation Mexican-Americans are different from the first generation. The first generation is more family-oriented and the decision has to be made together. The ties in the family may be more fragmented in the second generation; families are usually more Americanized by then.

Flora Fortis, School Psychologist

When in doubt about who to talk to, talk to them all. Mexican families have a great sense of inclusion—grandmother, parents, etc. I even ask the parents if they'd like their child to come to our meeting. Usually this is with older children (at least 9 or 10 years old). Families mostly regulate the extent of the privacy they want around an issue. We let them decide who should be included.

Alice del Pinal, School Psychologist

What are helpful ways to explain a child's test results to the parents?

You have to be very sensitive, assess their educational level, and gear your explanation to their level of understanding. You might have one Hispanic parent that doesn't know how to write her name and another that has a master's degree. You have to get a feel for where they are coming from, and you have to treat all of the parents with the same respect. When meeting with parents, you have to have done your homework and be ready with all of the questions and answers to any questions—even ones that aren't asked. You also have to be supportive and explain that the purpose of special education is not to label the child but to help the child with his learning. You have to explain what the child's disability is, the different programs, and how they will help the child.

Flora Fortis, School Psychologist

We must get beyond our professional terms and describe their child's education or health problem clearly and simply. (There's a lot of Latin in Spanish, so some of our Latin medical terms may be understood.) Describe what was done in the psychological testing or any other kind of testing.

Alice del Pinal, School Psychologist

How do Latino parents view teachers, psychologists, and social workers?

In my experience as a school psychologist, I am viewed as OK. I explain my role in testing their child. By the time the parents see me, they are ready for their child to get some help. Teachers are viewed very highly by the parents. They also respect the social workers who work with their preschool children. It's important to explain your role to parents and assure them that you are not there to analyze them or their child.

Flora Fortis, School Psychologist

Teachers, psychologists, and social workers are considered knowledgeable. All of them are called *maestro* [mah·EHS·tro: teacher] by the Latinos. They have trust and respect for education.

Alice del Pinal, School Psychologist

How can we get families to carry out recommendations?

I tell the families that it is important for them to show their child that they care about him or her. Many parents can't really work with their child on academic skills because they can't read or write English, but I encourage them to show an interest in their child and in their work. Parents can read to their children, talk to them, and take an interest in their schoolwork—even if they can't read or speak English themselves. They can talk to their child about what they do—the ordinary things they do together, like shopping or just going around the neighborhood. They can tell their child stories about themselves and their growing up. I tell parents to ask their child questions, to get involved in their life. I encourage them not to be ashamed of their lack of education and recognize what they can give their child by showing interest.

Professionals need to treat all parents with respect, but also recognize the level of each parent and talk to them at that level. They need to explain everything very thoroughly and not assume that parents will understand information just because it's written in Spanish. It's important to show the parents how their child will benefit from the program and to be in touch with the parents frequently. Parents need a lot of encouragement because it's hard for them.

It seems to me that the schools that are most successful in getting parents to come to meetings and be involved are the ones that provide transportation for both the child and the parents. Also, it's important for Mexican parents to have someone who can understand them and who can talk to them in their own language.

Flora Fortis, School Psychologist

It's not much of a problem for parents to carry out the school's recommendations when the services are at school because it's usually not too difficult to stay at school or come to school when it's right in their neighborhood. So educational services are easier to follow through on than other types of recommendations.

Parents can follow through more easily with younger children; with older children it's not as easy because parents may not have as close of a bond and often have less influence over their child. Older children are often not as cooperative with parents. Parents can more easily get a first-grader to tell them what he learned in school that day. But older kids want more independence, and it's usually harder for parents to find out how he's doing and what he's thinking.

Alice del Pinal, School Psychologist

Are the parents required to be involved in the child's special education program?

Most of the time we don't require it. It depends on the teacher. If the teacher is aggressive and seeks them out, she has good results. But the parents are often reticent and they don't volunteer. Parents don't come to the regular schools either. We have another problem in that our school district is desegregated, so children may ride up to an hour-and-a-half on the bus to get to school and the parents may not have any way to get there. But I have a good turnout when I have parenting classes.

Flora Fortis, School Psychologist

What do you do about families not keeping appointments?

We try to teach the family about the importance of appointments by calling them the day before to remind them, and then we call them at the appointment time if they're not here. They eventually get better about keeping appointments.

Alice del Pinal, School Psychologist

The highlights of this part of this chapter include making sure parents know you believe their child is not retarded, is not someone to be ashamed of, and is not willfully being difficult. It's important that you let them know that you believe the child truly has special needs. It's important to ask for the parents' observations, to explain the evaluation results and treatment recommendations thoroughly, and to follow up on other related issues. It's also useful for the parents to know specifically what you expect of them in terms of their working with their child. A good communication technique is to demonstrate what you are asking the parents to do. Special services from the school are probably the easiest for Mexican parents to welcome and accept, partly because there usually is not an additional cost and partly because the services usually are right at the school—a familiar and often convenient place for the parents.

How do families view mental health services?

Latin Americans don't have much experience with mental health services, except in big cities. They would more typically talk to older relatives, friends, and clergy. They're appreciative for having someone to talk to, but there's a stigma around being crazy. A *consejero* [kohn·seh·HEH·ro: counselor] is seen as someone who will give you guidance, and that's not so bad. When you talk about a psychologist or psychiatrist, it's assumed mental illness is involved—that the child is crazy or retarded—and there is more of a stigma. However, when a doctor recommends a service, it's usually taken fairly well. Still, the concept of mental health services is so foreign. The Mexican community is generally living at such a survival level, dealing with concrete issues (shelter, food, clothing), that a child's sensitivities and problems with school and learning may not be a priority. A mother might sometimes ask for psychotherapy services once it's explained to her, but the father might refuse or might just come in but not buy into it at all. Males have a lot of resistance to seeking help. There's a sense of shame and secretiveness. This attitude is not uncommon in Anglos either. The Latino community's attitudes about mental health services is similar to the attitudes the U.S. community held in the recent past.

Alice del Pinal, School Psychologist

Parents believe that problems that happen at home need to be kept at home. This is a real deep belief. They hardly ever ask for help. They may trust the priest at church or maybe the grandmother, but usually it's kept at home. I am a mental health specialist, but I don't like the label because when you introduce yourself as a mental health specialist in the Latino community you are rejected. They think they don't need you because they are not crazy. They don't see you as someone who can help prevent problems. They only see you as someone who treats crazy people, who sends people to hospitals.

Maty Brito, Mental Health Outreach Counselor

With Mexican families, problems are private. You don't expose yourself to anybody. It's best to keep it within the family. You talk to the person you're close to—a sister or a mother. It might be a friend or a neighbor that you see each day and feel very comfortable with. You certainly don't go to a mental health professional. As our parenting groups become real support groups, parents start to reveal more and you realize there's a lot more going on in their lives than you thought. They have to trust you, feel very comfortable, and be sure you're not going to hurt them or embarrass them. Information will be most useful when it's presented in a way that is relevant to their daily lives. Most of them will probably not read things you might give them. We use a lot of pictures in their lessons.

Carmen Cortez, Associate Director, Parenting Program

Parents respond to modeling, so it's good to show parents what you want them to do with their child and how they can do it. Teach them that what they do affects the child and the child's education.

Alice del Pinal, School Psychologist

Professionals could go to the community to let them know of the services by talking to them in person, not by mail. Mexicans often don't feel invited by that. They don't relate as well to the mail. (Besides, frequently they can't read what you send them.) I call families by phone to invite them to parenting classes. That's more effective than the mail. They hear my voice and my language, and it sounds familiar. It's even better when you can go to their home and talk to them. After that, I let them make their own decision about whether they want to participate in the parenting classes, etc.

Raul Rojas, Parent Educator and Community Outreach Coordinator

Families usually don't go to a psychologist or psychiatrist because of the money. They may think talking to a counselor would be beneficial. In Latino culture (even in the U.S.), there are informal people you go to for help. It's usually a woman—like a *doña* [DOHN·yah: a wise, respected woman who has the esteem of the community.] She can provide counseling. She's usually involved in the church, very upstanding, and vocal about her values. A *doña* has a respected role. She's usually very discrete, and she will talk to the other family members, too. You don't pay her; it's informal—a position of honor. You ask and people will tell you who to go to.

Dolores Ramirez, Multicultural Director

When we train as therapists, we have certain kinds of expectations about what kinds of changes need to happen and how quickly. We're more intellectual about things. I'm not saying that's better. We make certain assumptions. Because we have cars to get from here to there, we assume everyone does. But Latinos may not. We may make suggestions like, "If you hate that job so much, why don't you change your job?" Well, that's easier said than done. We may not tolerate a boss yelling at us, but some people have to for survival. We also might have assumptions about a lot of people living together in one household. We might think, "It must be bad for the children." Well, it could be good for the children and the family to have all that support.

Jorge Gonzalez, Psychiatric Social Worker

Once you've helped them with their pain, they'll be very grateful about it and try to give you something back—maybe they'll bring you food, which is a big thing to them. So it will probably be harder to establish a "professional" relationship with a Latino client than it is with an Anglo client because we observe more boundaries and space in Anglo relationships. With Latinos, once you've proven that they can trust you, they'll try to get closer to you.

Ana Morante, Outpatient (Mental Health) Case Worker

Chapter 37

Teen Years

What are the issues for a Mexican adolescent in the U.S.?

How does earlier child rearing impact the Latino as an adolescent?

What about some of the well-known concerns, like students dropping out of school or students becoming part of a gang?

What is being done and what can be done to better help the adolescent and his family?

Here we see some of the parent and adolescent struggles that are impacted by biculturalism, early child-rearing practices, poverty, the school experience, and the difficult stage of adolescence. Looking at the specific experiences that family members have during the teen years helps us understand not only what parents and adolescents need during these years but also what changes might be beneficial during earlier child-rearing years.

What happens to the Mexican child within the family as he becomes an adolescent?

There are three different stages of acculturation. The immigrant stage, the transitional stage, and the bicultural stage. A child who's been in U.S. schools for a couple of years and seen the participatory family role of American class-mates might question his Mexican-born, traditional parents about why he doesn't have any say in family decisions. This causes some pressure in the family. But the parents are not going to change their traditional ways if they feel they are going to lose some of the power and control and responsibility that has been inherent in their tradition. So as the child's insistence gets stronger and he reaches adolescence, all hell breaks loose. It's important that Latino parents teach their children what they believe their parental role is. It's also important for the child to teach his parents what it is like to be an adolescent in California today. They both learn a lot about the other this way, and they begin to compromise—always keeping the parents in control. As Latino parents, we have two dilemmas when raising bicultural children. One is the universal generation gap that all parents, regardless of culture, suffer through. The other is the acculturation gap. When you add those two dynamics to the dynamic of adolescence, it's an enormous task for parents. Adolescence poses the greatest challenge to all parents. In the Latino population, it is coupled with the breakdown of power and authority and with parents not understanding their child's need to break away. The process is explosive.

Josie Romero, Clinical Social Worker and
Director of a Family Institute

Adolescence is a difficult age in any culture. It's a time of pulling away from family. When, on top of this, you have parts of you saying you must be loyal to your family, loyal to your peers, loyal to your culture—and they're all telling you to do different things—it's even more difficult. This is especially true for Latino boys. There's a challenge to the father about who is going to be the boss. And, in the U.S., traditional roles of the Latino father are often usurped by the sons. A child who learns English quickly finds himself interpreting for the family by the time he's five years old. So when he and his parents go out to buy something, the father, who would normally take command of the situation, has to watch his five-year-old interpret for him and become, in a sense, the "father" and in control. So by the time this child is a teenager, he is well in control if the father has not learned English or if there is still a lot of poverty. If you're doing OK, it's easier to have your child do better than you. But if you have struggled your whole life and your child is telling you that he is going to have more than you and that the way he is going to do that is to become more Americanized and lose his culture, it is hard to be supportive of that growth.

Yolanda Torres, Child Care Consultant

In the Latino culture, the grandmother has a lot of influence and first generation children will listen to her. The second generation is mixed with American culture, and the family ties are not as strong. Another problem that I see is that a lot of the families are headed by single mothers. Now remember, in the Hispanic family the man rules. And when these children become teenagers, they don't see their mother as the authority. That is why we see so many problems. It's why teenagers join gangs. What do gangs offer these kids? Discipline, structure, punishment (if you mess up), rewards—everything that we used to find in the family. It's not that these single mothers don't want to be the authority, it's that they don't know how to be. And if they have boys, the boys assumed the father's role and became the authority in the family at an early age. When these boys become teenagers, they don't want to listen to their mother because she has no authority. The lack of respect for mothers amazes me. Children look at their mother like the husband would: "You don't know what you are talking about." She's loved and cherished, but it is the father that traditionally deals with authority and decision making. But, when there is no father, children are left with women who were not raised to make decisions. That's how this problem starts. The son stops respecting the mother because she is not strong enough to tell him to "Do this, or else!" I see this all the time. The children run around and stop respecting anyone.

Flora Fortis, School Psychologist

Sometimes a child's feelings for his mother and the family help keep him from doing things that can get him into trouble. The children don't want to make their mother suffer.

Beatriz Cerrillo, Family Resource Specialist

I hear boys in junior high say, "Oh, but my poor mother." I say to these boys, "Can you imagine how your poor mother must be suffering, how she feels about your doing this?" A mother's feelings are important and this makes a big impression. It can be a way to keep the youth out of trouble or get them out of it.

Victoria Orozco, Family Resource Specialist

Why is the dropout rate so high?

Many of the children get to middle school and feel that they can't keep up with the other children. Their language acquisition is still very limited. Sometimes they go back to Mexico; sometimes they have to go to work to help their parents. Mainly, I think that those who drop out are those who don't feel good about themselves. They don't feel that they belong, that they can compete with the rest of the children.

Flora Fortis, School Psychologist

What has happened to make them feel that way?

A lot of these people move a lot, so they don't have a sense of belonging. Programs change from school to school, especially if the child is trying to acquire English as his working language. The education is fragmented. The child may have had to stay home to help the mother. This further delays language acquisition and to succeed in the U.S. you need to learn English. So when a child doesn't have the necessary skills, he feels more and more lost. And because so many of the parents don't have education themselves, it's difficult for them to support their child's higher education. On top of this, there are drug problems and gangs. I see more dropouts in middle school and high school. But we do have children dropping out of elementary school.

Flora Fortis, School Psychologist

People talk about school dropouts as being one of the major problems with the Mexican population. There are possibilities in life for happiness other than obtaining a graduate degree or even going to college. We need to start with a vision that different behavior is not a product of deficit—that not going on to college does not mean Mexicans don't have motivation or knowledge or skills. We need all types of children in this society—the silent observer, the active participant. We need dependent people as well as independent people. We need to have interactions that are respectful, and teachers must begin to understand what is going on in Mexican families and why parents do what they do and what the children are being socialized for.

Rafael Diaz, Professor of Education

A lot of the people that immigrated here had the idea that they had to work hard. A lot of it had to do with poverty. Their children had the idea that once they graduated from high school they wanted independence, their own car, and their own money. So the children weren't motivated toward becoming professionals. Instead, they wanted to go out and work. What especially interests me is how to motivate women to motivate their children to go on to higher education. Confidence and self-worth are very important. A lot of the children lack a sense of self-worth. Much of this is due to all the changes that occur once they move to the U.S. from their native country. I think this low self-worth is part of the reason young women become pregnant. It's an escape. They don't love themselves enough to continue their education, to make something better for themselves.

Luz Agudelo, Radio Call-In Show Hostess

Higher education is not valued as much in the Mexican culture. It is not seen as a means to an end because it's hard to see a way out of the poverty.

Carmen Guedea, Parent Educator

A high percentage of Mexican teenagers drop out of school. They want to get a job to buy a car. There is not much help for those kids. They have to go to counseling. If they had people come to their house and talk to them it might help. They don't go to the agencies or institutions; they are afraid of what people will say to them.

Rosa Carreno, Community Health Worker

We come from a poor underdeveloped country and when we come here, things are better no matter how bad they are, so we appreciate what we have here. But in my experience, the *U.S. born* Mexicanos seem angry all the time, and I think that what happens is that they suffer a life time of racism and by the time they are in high school, they are so turned off to school; they seem to hate their teachers. Something happened to those kids and I think it was racism and loss of identity. You're called a "beaner," a "wetback." When you've lived your whole life here and all your experience is the same poverty, it's hard to appreciate anything. If you grow up in a housing project with graffiti all over and broken down cars, it's hard to see anything different for yourself.

Gil Villagrán, Child Welfare Social Worker

Certainly we have our share of problems. We suffer from more unemployment, poverty, less education. But if a father had a terrible experience and his son also was having a bad experience, he might tell his son that it was OK to come to work with him and not go back to school. The father would do this out of love for him because he wanted to protect him from getting hurt like the father may have been. Unfortunately then, people assume that Mexicans don't value education. Teachers should take a look at how children are being hurt at school; it's too painful for them. Why would someone stay home when they know that education is the only way to get a better job?

We need to train the parents to get involved in their child's school and learning even if they themselves can't read. We need to give validity to what they do know.

Gil Villagrán, Child Welfare Social Worker

If children are brought up in authoritarian homes, what happens as they get older? Is there a connection between this and joining gangs?

Being raised in an authoritarian home is one of the reasons it is so comfortable for them to go into another controlled environment: gangs. In gangs, it is their peer who is making the decisions for them, which seems more acceptable. Also, there may be a lot of rebellion from teens.

Renee Martinez, Professor of Child Development

As they become adolescents, it's common for boys to intimidate their mothers. This is related to the authoritarianism and the violence Latinos are exposed to. A lack of cultural identity leaves you without a group you can identify with, except maybe in the school. The need for roots and identity is not met by things like a sports team. They need a sense of identity and loyalty and the gangs are there. Lots of kids feel threatened, so they fight and need to protect themselves. If anyone threatens you, your gang will protect you.

Ana Morante, Outpatient (Mental Health) Case Worker

When their children join gangs, parents often blame it on leniency in discipline. They feel that, if they were in Mexico, they could have been stricter and just beat the kids up without risking arrest. There's no such thing as child abuse over there. They feel the kids are brainwashed here. A child can call the police on the parents. Parents just hate that. Children become less manageable; they stand up for themselves; they become disrespectful. They may join gangs. All the relatives feel the same way about disrespect.

Carmen Guedea, Parent Educator

Gangs are increasing for girls. It's a way of fitting in with their peers. It has to do with their definition of love and friendship and with wanting to be accepted by the boys.

Renee Martinez, Professor of Child Development

The gangs are about protection of each other. It's Mexicans against Chicanos. They are fighting each other in order to feel better about themselves. If I am a Chicano, I pick on the Mexicans because all they speak is Spanish so they're not as good as I am—even though the way I speak English is not like the mainstream white kids who still call me a "beaner," a "wetback," and don't accept me. So fighting with the Mexicans is a way of protecting myself from the humiliation of what I feel from the racism. We all need to realize that the enemy is not each other but the poverty and the lack of education that we are suffering from.

Gil Villagrán, Child Welfare Social Worker

What is being done about the gang influence?

We are trying to introduce uniforms for students. In one of our schools where students now wear uniforms, the gang influence has gone way down and discipline has really improved. We have people that come into the schools to talk to the teachers and children. But sometimes the problem is in the family. These gangs have gone on for generations in some families. Sometimes children just need to belong. The influence of friends often seems more important at that age than adult influence.

Flora Fortis, School Psychologist

Parents intimidate children and children, in turn, want to intimidate others. Children who are attracted to gangs have violence at home. Children lack safe opportunities for recreation and for getting together to learn different ways to adjust to the U.S. culture. They face job discrimination and lack the opportunities to get a job. The family's lifestyle is important. We can't change a family's whole lifestyle in an eight-session parenting class, but we can at least plant a small message in their minds about change.

Raul Rojas, Parent Educator and Community Outreach Coordinator

Gang membership meets a lot of children's need for recognition. Not all gang behavior is destructive. Some very strong leadership skills are used in these gangs. In our community there's a tortilla factory run by gang members called Home Boy Tortillas. They've done some very innovative things. I saw gang members working there and doing very productive work.

Renee Martinez, Professor of Child Development

Gang prevention programs for 13- and 14-year-olds are too late. We need to do it when kids are eight or nine. We need to help kids develop talents in art, music, sports, woodwork, auto mechanics, carpentry, cooking, writing, dance, etc., to provide as many experiences as possible to open the world up to the child.

Maria Reyes, Social Worker

I work with a group of youth at risk of becoming gang members. I assigned them the task of finding names for their small groups. We tried to set up a competition between the groups and asked them for suggestions of good ways to compete. Many of them said, "We want to fight; we need to fight and be physical." I tried to suggest other ways of competition because we had no way of letting them fight safely, but the kids insisted that the only way was to use force, to fight each other. Finally, the young women in the group suggested that I give them some questions that the groups could think about and discuss. I said, "Great, this is another way to compete." Too many kids use power, force, and intimidation. It's considered very macho to have the power to intimidate others.

Raul Rojas, Parent Educator and Community Outreach Coordinator

What about Latino teenagers going on to college?

The Mexican population has a big college-dropout rate. I think a lot of it is their loneliness for family, for really knowing who they are and not having to think about how to fit in with the U.S. culture—about what is considered right or wrong. America is very future oriented and the Mexican culture is very "here and now" oriented.

Yolanda Torres, Child Care Consultant

Latino women have only been readily accepted into universities and paid attention to in the classroom for the last 15 or 20 years. Latino men did not accept that women could know more than they did. This is still a problem in the rural areas, where families give little or no encouragement to girls to pursue any type of education.

Rita Rossi, Librarian and Resource Center Staff

What are some of the more pervasive problems in the Mexican families that you see in your work?

I think a lot of the problems have to do with the cultural clash. For example, for teenagers there's a conflict between what the parents do (what was done in the old country) and what the teenagers feel works in the U.S. Parents are either unable to make the shift or don't have the information they need to make a shift. When most people talk about assimilation, they mean people assimilating *into* the U.S. culture. I look at it differently. People assimilate aspects of the culture into themselves. Nobody just makes a switch to another culture. Kids assimilate certain aspects of the U.S. culture, and parents don't understand that they need to make a shift, too. They don't understand that the adoption of certain values is a natural process. So there needs to be a lot of teaching and orientation for the parents about that. The tradition is to have the man come to the U.S. and send money home. But in the last few years, a lot more single women have been coming to the U.S. These women are either coming by themselves or with their children. Those who come undocumented go through a lot of trauma. They have a really tough time. If an institution lacks the proper staff, the Mexicans can't relate to them. When it comes to talking about what they feel, they need to speak in their native tongue. Another issue in the typical Mexican family is class differences. Those of us who have been through a middle-class education have middle-class ways of saying things, a set of expectations and timelines that may make no sense to a working-class person.

Jorge Gonzalez, Psychiatric Social Worker

What do parents in your parenting class need help with?

They need help with exactly what other parents need help with: how to understand their child's development at this stage; how to take care of their child; what behavior to expect and what it means; how to learn more about their child; how to establish adequate communication with their child; how to teach discipline to their child; how to discipline with love and how to understand that punishment and discipline are two different things.

Raul Rojas, Parent Educator and Community Outreach Coordinator

What would a good parenting education program for Mexican families look like?

We need to address programs and services from the perspective of an evolving culture, of a bicultural experience. Not every family is at the same stage of acculturation—it depends on the generation and on the family. This presents a challenge. We also need to start at a very early age. It would also help to look at the parents' lives from a holistic point of view. Parenting is only one part of being a parent. Being a parent also involves survival, employment, education, and housing. The best educational program in parenting will be ignored if it doesn't deal with the parents' most immediate survival needs. So the parenting program has to be linked to many other kinds of services to meet the family's survival needs.

Josie Romero, Clinical Social Worker and
Director of a Family Institute

As the Latino professionals discuss some of the adolescent struggles in this chapter, we keep hearing about issues that have gotten increasingly out of control since these children were infants. Comments about children who don't find satisfaction in school and who lose respect for their parents raise the issue of parents listening to and valuing the views of their children beginning at infancy. They also highlight the importance of parents becoming familiar with the U.S. school system, learning some English, and learning more about child rearing through parenting classes and support groups.

PART V

HEALTH CARE
CONCERNS[14]

---

[14]Most of the information in this Part is *also* very relevant for professionals working with Latino families in social services; education, including special education; early childhood and parent education; and mental health.

Chapter 38

Establishing a Good Relationship with Latino Families

What is important in establishing a good relationship with Latino families?

In this chapter, the focus is on what we can do as professionals to be more welcoming to Latinos and to establish the kind of relationship that is more likely to increase their comfort level and feelings of acceptance.

The personality and attitude of the professional is important. It has to come from the heart. Is the professional interested and sincere? Is he or she taking the time to be human, not rushing, and not being fearful just because the Latinos come from a place the professional doesn't understand?

From a meeting of Latina/Chicana social workers
at a county social services agency

You need good quality people that will treat Latinos with respect and dignity. Latinos are very proud people. They need to have their dignity respected.

Amalia DeBord, Clinical Social Worker

Respect. Look at them and be sincere. Eye contact is very important.

Latinos want to be treated with respect, no matter how they look, talk, etc. It's important not to ignore them and to help them feel you care. This begins with the receptionist.

From a meeting of Latina/Chicana social workers
at a county social services agency

Professionals need to spend time with the families. They need to listen to them and develop a trusting relationship.

Rosa Carreno, Community Health Worker

Latinos want to have more time—not just the billable hours. Touch them; find out about their family and what they have been trying.

From a meeting of Latina/Chicana social workers
at a county social services agency

Those who like going to the pediatrician are those who have a pediatrician that takes time with them. The families feel especially comfortable when the pediatrician remembers their names and some special tidbit from the past. This makes them feel special, which makes it more likely that they'll follow his recommendations.

Carmen Cortez, Associate Director, Parenting Program

A lot of Latinos like to have their hand shaken when they come into the room. They like a very easy, non-condescending approach. Try a humble approach. Genuine sincerity will go a long way.

Juan Carrillo, Pediatrician

Professionals might ask a family, "What brought you to the U.S.? What was your life like before you came?" Some families came from a civil war or from an otherwise violent background.

Dolores Ramirez, Multicultural Director

Many non-Latino health care professionals move too fast, wanting to get right into business before they've established a relationship. That's important to know because an action plan or advice is only going to be as valuable as the perceived relationship. If the professional has not taken the time to develop that relationship, the advice or plan has no value.

Josie Romero, Clinical Social Worker and
Director of a Family Institute

At the beginning, the family will be distant and formal. It will be hard for them to talk openly. Once you establish a relationship, the family might be very informal and may treat you more like a relative than a professional. It's a different way. It's important to be willing to accept the relationship that the Latinos expect. Touching and hugging are part of what is expected. Physical contact is important to Latinos. They need less personal space than Anglos. They tend to stand closer. This varies, of course, depending on a number of factors: the level of acculturation and assimilation to this culture; whether or not they were born here; whether they came as an adult or as a child; how rooted in or alienated from their culture they are. It's harder for Latinos to change if they come here as adults. Their kids will probably try to be more American. This causes a huge gap between the generations.

Ana Morante, Outpatient (Mental Health) Case Worker

What else is important for professionals working with recent immigrants from Mexico to know?

Well, I always try not to stereotype. I find it useful to look at Mexican people in a modern/traditional continuum and find out where the family falls. How traditional are they? If someone comes from Mexico City, I already make some assumptions—it's a cosmopolitan city. I try to find out how long it has been since they worked the land. Those who work the land would be more likely to be on the traditional end of the continuum. Working-class Mexicans are generally problem-oriented and concrete, so the advice we give them has to be very specific and concrete.

Jorge Gonzalez, Psychiatric Social Worker

The lack of a common language makes a Latino uncomfortable. This is made worse if the professional does not try to understand your situation, does not make you feel welcome and important, and does not make you feel like a human being who needs services and help. All these barriers are great. The doctor is a very important figure to the Latino—like the parent is to the child. Latinos leave the responsibility for their health in their doctor's hands.

Raul Rojas, Parent Educator and Community Outreach Coordinator

It's important to be aware that these families are like everyone else. They may speak Spanish, they may have less education, and their skin is darker, but if their baby gets sick, they worry; if someone dies, they cry; and when their child comes home with an A, they are happy. We have to be really cautious about stereotypes.

I think any professional has to figure out if he or she has respect for these people and if they don't, then they should not work with them.

Gil Villagrán, Child Welfare Social Worker

It's important that we realize that, even though a person is an immigrant and may not speak the language, they do know what they are doing. Sometimes I run into colleagues who assume these people don't know what they are doing and it always ends badly. Patients are going to teach us about themselves. I always assume that I don't know. Mexicans like to be given advice. You are the expert. You need to be humble, but you also need to let them know you have something to offer them. You need to do a dance between being a very warm person that understands and listens and distancing yourself enough to say, "This is what I recommend." You still have to show warmth; they have to like you. For Mexicans, the relationship with the person is the important thing. Even teachers have to establish some kind of relationship where the parents and the child like them. This is true to some extent in any culture, but it is more true in the Mexican culture.

Jorge Gonzalez, Psychiatric Social Worker

Chapter 39

Deciding to Use a Doctor

When do families go to doctors and what are their views about doctors?

Here we see what influences the rural Mexican family's decisions about using health care professionals. We also get more insight into their views on preventive care.

If the problem is mild, people from Mexico tend to use home remedies such as teas and certain kinds of food. If the problem continues and gets worse or if it keeps them from work (like a back or arm pain), they'll go to the doctor. There are very few physicians in rural and semi-rural Mexico, so families from Mexico usually have not had much experience with physicians.

Carmen Guedea, Parent Educator

Most families do not see a need to go to a doctor for preventive care. If there is no problem, they don't go. Their attitude is, "Why worry about something that has not happened yet?" For example, pregnancy is not considered anything to be concerned about.

The problem has to be serious to go to the doctor. Because of the cost, they just don't run to the doctor for every little cold. Men, especially, have problems seeking medical care. It's not manly to be sick or admit weakness. And they can't afford to miss work. By the time they get to a doctor, the condition may be very serious.

Going to a doctor means going to someone who doesn't understand them or their culture. They have to try to explain the problem, and they are timid about revealing something that may be humiliating—it's uncomfortable or a sign of weakness. They may also fear the unknown: whatever is wrong with them, whatever is going to happen.

When I took migrant workers to get help, they were willing to go. They were not afraid of doctors, but they had to be almost dead to go (for example, they were having trouble breathing). Their fear was of losing work. So they only went when they could not function. It's a very male thing; they have to keep getting a paycheck. It's a little different with women. They tend to go to a doctor more quickly with their children, but they have to justify it to their husbands. The women are timid and are used to having someone tell them what to do.

Dolores Ramirez, Multicultural Director

Families think that doctors are very expensive. They think they should only go to the doctor when they are very, very sick, not for preventive care. Preventive care is not seen as very important. If there is someone with the doctor who speaks Spanish, it's easier for the family. They don't always understand instructions that doctors give them for medications and other treatments.

It's difficult for Mexicans from rural and small town areas to deal with the system here. If they call up a doctor or a social worker and get the voice mail, they get upset that they can't talk to the person. They don't know what to do.

Rosa Carreno, Community Health Worker

Families don't go to a doctor unless they are very ill. They don't go for preventive care. They don't have insurance, and it's just not something they do. Besides, they don't know where to go. They don't check with a pediatrician. They also don't see dentists, and, with all the sweets they eat, that's a problem.

Linda Espinosa, Professor of Education and
Former Director of a Parenting Program

By the time parents go to a doctor for their child, the child is pretty sick. They've already tried everything else; a doctor is their last alternative. A lot of times you see Latinos in the emergency room. The children may have to be hospitalized. (Colds lead to ear infections, pneumonia, and bronchitis; diarrhea leads to dehydration.) Their reluctance to go to doctors sooner changes with more education and information about preventive health. It helps when we take time to explain the importance of preventive care to patients—individually and in parenting groups.

Carmen Cortez, Associate Director, Parenting Program

What are the barriers to using physicians?

The main reasons Mexican families hesitate to use physicians are their belief in other kinds of remedies, their limited experience with physicians, a lack of money or insurance, and the shortage of bilingual/bicultural physicians (that is, someone they feel will really understand them). If patients are insured, they often select their physician by looking through the insurance directory of physicians for those with Spanish surnames.

Juan Carrillo, Pediatrician

People from rural areas look first within their community and friends before going to anyone else. Many of them don't have access to health care because they don't have insurance and they are undocumented.

Rafael Ramirez, Elementary School Principal

Some Mexicans ask me whether certain medications are safe. They feel something natural is best and may have a strong resistance to taking drugs. They fear that the doctor will treat them for something that's not that bad with something that will make them feel worse. Mexicans are an earthy people. There may be a difference in attitudes depending on whether they are rural or urban, educated or illiterate. Mexicans have a long tradition of using natural healers who use teas and folk medicines. They can usually find an herbal specialist—someone knowledgeable about what to take and how much. Also, Mexico doesn't have strong laws on drugs. You can buy penicillin in Mexico without a prescription. And you can get snake venom capsules for arthritis. You can get syringes easily, too.

Dolores Ramirez, Multicultural Director

Do many Latino families use folk healing first?

If families are new immigrants and don't have health care, they would tend to use folk remedies first. In Mexico and other Latin American countries, you can get a lot of medicine over the counter in pharmacies that would only be available as prescriptions in the U.S., so there's a lot of self-prescribing. Some people go to Tijuana from the U.S. just to get the medicine. If they can figure out what they have from the symptoms, they just buy the medication. They also use a lot of natural medicines and herbs. I use some herbs made into teas for stomach aches. These are things my mother used. People use family remedies.

Ana Morante, Outpatient (Mental Health) Case Worker

By the time families bring their children to me, they have already gone through various family members for advice—either directly or indirectly. Most family members have contributed their ideas, for good or for bad, and when the child doesn't get better, the parent seeks help elsewhere—depending on their level of sophistication with the American medical system. I think some would go to healers (*curanderos* [koo·rahn·DEH·rohs: folk healers], *sobadoros* [so·bah·DOH·rohs: masseuse]) because that's their tradition. A lot of patients have gotten good results and they believe in it. Faith is a very strong element in the healing process. Who they go to for help has to do with the severity of the problem. Aside from a few dangerous maneuvers, I think what *curanderos* and *sobadoros* do isn't such a bad thing—it's benign. It gives the Latino the feeling of getting some relief or benefit. If the *sobadoros* or *curanderos* don't fix the broken leg or the pneumonia, parents start looking elsewhere—sometimes out of desperation. They'll speak to family members or friends and ask who they can take their child to. The Latino families I see in private practice are the ones who know me by word of mouth. Most patients from Mexico will choose to go to community clinics or community medical centers. If they know of me, they'll come to me. A lot of Mexicans feel comfortable with general practitioners because they've had good success with them. Families that are from a city in Mexico tend to be more sophisticated and more likely to use a pediatrician or a general physician instead of other remedies.

Juan Carrillo, Pediatrician

The barriers to using health care services for families from rural and semi-rural Mexico are clearly enormous. Using welcoming approaches to establishing good relationships with Mexican families, such as those described in Chapter 38, p. 220, and increasing our understanding of folk healing methods, described in Chapter 40, p. 229, are extremely important. Major barriers for families include knowing who and where to go to for medical treatment, being able to get there, and being able to afford both the care and the loss of income.

Folk Healing

What is folk healing?
What are commonly used folk healing practices?
Who are the folk healing practitioners?

This chapter offers an excellent introduction to folk healing. In addition, several Latino professionals share their own experiences with folk healing methods. It is important for health care professionals to learn about the basic beliefs of these time-honored and continuing physical and spiritual health systems.

Excerpts from "Folk-Healing Among Mexican-American Families as a Consideration in the Delivery of Child Welfare and Child Health Services," by Elvia R. Krajewski-Jaime, from Child Welfare, 70(2), pp. 157-167, 1991, reprinted by special permission of the Child Welfare League of America:

Definition of Folk Healing

Curanderismo, or folk healing, is the treatment of a variety of ailments with a combination of psycho-social interventions, mild herbs, and religion [Chesney et al. 1980].[15] Some of the ailments that *curanderos,* or folk healers, focus on are thought to be equivalent to those treated by psychiatrists. This commonality has led some authors to suggest that the *curandero* and the providers of psychiatric services be more closely integrated [Abril 1977].

---

[15]The references cited in this excerpted article can be found at the end of this chapter.

The health and sickness folk belief system, particularly the Mexican-American, shares its heritage with today's scientific medicine in classical Hippocratic concepts [Kosko and Flaskerud 1987; Ripley 1986; Chesney et al. 1980]. Folk medicine originated in the humoral medicine of Western Europe, in which a state of health requires a balance between the various bodily humors and between heat and cold. These views were brought to the New World by the *conquistadores.* Ripley [1986] observes that 30 years before the first log cabin settlements by the English at Jamestown, the first North American medical school was opened in Mexico City in 1580, barely 60 years after the Spaniards colonized that city. The *conquistadores* mixed their views of health and sickness with those of the American Indian natives. The Spaniards themselves owed their knowledge of medicine to the Moors who ruled the southern part of Spain and who had much earlier opened the first European school of medicine, at Salerno, when the rest of Europe was still deep in the Middle Ages.

Descriptions of folk medicine among Hispanics have identified three central aspects:

The role of the social network, particularly kin, in diagnosing and treating illness;

The relationship between religion and illness, which includes the use of religious ritual in many healing processes; and

The remarkable consistency of beliefs among Hispanic communities about symptoms, etiology, and regimens of healing; this consistency, however, does not imply uniformity of belief among individuals who are Hispanic.

Folk healing, however, *must not* be confused with *spiritism, santerismo,* or *witchcraft. Spiritism* is a system mainly used by a significant number of Puerto Ricans. It consists of an invisible world, populated by spirits, that surrounds the visible world. These spirits can penetrate the visible world and attach themselves to human beings. Some spirits are currently incarnated (as human beings) and some are not. Non-incarnated (disembodied) spirits communicate with the incarnated (embodied) through mediums or people who have developed *facultades spirituales* (spiritual faculties) and may directly intervene positively or negatively in the existence of the incarnated [Torrey 1986].

Santerismo is mostly used by some Cubans and other Caribbean populations. It invokes the intervention of different saints to heal illness. At times, however, it also uses a combination of spiritism and religion.

Witchcraft is considered evil and not good to use in the practice of healing. Witchcraft calls evil spirits to cast usually negative spells on people. Since the use of witchcraft is not a positive force, people seeking to be cured stay away from it.

Folk Illness and Etiology

Some people among Hispanic populations, especially Mexican-American and Puerto Rican, have their own beliefs about the causes of disease and illness [Ripley 1986; Chesney et al. 1980; Abril 1977; Clark 1970]. They perceive illness as a state of physical discomfort. Researchers have found that the most common criteria of good health among Hispanics include a strong body, the ability to maintain a high level of normal physical activity, and the absence of persistent pain and discomfort [Abril 1977]. If an individual has no symptoms, as in early anemia, diabetes, tuberculosis, or heart disease, the person is believed to be well and healthy; prevention, therefore, is a challenging concept to convey.

In general, three of the most common beliefs are (1) natural and supernatural forces; (2) imbalances of heat and cold; and (3) emotions as a cause of disease [Chesney et al. 1980; Klein 1978; Abril 1977; Keiv 1968].

Natural and Supernatural Forces

Exposure to the forces of nature, such as moonlight, eclipses, cold, heat, air, wind, sun, and water, are believed, especially by poor immigrant families, to cause illness [Abril 1977]. *Mal aire* is a folk belief in which "bad air" affects children and adults, causing pain, cramps, and most commonly, facial twitching and paralysis [Clark 1970]. Individuals are reluctant to go from a warm room directly into the cold, especially when they have just awakened or taken a warm bath. When a child is born with a cleft lip or palate, it is believed that the mother was exposed to a lunar eclipse when she was pregnant. To prevent this from happening, after exposure to an eclipse a pregnant women wears a belt to which a set of keys is attached in such a way that the keys lie right over the womb; she wears this belt until the child's birth [Abril 1977].

In terms of the supernatural, some people believe that some ailments are caused by magical powers such as the "evil eye": If someone with *strong vision* admires someone else's child without actually touching him or her, the child may fall ill—the evil power is transmitted through the gaze of that person. Symptoms of this malady include insomnia, aches and pains, excessive crying, fever, severe headache, and restlessness. The simplest treatment for evil eye is to have the person who exerted the influence touch the child to break any possible evil bond. Some parents may even expect that person to make the sign of the cross over the child [Abril 1977; Chavira 1975] If the person who exerted the influence is not located, the child is taken to a folk healer. The treatment consists of rubbing an unbroken raw egg over the child's body; the egg is then broken and the yolk examined. A red spot on the yolk is a diagnostic sign. The same egg is put into a small bowl of water and a cross made of blessed palm is laid over it. The bowl is then placed under the head of the victim's bed. This is thought to help draw out the evil force. The following morning the egg is buried, away from plants to avoid the force of any evil from it wilting them [Abril 1977; Clark 1970].

Imbalances of Heat and Cold

To be healthy requires a balance between heat and cold and the various bodily humors. With the domination of Christianity over the pre-Hispanic beliefs, the various humors or spirits of the body became rationalized into "good spirits," with evil trying to gain entry at every opportunity. Ripley [1986] notes, however, that Hispanics are not the only ones to do their best to keep the evil spirits at a distance. Noting that many Anglo-Americans today still say "God bless you" when they hear a sneeze, he claims that our collective preconscious recollection of fear that the soul will leave the body momentarily is still strong!

The state of health is seen as demanding a balance between the hot and the cold and maintaining a strong defense against the entry of evil [Ripley 1986]. Some diseases are hot and some are cold. Foods and herbs are also classified into hot or cold for treatments [Abril 1977]. Sickness that enhances the cold within the body requires a hot treatment to restore the balance, and vice versa. To avoid a hot sickness, the person must not become cold, therefore, the individual must not walk barefoot on cold tiles for fear of catching tonsillitis [Ripley 1986]. Similarly, if the feet get wet, it is important to get the fontanel area of the head wet as well or the imbalance will lead to a sore throat. People are given chili, a hot food, or chicken soup, for a cold disease such as pneumonia or a common cold, and lard, having "cold" properties, is used on burns [Abril 1977].

Emotions as a Cause of Disease

Two common emotionally based illnesses are *mal del susto* and *espanto*. *Susto* (fright) is usually the result of a traumatic experience that may be anything from witnessing an accident or death to a simple scare at night. *Espanto*, another form of *susto*, is thought to be caused by fright due to supernatural causes. In *espanto*, the spirit leaves the body as a result of the scare. Symptoms of these illnesses include anorexia, insomnia, hallucinations, weakness, and various painful sensations [Chesney et al. 1980; Abril 1977]. Treatment by the folk healer includes having the patient lie down on the floor with arms outstretched in the position of a cross. Sweeping the body with branches, herbs, and prayers, she coaxes the lost spirit to reenter the victim's body. Cases of *susto* or *espanto* delayed by using a practitioner not equipped to handle such conditions (such as a doctor), are believed eventually to prove fatal [Rubel 1960]; patients and their families may strongly resist referrals for professional help [Abril 1977].

Finally, two diseases identified in folk medicine that do not fall into any particular category are *empacho* and *mollera caida* (fallen fontanel). *Empacho* is believed to be caused by a bolus of poorly digested or uncooked food sticking to the abdominal lining, causing swelling. Symptoms include lack of appetite, stomachache, diarrhea, and vomiting, and in children, crying [Chesney et al. 1980; Abril 1977]. This ailment is diagnosed by feeling the calves of the legs for bundles of knots along the nerves. If lumps are found in the calves, the abdomen is palpated and a large hard ball in the stomach may be felt [Clark 1970]. This condition is attributed to excess intake of cheese, eggs, bananas, and soft bread, especially in children. The goal of treatment is to dislodge the bolus of food from the wall of the stomach. Treatment includes rubbing the stomach and pinching and pulling up on the skin of the back in small folds at every third vertebra and then releasing it. This is repeated until three pops are heard, signifying the dislodgment of the bolus. A purgative tea *(estafiate)* is usually given to the patient to help "clean out the stomach" [Chesney et al. 1980; Abril 1977].

Mollera caida is of special interest to child welfare and child health care providers. This condition, which has fallen fontanel as its most prominent symptom, is believed to be caused by dropping or bouncing a baby too hard or by removing the nipple too roughly from the baby's mouth. This, in turn, causes the fontanel to sink, making the palate bulge, which interferes with the infant's eating. Symptoms include failure to suckle, sunken eyes, vomiting, diarrhea, excessive crying, and sometimes fever. Treatments include holding the child upside down over a pan of water, applying a poultice to the depressed area of the head, and/or inserting a finger in the child's mouth and pushing up on the palate [Chesney et al 1980; Abril 1977].

Researchers claim that of all conditions listed so far, fallen fontanel is the most difficult for the family practitioner or health care practitioner to handle. The cultural belief in the cause and treatment of this illness is very strong, and much ingenuity is needed to prompt the mother to seek medical intervention. Abril [1977] contends that in too many cases, when the mother finally seeks medical attention, the clinical symptoms of dehydration are already apparent.

Acceptance of Folk Beliefs and Practices

Hispanics in the United States are a heterogeneous population that includes Mexican-Americans, Puerto Ricans, Cubans, and many other Hispanics from Spanish and Latin American countries. Each of these subgroups has its own cultural ways, beliefs, and historical background. Belief in folk healing, therefore, must not be generalized to all Hispanic populations, or even to one Hispanic group. Chesney et al. [1980], for instance, in a study of Mexican-American folk medicine, found that between 20% and 30% of their sample did not believe in folk illnesses or folk healing. Although it has been found that the lower the socioeconomic level the stronger the belief in folk healing, it is also important to take into consideration that the degree to which these folk beliefs and practices are accepted varies from generation to generation, and depends largely on the extent of education and level of adaptation to the Anglo-American dominant culture [Kosko and Flaskerud 1987; Abril 1977].

Within the Mexican-American population many attitudes and practices, including attitudes toward health and illness, have filtered down through the years. With time, these practices have become diluted and are now considered "traditional" by even fourth or fifth generation individuals [Tripp-Reimer 1982; Abril 1977; Ragucci 1972].

The literature on folk medicine, especially among Mexican-Americans and Puerto Ricans, suggests that the choice of conventional care and/or folk medicine depends upon the symptom, that families often use both folk and conventional medicine, that they are more likely to seek medical help for anxiety than for depression, and that knowledge of folk medicine is best acquired by asking about specific folk diseases [Torrey 1986; Ailinger 1985; Chesney et al. 1980].

Implications for Child Welfare and Child Health Care Practitioners

Folk medicine and modern scientific practice have coexisted for many years. Professionals trained in the modern biomedical sciences, however, may not be aware of the patient's or client's beliefs or participation in folk medicine. The literature suggests that many Mexican-American patients or clients may concurrently receive treatment from both the conventional and folk medicine systems. This is especially important for child welfare workers and health care practitioners such as medical social workers, physicians, nurses, and any other professional practicing with Mexican-American families [Ripley 1986; Chesney et al. 1980]. It is important to recognize that health-related cultural issues apply to treatment or intervention with this population.

One implication of folk medicine in family intervention has to do with the strong ties with the extended family among many Mexican-Americans. It is noted that when a person is ill, many of the family members are involved in deciding if indeed the patient or client is ill in the first place, and the extent of the illness, the treatment to be given, and by whom.

Most social workers and physicians receive special training in interviewing and communication [Chesney et al. 1980]. A supportive and accepting approach using the kind of empathy taught in communication courses may build trust and a mutual sharing of ideas and information. ***In many cases, practitioners must demonstrate some knowledge of folk medicine before patients or clients are willing to discuss it.*** [emphasis added]

Knowledge of folk healing practices enables practitioners to know that many Mexican-Americans consult a folk healer before even considering a visit to a medical doctor. As a second choice, families often consult chiropractors, naturopaths, homeopaths, and herbalists rather than medical doctors. Mexican-American families find these practitioners to be more compassionate and kind, and to possess a more understanding acceptance of traditional beliefs and practices, than physicians [Clark 1970]. In addition, treatment by these practitioners involves massage, manipulation, and use of herbs, treatment congruent with that of folk healing.

In most instances, however, the folk healer is consulted because he or she has known the family intimately for many years, speaks their language, and *does not dictate orders for care but makes suggestions, leaving the ultimate decision up to the patient and family.*

Success in intervention with Mexican-American families also involves keeping other considerations in mind. For example, since many Mexican-Americans prefer to consult family members about treatment, especially in cases of hospitalization or prolonged therapy, before making a decision, practitioners who assume a dictatorial or authoritative manner will just bring about noncompliance because final authority rests with the immediate family.

Language is another consideration. Although many Mexican-Americans are bilingual, when it comes to expression of pain, many may have a strong preference for speaking in the language with which they feel most comfortable. If a patient speaks Spanish only, or prefers this language, a Spanish-speaking child welfare service provider, medical social worker, doctor, or nurse must be available. Directions for medications or treatment should be explained in detail, and Spanish literature might be used to reinforce these verbal instructions. If no Hispanic professional is available, the use of trained bilingual aides is best. Caution must be exercised in using untrained interpreters, such as members of the family, since much is lost or misinterpreted, especially in health care settings.

Sensitivity, an open mind, and an understanding of the patient's or client's perception of the illness and his or her ideas about what constitutes effective treatment are other caveats in intervention with Mexican American families. Conflicts with, or rejection of, these beliefs by non-Hispanic professionals leads to fear, distrust, and eventual rejection of their services [Chesney et al. 1980; Abril 1977]. A fairly large group of scientifically identified diseases, such as tuberculosis, cancer, pneumonia, and chicken pox, are recognized by Mexican-American people who believe in folk healing. Although the etiology and treatment of these illnesses may be different from conventional medicine, some practitioners do not find an integration of both systems incongruent or damaging. For instance, understanding and support of the use of the belt with the set of keys for the mother who believes that exposure to a lunar eclipse will result in a cleft lip/palate of her unborn child does not affect conventional treatment. On the contrary, the practitioner will help to validate a strong belief while alleviating guilt feelings and providing much-needed emotional support [Abril 1977].

Another way to integrate folk beliefs with conventional medicine is keeping an infant or child partly covered during a physical examination. This may reduce some of the mother's fears about mal aire. Similarly, while the mother may be encouraged to give a child warm herbal teas to balance out the cold disease process of a sore throat, the mother may also be informed that, to be on the safe side, a throat culture to rule out a possible strep infection will also be included in the treatment. Again, introducing ice for the treatment of burns is usually congruent with the folk healing belief in the hot and cold classification of disease [Abril 1977].

In conclusion, an understanding of the view of illness between the professional and the client or patient greatly enhances the intervention process and prevents misdiagnoses and incorrect assessments. The fact that the professional "knows" what is wrong affords considerable relief to the worried client or patient, and the naming process itself thus becomes therapeutic [Torrey 1986]. As Abril [1977] stresses:

Rather than openly deny the existence of folk illnesses and the effectiveness of traditional home remedies, the health care worker should try to incorporate them into the plan of care. It is not necessary to destroy a people's culture to improve their health and well-being. [emphasis added]

Do families you see still use folk medicine?

Yes they do. We can never dispel the myths, misconceptions, or the people's belief in that system. That belief is a very hard thing to dispel. I don't think it's so much an educational process. It would be futile to try to educate them all into Western ways of thinking. It just won't hold. New families are coming all of the time from Mexico who have never been to a Western doctor. They just want their child to be healed, and everything sounds so foreign. They might also be feeling worried and anxious. So it's not a good time to educate them. There's a big gap because some of them operate on a belief system of *curanderismo* [koo·rahn·dehr·EEZ·mo: folk healing] and folklore. I can't begin to dispel some of those myths; I prefer to just work alongside it. I don't criticize. Maybe they took their child to the *sobadora* [so·bah·DOH·rah: masseuse] and what the *sobadora* did didn't work. I have to agree with them that there will be times that what I do isn't going to work either. Then we go on to another way of managing it. I don't want them to feel put down. They are doing all that they can to correct the problem. They're genuinely concerned. They're operating on their own belief system and that system may or may not work. Now they're coming to you for a solution. They don't need to be berated for what they've done.

Juan Carrillo, Pediatrician

Families may go to a pharmacist they feel comfortable with for advice. Pharmacists are well-respected and may be found at a *botica* [bo·TEE·kah]. A *botica* is like a drug store and has a lot of folk remedies, teas, ointments, big bandaids for pains and aches, candles, and soaps.

Carmen Cortez, Associate Director, Parenting Program

I think it is important to acknowledge the importance of folk remedies. The people have faith in them; the remedies have worked and they are part of the history and culture. Folk medicine, like the teas and the ointments, are a type of prevention. It may not be the type that we use in the Western World, but it is definitely a type of prevention. In the past there were no physicians where these families came from but the herbs were available. It is very important to give the mothers very positive feedback for what they are doing in using folk medicines and then build from there.

Rosalie Prado de Ramirez, Public Health Nursing Supervisor

Families use a lot of herbs to heal themselves. In rural areas they use a *curandero* as a healer. *Curanderos* [koo·rahn·DEHR·rohs] do spiritual healing and use herbs. *Sobadoras* do massage. A *curandero* has to have some really good training and the faith and trust of the people. You can find several in the nearby cities where there is a large Latino population. There are some in our smaller city, too. The knowledge is often passed down from one generation to another.

Rafael Ramirez, Elementary School Principal

Curanderos are psychological, religious, spiritual, and physical healers. It's an informal position and they are found within the community. If you need them, you can find them.

From a meeting of Latina/Chicana social workers
at a county social services agency

There are not too many *curanderos* around. When I was growing up, there were a lot and they were highly respected. My own parents and grandparents went to *curanderos*. A *curandero* was like your psychologist, physician, and advisor all rolled into one. They were messengers of God—blessed by God with a special ability to intervene. They had a lot of powers in terms of mental telepathy and a lot of ability to heal. A lot of that healing was emotional and deeply rooted in faith. They knew folk remedies and gave advice on what to take.

Carmen Cortez, Associate Director, Parenting Program

Some of the maneuvers of *curanderos* are somewhat dangerous, like lifting the soft spot. There's a lot of misconception about what the soft spot it. This has led to unfortunate cases where the measures they used caused damage to soft or intracranial tissue. These measures include putting a thumb into the hard palate and pressing as hard as they can to push the soft spot up, or turning the child upside down and spanking the soles of their feet. This can cause some micro-hemorrhage at the capillary level in the brain itself.

Juan Carrillo, Pediatrician

Do you think physicians should learn more about Latino folk medicine?

It wouldn't hurt. I could probably stand to take a course or two myself.

Juan Carrillo, Pediatrician

What kinds of folk healing methods do you still hear about from families you work with?

Pregnant women should not touch anything cold. For colds and coughs, they should drink boiled red onion juice and eat no sweets. Cough medicine is sweet, so it's believed to increase the cough. If you have a cold, stay warm. Hot/cold theories are very prevalent, especially for those just coming to the U.S.

Carmen Guedea, Parent Educator

There's a belief that a fallen fontanel means something is wrong with the child related to the palate and sucking, etc. They turn the baby upside down and shake him so that the fontanel will pop back out. There are other things that they do for this, but they require a special person to do it—someone who knows what they're doing. For example, putting a paper cone in the ear with fire is done to get the cold air out of your ear. I still hear of people believing in cold/warm/hot theories.

Carmen Cortez, Associate Director, Parenting Program

Sobadoras use back-rubs. *Curanderos* use home remedies, teas, and massage to take away bad spirits; they cleanse the body with weeds. They'll cure a baby with a fallen fontanel or one who has a spell on him. These types of cures usually cost $10 to $20 for a child, $15 to $25 for an adult. For a woman who can't get pregnant, it would cost $20 to $50 to get her uterus back in place. To get evil spirits out, it costs $100 to $300. *Curanderos* also treat *empacho* [ehm·PAH·cho] (That's when a child eats gummy stuff and it sticks to the intestines). The *curandero* will cleanse that, using a back rub or pulling skin to loosen what's in the intestines. If the problem continues, the family will then go to the doctor.

Carmen Guedea, Parent Educator

Sometimes you see a child with a red thread or ribbon around his wrist or under his clothes. It's to protect him from the evil eye. If you go to a home and don't touch a child enough or don't greet it, and that child later becomes sick, the family will think you gave the child the evil eye.

Rosa Carreno, Community Health Worker

A mother called me and told me she was having trouble with her teenage daughter; she was staying out late and not listening to her. I contacted Children's Protective Services [CPS] because the parents were hitting the daughter. I told the mother that she had to go to some classes to help her learn how to talk with her daughter. She told me she had gone to the *curandero*, who gave her some salt, aromatic herbs, and prayers. I didn't see any harm in this. After she finished the classes, I called her and learned her daughter was better. The mother told me, "See I told you the herbs would work." She didn't think it was the classes.

Rosa Carreno, Community Health Worker

It continues to be very important for health care, social services, education, and other professionals to understand the basis of folk healing or *curanderismo* [koo·rahn·dehr·EEZ·mo]. As you can see, there is a long and strongly valued belief in many methods that continue to be found therapeutic. Almost every Latino professional we interviewed continues to *personally* use some methods (especially certain types of teas) that they have found to be of help for specific ailments. Being able to ask about and, as much as possible, work *with* those methods that Western medicine has not found to be harmful helps professionals make a family from rural Mexico feel welcomed and respected.

References cited in *"Folk-Healing Among Mexican-American Families as a Consideration in the Delivery of Child Welfare and Child Health Services"*

Abril, I.F. "Mexican-American Folk Beliefs: How They Affect Health Care." *The American Journal of Maternal Child Nursing* (May/June 1977): 168–173.

Ailinger, R.L. "Beliefs about Treatment of Hypertension Among Hispanic Older Persons." *Topics in Clinical Nursing* 7, 3(1985) : 26–31.

Chavira, J. *Curanderismo: An Optional Health Care System*. Edinburg. TX: Pan American University, 1975.

Chesney, A.P., Thompson, B.L., Guevara, A., Vela, A., and Schottstaedt, M.F. "Mexican-American Folk Medicine: Implications for the Family Physician." *The Journal of Family Practice* 11(1980) : 567–574.

Clark, M. *Health in the Mexican-American Culture: A Community Study* (2nd ed.). Berkeley, CA: University of California Press, 1970: 173.

Keiv, A. *Curanderismo: Mexican-American Folk Psychiatry*. New York: Free Press, 1968.

Klein, S. "Susto: The Anthropological Study of Diseases of Adaptation." *Soc. Sci. Med.* 12(1978): 23.

Kosko, D.A., and Flaskerud, J.H. "Mexican-Americans. Nurse Practitioner, and Lay Control Group Beliefs About Cause and Treatment of Chest Pain." *Nursing Research* (July/August 1987): 226–231.

Ragucci, A.T. "The Ethnographic Approach and Nursing Research." *Nursing Research* 21(1972): 485–490.

Ripley, G.D. "Mexican-American Folk Remedies: Their Place in Health Care." *Texas Medicine/Folk Medicine* 82(November 1986): 41–44.

Rubel, A.J. "Concepts of Disease in Mexican-American Culture." *American Anthropology* 62(October 1960): 795–814.

Torrey, E.F. *Witch Doctors and Psychiatrists*. Northvale. NJ: Jason Aaronson, Inc., 1986: 155–168.

Tripp-Reimer, T. "Retention of a Folk-Healing Practice Among Four Generations of Urban Greek Immigrants." *Nursing Research* 32(1982): 97–101.

Chapter 41

Patient Communication

How can health care professionals learn whether a family is using folk healing methods?
How acceptable to the family is the advice you are giving?

This chapter offers valuable suggestions on communicating with Mexican patients, including how to talk to families about folk-healing methods and learning whether your medical advice is acceptable to the family.

I always ask if they have consulted the neighbor, or the *señora* [sehn·YOR·ah: that is, the older lady in the community]. "Oh, yes," they say. I try to find out what they have tried or been told to do. Especially with new mothers—they are very confused because they have lots of different people telling them what to do.

Amalia DeBord, Clinical Social Worker

It's important to find out what the family's customary treatment is for the particular problem. If you want to give a treatment for something and are not sure how it would be received, ask, "What did you do in your family for this? What is customary?" Being asked is flattering to the family. With their limited

English, they have to listen a lot and are rarely asked their opinion. These questions show that the professional is interested and gives value to what the family is saying.

Dolores Ramirez, Multicultural Director

Ask the patients what other advice they've been given. What have they tried? What have they been advised? Say, "That's interesting. What does that method involve?"

From a meeting of Latina/Chicana social workers
at a county social services agency

In Mexico, people are used to the doctor diagnosing them, giving them information, and so forth. The patient isn't used to asking questions. I try to teach them that, here, we place the responsibility on the parent, that parents have to be informed. I teach them what that means when they come to the clinic because they have no idea. I give them a pamphlet where they can write down the name of the doctor they saw, the date of the clinic appointment, and what was discussed. Some understand this right away, but I usually have to explain the use of this information four or five times. Once they start experiencing doctors asking them questions that they can't answer, they realize, "Oh, this is what she meant."

Amalia DeBord, Clinical Social Worker

It's easier for Mexicans to work with Latino professionals. It's important to Latino people to respect elders and authorities. They will respect professionals. So, even if they don't believe the person, they will not contradict them. They will not say, "I don't think it will work." Americans see it as a lack of assertiveness. However, when it comes down to doing what's recommended, the families will do the things their own way. It's important for professionals to inquire to make sure that what is being advised makes sense to the family.

Ana Morante, Outpatient (Mental Health) Case Worker

It's important to teach the Mexican families that they have the right to participate in the decision making with the physicians and other health professionals. The families should participate in order to get better results. This will be a learning process for Latinos and for Anglo professionals. It's difficult for the doctor to be patient. The doctor should not expect the family to immediately offer opinions; they may need to go home and discuss the matter with their extended families. Try to teach the patients that they have options and a right to participate in this process.

Raul Rojas, Parent Educator and Community Outreach Coordinator

How can the health care professional find out if a person doesn't understand?

Be positive. Ask, "What did you understand about what you were just told?"

From a meeting of Latina/Chicana social workers at a county social services agency

Once the family gets home, there may be a problem implementing the advice they've been given. You won't know this unless you ask. Before they leave your office, ask if they think they will have any trouble following your advice. "Now, do you understand what the instructions are? Can you tell me or repeat them to me so I'm sure my instructions are well-understood?" You could also demonstrate—slowly—what you are asking them to do. It's important that you, as a professional, don't imply that the listener is stupid. Ask, "Do you think you can do this? Will this be difficult to do? Do you think there will be any problems?" You might find out, for example, that the recommendations aren't affordable.

Dolores Ramirez, Multicultural Director

Chapter 42

Other Issues for Mexican Families in Getting Health Care

In what ways can professionals meet the special challenges of working with Mexican families?

In this chapter, we further address ways to improve our relationships with Mexican families—especially in the arena of health care. Understanding some of the expectations Mexican families have about such things as medications and making appointments can enhance our communication—as will recognizing the role of the extended family in their decision making. Keep in mind that maintaining the patient and family dignity is paramount. We must look at our recommendations in the context of the family life and survival priorities. This chapter further points out that, even when a language barrier requires the use of a translator, there are things the professional can do to establish a warm relationship.

What do you think about folk medicine in general? Do you feel that some of it is of value?

I think so. A lot of medication came to be because of the herbal properties and medicinal properties in these teas and other remedies. I think it's just our standoffish approach that gets in the way. When they really study *manzanilla* [mahn·sah·NEE·yah: chamomile] tea in a controlled way, they may show that it does work, and here we were all along thinking it didn't. To me, as long as I don't see anything harmful in the way of folk remedies, I don't berate the parents, and I encourage them to continue trying other methods because one approach may not work all the time.

Juan Carrillo, Pediatrician

What do you do if parents give things to a child you don't want them to give?

It depends on how much I want to push and how much the patient is willing to try a different approach to the problem. For example, when a colicky baby's being given *manzanilla* tea by the grandmother, I used to say, "Stop it, don't do that. The baby should only have milk and water for the first four months." But if the baby is thriving and has no other physical problems, now I just say, "Dilute it. Never put honey in it. If you need to put sugar in it, use just a little." I tell them that we recommend milk and water for the first four months, that anything given before that time may cause allergies or other digestive problems down the line. Then I wait to see what happens. Usually the grandmother will smirk and doubt that I know what I'm talking about, possibly thinking, "Who are you to tell me how to treat colic?" The mother will probably try both methods. After all, I only have the mother for 10 or 15 minutes; the grandmother has her all the time. But my telling the mother this will probably make her think. There are so many misconceptions. I try to dispel them sensitively in whatever way I can and, as long as the methods they're using are not really harmful, I don't push it. You don't want to alienate patients or have them lie to you or not come back. Our western method isn't always the perfect one.

Juan Carrillo, Pediatrician

If Mexican families come for medical help and aren't given any medications or prescriptions, do they feel they haven't gotten the help they came for?

Yes. And it used to be that if they didn't get an injection of antibiotics, they felt they hadn't been helped. These injections are overused. Mexican families use antibiotics, like penicillin, for treating colds and flus, not for proven bacterial infections. Sometimes I explain that penicillin won't help and, when the child gets better without it, I win those parents over. Some parents are very resistant to my advice. I've prescribed penicillin for a mild otitis that I can justify a mild antibiotic for. But I try to talk these parents out of giving injections. You see, they have the supplies for injections at home and just want your OK for them to give it. Some patients are pushing hard for antibiotics and self-treating. When I can't justify an antibiotic, I give them a cold remedy that I have on my shelf. It's similar to what can be bought over the counter and I explain that it may or may not work. I win over a lot of patients by explaining the disease process from the Western point of view. Sometimes it works, sometimes it doesn't. There are probably a lot of patients that didn't come back to me because I didn't give them penicillin for their child's cold.

Juan Carrillo, Pediatrician

Patients often think that if the doctor doesn't give them medicine, seeing him was a waste of time.

Rosa Carreno, Community Health Worker

Mexicans believe that when you give medications, the more the better. If it's an injection, it's better. If it's an I.V. [intravenous solution] that goes straight to the vein, it's better still. If you are sick, you always have to have some medicine from the doctor. If a doctor tries to explain why a virus doesn't get better with medicine and a bacterial infection does, it often doesn't get through. If a doctor tells a mother to feed her sick baby just water and no milk and to come back in three days, she'll come back the next day saying her baby is still sick and that she wants some medication. That's very difficult. Sometimes they bring powders to mix with the formula when the baby is having diarrhea. Sometimes you have to just work with their methods.

Amalia DeBord, Clinical Social Worker

Who in the family makes the decisions about children's medical treatment?

Sometimes parents don't make a decision until they've consulted with a lot of different people—relatives, godparents, friends, people they have emotional attachments to. We need to give families time to discuss their choices with the extended family. It's a family decision and other people are involved.

Carmen Cortez, Associate Director, Parenting Program

Should health care professionals invite the extended family in?

Only if the illness is very involved or complicated. Otherwise, the parent will just take it back to the extended family and discuss it at the appropriate time.

Carmen Cortez, Associate Director, Parenting Program

What would encourage parents to cooperate with a health care provider?

We all go to people who we have faith in. Providers need to behave in a way that generates this faith. In the Mexican culture, doctors and teachers are seen as the experts. Their advice will be followed, but their suggestions need to make sense within the Mexican culture.

Jorge Gonzalez, Psychiatric Social Worker

What should physicians be trained to do differently?

It's important for physicians to become more aware of poverty and of other things going on in a family's life. Mexican families are often living with a lot of stresses due to poverty. It's important that physicians not just focus on the symptoms of the disease. If your Mexican patients are not following your instructions, you need to be asking what other problems they have. There is something else that needs to be explored.

Amalia DeBord, Clinical Social Worker

Many professionals are quick to judge problems and give solutions. It's important that they first show that they value things the parents are doing right and that they reinforce these things. This is important for the parents' dignity.

Josie Romero, Clinical Social Worker and
Director of a Family Institute

How do you approach parents with the concerns of the doctors?

I address the stress level of the parents first. Let me give you an example. The doctor is concerned that a child is not gaining enough weight, and he wants me to find out about the baby's home environment and feeding habits. So I start with stress. I try to ask the mother questions that will help me see if she is under a lot of stress at home or if she is feeling uncomfortable with the problem or the advice. After you empathize with the mothers and their level of stress, the conversation flows. After I identify the problem and the stress for the mother or the family, I can teach the mother what the clinic's expectations are and what the doctor wants the family to do about the problem. There would be a problem if I just went to the mother and said, "I want you to learn what we do in the U.S." That just doesn't work. You need to empathize with them. And you need to give very basic information about why the doctor is worried.

If the parents are in the clinic, I introduce myself and let them know why I am there. We talk awhile and I try to let them see that I am concerned about their whole situation. Sometimes the thing that the doctor is concerned about is only one of many problems that the family faces. Sometimes the doctors just try to reason with a family about why the medication or treatment they've pre-scribed is important, without finding out what might be preventing patients from following their instructions.

Poverty is a big factor. You need to address the family's basic needs before you can expect them to deal with anything else. How can we ask a mother to sit with a child and read when she has six children and they don't have a bed to sleep in? We have to take care of the family's basic needs first. I try to establish contact with the social services they may need. I get the school involved and arrange for transportation or housing or Children's Protective Services.

I have seen a tremendous problem with the young mothers here who have no family around to help them. They are 17 or 18 and living with young males; they have no older aunts or cousins. When they first come in, I always ask who is helping them. They are totally isolated. The males may help with things like transportation, but these young mothers are extremely isolated. Sometimes they reach out to the older neighbors, but most of the time they don't. It is a puzzle to me how these young kids are surviving without their extended family. I also try to do a lot of parenting training with these families. They need very basic information about their babies and how to care for them.

Amalia DeBord, Clinical Social Worker

What structure would help families take advantage of parenting information and health care services?

We are thinking about beginning a program in the neighborhood that mothers could walk to with their babies. We'd work out of a van that we could park in an apartment complex. We'd give vaccinations and basic information. We would establish a clinic that meets maybe twice a week. And people would come because it is in their area and it's free and nobody asks questions about immigration or money or income. We are also thinking of going to their neighborhoods so they don't have to worry about transportation. Latinos also respond to classes. If you set up classes rather than a support group, they do come.

Amalia DeBord, Clinical Social Worker

What about the problem of coming on time for appointments?

In Mexico, you go to a clinic. You may have to sit for two hours, but you will be seen. You don't make appointments. You just come in. Mexicans take this for granted in the U.S. If they make an appointment and show up two hours late, they expect to be seen. They don't really understand why people make appointments or why Anglos get so frustrated with them when they are late. Mexicans take things as they come. They might be unable to respect the policy of the medical clinic they go to because they don't understand it. They can't understand why they have to pay for an appointment they don't show up for or why they have to pay a late charge. All this needs to be carefully explained.

Carmen Guedea, Parent Educator

I discourage families from just dropping in without appointments and from coming late to appointments as much as possible. Sooner or later, they get the message. I know they want their children to get taken care of and they're not used to making appointments in Mexico. If you don't teach them that they have to make appointments or come on time, they won't learn it. Usually they understand this after you've reminded them two or three times. If they do it more than a few times (other than emergencies), we'll nicely tell them that they'll probably need to find another doctor. We point out to them that they wouldn't like to be kept waiting for an appointment. It is very infrequent that this problem persists.

Juan Carrillo, Pediatrician

What is hard advice for parents from the small towns and rural areas of Mexico to take about their child and themselves?

The biggest is diet. I try to discourage bottle-feeding as the child gets older because often a two-year-old child is getting only the bottle and nothing else. But I don't push it if a baby wants to drink a lot of milk and he's not ready for solids. Also, Mexican people often feel being rotund is healthier than being thin. It relates to their own perception of health. Lots of people in rural areas are thin—those who are sickest are the thinnest. Everyone wants his child to be plump, with rosy cheeks. It's an acculturation issue.

Juan Carrillo, Pediatrician

It's hard for farm and factory workers to follow advice on diet and rest.

Carmen Guedea, Parent Educator

It's hard for them to follow advice about their diet, about eating certain foods. Even if it's for diabetes, they often don't make the recommended changes in their diet and the situation gets worse. Our parenting program is going to try a new class about nutrition-related diseases. We've tried to make it very relevant so they can say, "Oh yes, my mother-in-law has this problem and she eats a lot of that," etc.

It's also hard to have Latinos take advice on drinking and smoking—especially males. We're thinking of teaching a class on drinking and smoking. It will be a problem, though, because it is insulting to a male to be asked to stop.

Carmen Cortez, Associate Director, Parenting Program

How can professionals deal with the language barrier?

Language is one of the biggest barriers for Mexicans; we have so many problems trying to express our ideas in English. When it has to do with health, it's hard to explain the problem clearly. Sometimes the interpreter might help. But sometimes the patient doesn't feel comfortable with the interpreter. The rural Mexican family often feels uncomfortable having someone else know so much about their personal lives.

Raul Rojas, Parent Educator and Community Outreach Coordinator

The thing is that we will never have enough people of Mexican or Latino descent to work with the Spanish speaking population here. We just don't have enough people going to college and becoming teachers, social workers, doctors. I have a lot of respect for the people who are not of Spanish descent that take the time to learn the language or the culture.

Gil Villagrán, Child Welfare Social Worker

Professionals think they can communicate with bilingual families because the family speaks English. But in times of need, Latinos are going to need to hear advice or get help in their primary language—a language that they can relate to, that gives them a sense of nurtured support and a feeling of love and attention. When people are in pain, they need to be taken care of in their primary language.

Josie Romero, Clinical Social Worker and
Director of a Family Institute

When learning a new language, people are in different stages and may only understand some of what's being told them. The speaker might think the listener is looking attentive, but the listener may have missed the most crucial word. Some families will understand. But if they don't, you have to take them step by step.

Dolores Ramirez, Multicultural Director

It is important for the professionals working with Mexican-Americans to speak Spanish. With a translator, there is something lost in the relationship. There is not the personal involvement between the client and the provider. Translators can be a positive or a negative, depending on their background and education. If there is a third person in the process, like the translator, all three have to have an active part. Often times, the professional who depends on a translator doesn't look at the client and this makes the client feel like a non-person. The translator has to be involved. She has to say, "let me explain it to them this way or it won't be acceptable." Everyone has to be involved in the conversation. It may be a taboo subject and the translator will know that you should not bring it up at the first meeting. Translators need to not only know the language but to be able to really use it so the essence of the communication gets across.

Rosalie Prado de Ramirez, Public Health Nursing Supervisor

It's hard with those families who speak only Spanish. However, when using a translator it can be helpful to have the physician be more active and involved. He should break into the conversation between the translator and the family so he seems interested. Using body language (proximity, looking interested, smiling, etc.) can help. Otherwise, the translator and patient will be the only people having the relationship. It's important that the physician and the family develop a trust and a good feeling about each other. That way the physician can give help and the family can more readily accept it.

Carmen Cortez, Associate Director, Parenting Program

Conclusion

This book has been mostly about sensitizing you to the experience of being Mexican and living in the U.S.—increasing your awareness of how families from rural and semi-rural Mexico look at things, what their life is like, what their struggles and worries are, what gives them joy.

We hope you have found this book interesting, informative, and exciting. We also hope that you have learned enough to begin to look at families from Mexico differently, with an increased empathy and a deeper understanding not only for what *is* but also for what *is possible*.

Through the Latino professionals quoted in this book, we have learned about early child-rearing practices, the school experience (including the use of special education), and the comfort of the family from rural Mexico in our health care system. The Latino professionals who were interviewed for this book all spoke to the fact that more bilingual and bicultural professionals were needed in the various disciplines to make any impact on the way Mexican families were served. While this need is paramount, we hope this book carries non-Latino professionals through the first steps to finding ways of being with Latino families that show a better understanding of their motivations and respect for their goals while helping them adapt to this new culture with its own set of rules, regulations, and institutions.

We, and the Latino professionals, were mindful that much of what was being described about rural Mexican families was as much a function of poverty, lack of formal education, limited exposure to the wider world beyond their very small communities in Mexico, and the influence of the Catholic church as it was a function of culture. With that caveat, we believe we have captured in these pages some of what it means to be from Mexico—even when that might also mean being poor, having a limited education, and being Catholic.

There was a great deal of information from many different sources that needed to be brought together in a cohesive way. *This book has tried to integrate the vast amount of information that was collected in a way that paints a vivid picture of the intimate details of Mexican life in the U.S.* Each interview built upon the next, validating and corroborating the growing picture of the life experience for low income, limited education families from rural and semi-rural Mexico.

Through this book, we have learned more about the process by which Mexican children become socialized to be interdependent, to be respectful of adults, and to stay within their gender roles. We have a better understanding of the role and impact that *machismo* plays in the lives of not only the men but of the women and children as well.

We have come to understand and appreciate the tremendous ambivalence that many of the Mexican families struggle with while living in the U.S. The distance from their rural communities to the modern urban or suburban existence in the U.S. can't be measured in mere miles. Coming to the U.S. requires a new way of interacting with the world around them. They are confronted with a new language, new foods, new rules and regulations, new processes for getting things done, new and more institutions, and new ways of interacting with these institutions. Maybe more significant and confusing are the intangibles—issues such as independence, speaking up, and personal space. These are beliefs and behaviors so natural to those of us who grew up in the Anglo culture that we are virtually unaware of their role in our daily interactions. We sense something is "wrong" when someone doesn't conform to our norms, but we probably can't pinpoint what it is.

As we have learned, the process of acculturation can be overwhelming and frightening. For lots of families who are uneducated and scared, their culture and the guidance of their church, family, and Latino friends and neighbors is all they have. They often fear losing their culture and traditions to a culture that seems diametrically opposed to theirs. They may fear losing their children to a more independent way of life. They may even fear losing themselves. We know this is not true to the same extent for all Latino families. What we have also come to understand is how important the individual families' experience and history is in this process. The more their basic needs are taken care of, the more resources available to them, the better their coping skills, and the more support they have, the less their fear.

One of the most striking things we learned was that many of the people moving here from Mexico have almost no other options for survival. Their poverty and limited education play an enormous part in their thoughts, beliefs, behavior, and reaction to the U.S. Living in the U.S. means learning a whole new set of standards, rules, laws, and behaviors for these people who have their own history and traditions. Learning the new rules and how to act is a very hard and very slow process. The close proximity of Mexico to the U.S. magnifies the ambivalence these families feel about their lives in the U.S. and slows the process and hard work of change. *To make things worse, Mexican families in the U.S. experience prejudice and discrimination a great deal of the time.*

We hope that getting inside the lives of rural Mexican families has made you more knowledgeable, sensitive to, and thoughtful about the many struggles they face as they try to make a go of it in this country. We also hope it has helped you recognize and appreciate the richness and beauty of their culture, values, and traditions.

We have given you enough information to better understand some of the subtleties in the building blocks that help children become family oriented and respectful. We have also looked at the building blocks of child-rearing practices and their outcomes; practices whereby children may not be played with, read to, or talked to enough for them to be sufficiently prepared to learn in school and be ready to successfully meet other challenges of living in the U.S. We have also looked at how children are expected to learn to listen to their parents and have seen some of the outcomes when children get older and start to question the way their parents demand obedience. The relationships between the authoritarian style and the use of power and violence were also described.

When writing about a culture, one naturally lapses into generalities. If we are not careful, those generalities can contribute to stereotyping. This was not our intent. The information and generalities found in this book can provide valuable background information on the culture of families from the very small towns and rural areas of Mexico. But they are merely pieces in the puzzle of the individual and the family and cannot stand alone. *Attesting to the fact that you cannot truly generalize about a culture are the many and often contradictory views and opinions expressed by our Latino professionals.*

The Mexican experience in the U.S. can be one of isolation from the non-Latino community. It can be one of traditional male and female roles, where males are more dominant, more powerful, and more important and women have many children. It can be one of children who are expected to be seen but not heard, who learn not to ask questions or give opinions, who learn to obey out of fear. These aspects of Latino child-rearing practices tend to get in the way of opportunity and success in this country—partly because of the impact on the child's self-esteem and confidence and partly because of the child's not learning the skills he or she needs to use in the Anglo culture of the U.S. This doesn't mean that Mexican families raise their children badly. It just means that some aspects of their culture may be working against increased opportunity for their children in the U.S.

The Mexican experience can also be one where the families have opportunities to modify some of their traditions and incorporate parts of Anglo and other non-Latino cultures into their lives. These opportunities will come through formal and informal channels. They will come when we show an understanding of and respect for the important values of Latino culture and find new ways of preserving those values in a way that offers increased respect, learning, and enhanced self-esteem for everyone. *In order to increase opportunities for Mexican women, we need to educate men about the advantages these changes hold for them. Enhancing a woman's competency and self-esteem should not automatically mean lowered self-esteem for men.*

As we learned about the values of families from rural and semi-rural Mexico, we found it useful to look at these values as important strengths and goals that we could work with rather than against. When some seem problematic within the culture of the U.S., we can reframe them in helpful ways for the parents. For example, we can find ways for children to show respect for their parents and elders other than blind obedience. Children can be respectful and "under control" and still express their opinions. Raising children in the U.S. does not need to be an either/or experience (i.e., absolute authoritarianism vs. total permissiveness). There are many shades of gray between these two extremes that can be learned by families and that still honor and uphold the values of the culture.

Too often goals and values get mixed up with behaviors. In order to change a behavior a person feels they have to change their goals or values. We have learned of the strength of many of the Latino values and the purposes they play in preserving the culture. It is not the goal that is the problem. More likely, it is the behavior used to get to that goal. Families may know of only one way of getting to their goal. We can help them expand their understanding and their approaches in order to find new ways.

We can be most helpful by starting with the family's beliefs and helping parents understand basic child development. We can help parents recognize their importance in the growth of their child. *There needs to be a lot of education around alternate forms of limit setting that maintain the parents' authority—forms that are authoritative rather than authoritarian. We can teach this by helping parents to see their role as "teacher" rather than as "punisher."*

It is always important for us, as professionals, to recognize that, when teaching parents new behaviors, we need to validate the parent's role and concern for the child. In addition, a lot of work needs to be done in the area of communication between parent and child. It is useful to help parents see that being a good communicator helps keep them in charge. This is important and will impact the child positively at home, in school, and in the community in general.

Each of us needs to look at family attitudes, needs, and child-rearing practices and recognize when they get in the way of helping children have a better life—a life with more opportunities, more self-esteem, and more education. We need to think about different ways to reach out to families at many points in the child-rearing process, and to offer them respect, information, and education.

Information during pregnancy, early child-rearing years, and school years all have value. Education linked to government subsidy programs, school, home visits, and community clinics—whether done individually or in groups, with bilingual staff or translators—can all have a positive impact. Finding ways to bring mothers and fathers in to talk to other parents of the same gender and to their spouses and children is equally important.

This book does not give a recipe for working with parents and children from rural Mexico. Rather, it informs, educates, and exposes you to approaches some people have found to be helpful. We hope it will act as a catalyst to your using your skills and experiences—together with those of the parents and children you work with—to develop your own approaches.*

There are many local and national Latino organizations, many Latino parenting programs, and many Latino professionals who are ready to work with you to help you better serve the Mexican community (see Appendices B and E). All the Latino professionals we interviewed volunteer their time and skills beyond their professional work to help Latinos with their struggles and their growth. They give to their communities because they see that there is much to do.

Let's take what we have learned and give our Latino colleagues and our Mexican families a hand. Our involvement can go beyond our roles as professionals to such things as informal family exchanges or adopt-a-school or adopt-a-church programs. There are many ways to join with Latino families and help each other. You will be rewarded with many new, close, and meaningful relationships with people from this important culture.

We have taken you on a cultural journey through the eyes of Latinos. The journey was filled with new information, insights, understanding, problems, frustrations, hopes, and fears. For those of us who allow ourselves to *feel* what we read on these pages, this journey can lead to change. Change is difficult and change is rewarding.

---

*We encourage you to continue your learning by meeting informally with other colleagues, both those who are Latino and those who are not, to share your beliefs, concerns, and experiences.

APPENDICES

In-depth Interview Questions

Pregnancy and Birth

1. How do couples decide when to have a baby — mostly planned? mostly fortuitous?
2. What does having a baby/becoming a parent mean to the woman? to the man?
3. What do couples think is necessary before you have a baby — marriage, education, job, housing — etc.?
4. What is the attitude about there needing to be a father or a husband in the planning for the baby *or* is it OK for a woman to get pregnant and just raise the child herself?
5. What is the age when it's OK to be a parent?
6. What about teen pregnancies — how are they received or viewed?
7. Does the culture suggest ways of encouraging a pregnancy if a couple is having trouble getting pregnant?
8. What is culturally common to do to prevent unwanted pregnancy by the woman? by the man?
9. When a woman becomes pregnant, what should she do for herself? (e.g., eat differently, go for check-ups, stop working)
10. When a woman becomes pregnant, what should others do for her? (e.g., encourage her, lift things for her, expect less of her, any specific folk medicine practices, etc.)
11. What is the male (or father's) role when the woman is pregnant?
12. Where does the birth take place? Who is there and what are their roles? Is a doctor necessary?
13. What is expected that the woman will do during birth (does the culture expect her to take drugs during delivery, scream, curse)?
14. How does the woman expect to feel after delivery?
15. What is she expected to do? (sleep, feed the baby, cry, etc.)
16. What are others around her expected to do just after the birth?
17. How long does it take a mother to recover?
18. Who else is involved with the mother in the first weeks after delivery and after that? What are their roles?
19. When do babies get baptized? What is the importance of baptism for the baby? for the family?

Child Rearing

1. What does the infant get fed at first and how frequently and by whom?
2. If baby has feeding problems, who do the parents talk to? What is generally prescribed? What are common feeding problems?
3. How useful is the doctor's opinion about feeding? When should a parent listen to it and when should a parent disregard it?
4. Who seems to know better than the doctor about feeding?
5. Why do babies burp? How and when should they be burped?
6. What will his family be feeding him during his first year of life and then on into his second?
7. What do mothers and fathers think of breastfeeding? Is it common to try to breastfeed? What do other families commonly think about breastfeeding?
8. Should babies cry? What do parents do when they cry? Why do babies cry?
9. Should babies be carried around? A lot or a little? By whom and how?
10. Do babies need a schedule? Why or why not?
11. How much do babies sleep? When do they start to sleep through the night? Is there anything a parent should or could do about it? Do babies need naps? Where do babies sleep?
12. How much do toddlers and preschoolers sleep? Who do they sleep with? What if they have trouble sleeping the way a parent expects? What - if anything - would the parent do? Would they ask anyone else for help? What kind of help?
13. What should babies be doing when they are awake? What's the parent supposed to do with an awake baby? Does this require any materials? Who else helps out with the baby when it is awake? What do they do with the baby?
14. What should one and two year-olds be doing when they are awake? With parents or others? Do parents think they require any toys, etc. - e.g.?
15. What about three and four year-olds — What should they be doing during the day? And with whom? What do they need — if anything — to play with?
16. What language is mostly used at home — between parent and child and also among most family members?
17. Do babies seem to be very much the same or each unique? If unique, in what ways?
18. Do young children seem very much the same or each unique? If unique, in what ways?
19. Do parents feel they can make a difference/influence how their child turns out? (i.e., what kind of a person he becomes?) If yes, what could a parent do to make a difference, and in what areas?
20. Can anyone make a difference in how a child turns out? Who and how?
21. What do people of this culture think are the characteristics that make for a good parent? (e.g., calm, patient, high energy, firm, etc.)
22. When crawling/walking babies touch things they shouldn't, why do parents think they do that? What do parents and other family members do and say? Why?

23. When a child gets to be two or three years, what things does he do that parents typically do not want him to? Why do they think he does that? What do parents typically do about it?
24. How does a child know when his parents or other adults are angry with him?
25. How does a child know when his parents or other adults are pleased with him?
26. When changing a baby's diapers and he starts to move around, why do parents think he does that? What do parents and other adults typically do?
27. When do parents think a child is old enough not to wear diapers? How do they get him potty-trained? Who else helps?
28. What do parents think about a child watching TV? What does he get out of it? Is there anything troublesome if he watches TV?
29. What do parents typically do when their child asks for food? Toys? The parents' time? Why do they think he asks for these things?
30. What do children do with their brothers and sisters and cousins? Do they fight very much? Why do parents think they do?
31. What do parents and other relatives do about it?
32. What responsibilities do children typically have at home and at what age did they start?
33. What differences - if any - are there in what is expected of boys and girls? What are the ways in which they are treated differently?
34. When do parents and other adults think a child should start school — at what age?
35. What do parents and other adults think he gets from going to school? What is the attitude of parents toward their child's school? What is the child's attitude toward his school? Are there any common problems that these children face at school?
36. What do families like to do on Sunday? Who comes? What happens? Do parents feel they need to go places without their children? Who takes care of the children then? What do parents want their children's caregivers to do for their children when they are taking care of them?
37. What do mothers, fathers think they should be doing with or for their children as their mother, father? e.g., feeding, bathing, dressing them; changing diapers; talking to them, playing, teaching; discipline; reading to them; earning money; keeping them safe?
38. In regard to the children, in what ways do mothers and fathers do things differently?
39. Who makes child rearing decisions and is that based on each of the parent's cultural roles (e.g., *machismo*) or more on each parent's strengths?
40. What are some things that there are frequently different opinions on between mothers and fathers and what are some things there is usually more general agreement? How do the differences get settled?
41. What are some things between the generations that there are frequently different opinions on? How do the differences get settled?

Family and Community

1. When parents have worries and problems, who do they go to for help? (personal problems, problems with children, problems with spouse, etc.)
2. Who else commonly lives with the parents and children? How frequently do families see their relatives?
3. How important is going to church? How does that help a family's life?
4. How does living in the United States for increasing years change a family's views and behavior?

Attitude toward Physicians

1. When would a family go to a doctor - for themselves or for their children?
2. Who else gives a parent help when she or he is not feeling well? What kind of help?
3. What is bad about going to see a doctor? What's good about it?
4. What advice do doctors give about adult problems that adults really find hard to follow? About children's problems that parents find hard to follow?
5. What do families think about physicians?
6. What are some common sicknesses and what helps cure them? (e.g. colds)
7. What would a family typically do if their child got very ill?
8. If a family member dies, what are some of the reasons that people might think that happened? (e.g., God is punishing them, etc.)
9. What do people think happens to you when you die? . . . especially for infants and children?

Background of Latino Professionals Interviewed*,**

1. **Luz Agudelo, B.A.**
   Radio Talk Show Hostess for
   Latina Call-in Program
   Address: KAZA Radio
           P.O. Box 1290
           San Jose, CA 95018
   Phone: (408) 984-1290 (work)
           (408) 281-7746 (home)

   Born: Rionegro, Colombia
   In U.S.: for 12 years

2. **Maty Brito, M.S.W.**
   Mental Health Outreach Counselor
   Garfield Elementary School
   in Redwood City
   Address: Garfield Elementary School
           815 Allerton Street
           Redwood City, CA 94063
   Phone: (415) 369-3759 (work)

   Born: Caracas, Venezuela
   In U.S.: for 10 years

3. **Rosa Carreno**
   Community Health Worker
   San Mateo County Department of Health Services
   in San Mateo
   Address: San Mateo Department of Health Services
           225 W. 37th Ave.
           San Mateo, CA 94403
   Phone: (415) 573-3470 (work)

   Born: Vina, Chile
   In U.S.: for 30 years

*When the address and/or phone number is listed, the professional would be willing to be contacted by the reader for further information or, in some cases, to possibly co-lead workshops for professionals or parents focussing on issues concerning Latino families.

**For the Latino professionals we interviewed that were born in Mexico, we have listed the state they came from. Appendix C has a map showing the names and locations of all the states of Mexico and their pronunciation. This is included to enhance your communication with the families you work with.

4. **Juan C. Carrillo, M.D.**
   Pediatrician
   Private practice
   in San Jose

   Born: Michoacán, Mexico
   In U.S.: for 34 years

5. **Beatriz B. Cerrillo, B.A.**
   Family Resource Specialist
   Family Focus for School Success
   in Redwood City
   Address: Family Focus for School Success at Fair Oaks School
   2950 Fair Oaks Ave.
   Redwood City, CA 94063
   Phone: (415) 368-8026 (work)

   Born: Durango, Mexico
   In U.S.: since infancy

6. **Carmen P. Cortez, M.A.**
   Associate Director for Program
   Services and Development
   Avance (Latino Parenting Program)
   in San Antonio, Texas
   Address: Avance
   301 S. Frio (Suite 310 and 350)
   San Antonio, TX 78207
   Phone: (210) 270-4630 (work)

   Born: Texas
   Parents Born: Texas
   Grandparents Born: Mexico
   and Texas

7. **Amalia DeBord, L.C.S.W.**
   Clinical Social Worker
   Packard Children's Hospital at Stanford
   in Palo Alto
   Address: Packard Children's Hospital
   725 Welch Road
   Palo Alto, CA 94304
   Phone: (415) 497-8649 (work)

   Born: Bucaramanga, Colombia
   In U.S.: for 20 years

8. **Alice del Pinal, M.S.**
   School Psychologist
   Redwood City School District in Redwood City
   Address: Redwood City School District
   815 Allerton Street
   Redwood City, CA 94063
   Phone: (415) 365-1550 (work)

   Born: Guatemala City, Guatemala
   In U.S.: for 10 years

9. **Rafael Diaz, Ph.D.**
   Associate Professor of Education
   Stanford University in Palo Alto
   Address: School of Education
   Stanford University
   Stanford, CA 94305

   Born: Havana, Cuba
   In U.S.: for 22 years

10. **Linda M. Espinosa, Ph.D.**
    Associate Professor of Education
    University of Missouri in Columbia, MO
    (formerly Director, Family Focus
       in Redwood City)
    Address: University of Missouri
             301D Townsend Hall
             Columbia, MO 65211
    Phone: (314) 882-2659 (work)

    Born: Washington
    Parents Born: New Mexico
    Grandparents Born: New Mexico
    Prior generations: Mexico

11. **Flora Englund Fortis, M.S.**
    School Psychologist
    San Jose Unified School District in San Jose
    Address: San Jose Unified School District
             1671 Park Ave.
             San Jose, CA 95126
    Phone: (408) 998-6070 (work)

    Born: Santa Ana, El Salvador
    In U.S.: for 25 years

12. **Jorge R. Gonzalez, L.C.S.W.**
    Psychiatric Social Worker
    Santa Clara County Mental Health
    —Children's Services in San Jose
    Address: Santa Clara County Mental Health—Children's Services
             650 South Bascom
             San Jose, CA 95128
    Phone: (408) 299-7939 (work)

    Born: Mexico City (Federal
       District), Mexico
    In U.S.: for 35 years

13. **Carmen C. Guedea**
    Parent Educator
    Monterey County Office of Education
       in Salinas
    Address: Parents as Teachers
             Monterey County Office of Education
             901 Blanco Circle
             Salinas, CA 93912
    Phone: (408) 755-0372 (work)

    Born: California
    Parents Born: Mexico (mother)
    and Texas (father)

14. **Maria Felix Kramer,**
    M. Library Science
    Branch Library Supervisor, Fair Oaks Library
    Redwood City Public Library System
    Address: Fair Oaks Library
             2600 Middlefield Road
             Redwood City, CA 94063
    Phone: (415) 780-7262 (work)

    Born: Tabasco, Mexico
    In U.S.: for 13 years

15. **Renée DeLeon Martinez, M.S.**　　*Born:* California
    Professor of Child Development　　*Parents Born:* Arizona (mother)
    East Los Angeles Community College　　and California (father)
    　in Monterey Park　　*Grandparents Born:* Mexico
    Address:　East Los Angeles Community College
    　　　　　1301 Avenida Caesar Chavez
    　　　　　Monterey Park, CA 91754
    Phone:　　(213) 265-8870 (work)

16. **Ana M. Morante, M.S., MFCC**　　*Born:* Lima, Peru
    Outpatient Mental Health Case Worker　　*In U.S.:* for 5 years
    Chamberlain Mental Health Services in Gilroy
    Address:　Chamberlain Mental Health Services
    　　　　　8352 Church St. (Suite A)
    　　　　　Gilroy, CA 95020
    Phone:　　(408) 848-6511 (work)

17. **Victoria J. Orozco**　　*Born:* California (raised in Spain)
    Family Resource Specialist　　*In U.S.:* for 16 years
    Family Focus for School Success　　(*Parents* born in Spain)
    　in Redwood City
    Address:　Family Focus for School Success
    　　　　　Redwood City School District
    　　　　　2950 Fair Oaks Ave.
    　　　　　Redwood City, CA 94063
    Phone:　　(415) 369-9427 (work)

18. **Rosalie Prado de Ramirez, R.N., M.S.**　　*Born:* Managua, Nicaragua
    Public Health Nursing Supervisor　　*In U.S.:* for 50 years
    Santa Clara County Department of Public Health in San Jose
    Address:　Department of Public Health, Narvaez Multiservice Center
    　　　　　614 Tully Road
    　　　　　San Jose, CA 95111
    Phone:　　(408) 299-4305 (work)

19. **Dolores Marie Ramirez, B.A.**　　*Born:* California
    (and teacher's credential)　　*Parents Born:* California (mother)
    Multicultural Director　　and Mexico (father)
    Mid-Peninsula YWCA in Palo Alto
    Address:　Mid-Peninsula YWCA
    　　　　　4161 Alma
    　　　　　Palo Alto, CA 94306
    Phone:　　(415) 494-0972 (work)

20. **Rafael T. Ramirez, Ph.D.**   *Born:* Zacatecas, Mexico
    Elementary School Principal   *In U.S.:* for 35 years
    Garfield School in Redwood City
    Address: Garfield Elementary School
                815 Allerton St.
                Redwood City, CA 94062
    Phone: (415) 369-3759 (work)

21. **Maria R. Reyes, M.S.W.**   *Born:* Texas
    Social Worker   *Parents Born:* Chihuahua, Mexico
    Santa Clara County Social Services Agency in San Jose
    Address: Santa Clara County Social Services Agency
                1725 Technology Drive
                San Jose, CA 95110
    Phone: (408) 441-5226 (work)

22. **Raul Rojas, B.A.**   *Born:* Mexico City (Federal
    Parent Educator and Community   District), Mexico
    Outreach Coordinator   *In U.S.:* for 3½ years
    Mayfield Community Clinic in Palo Alto
    Address: Mayfield Community Clinic
                270 Grant Ave.
                Palo Alto, CA 94306
    Phone: (415) 617-9722 (work)

23. **Josie Romero, L.C.S.W.**   *Born:* Coahuila, Mexico
    Executive Director   *In U.S.:* for 42 years
    Hispanic Institute for Family Development in San Jose
    Address: Hispanic Institute for Family Development
                1740 Cleveland Ave.
                San Jose, CA 95126
    Phone: (408) 288-7014 (work)

24. **Rita Rossi**   *Born:* Spain;
    Librarian and Resource Center Staff   (grew up in Jalisco, Mexico)
    Redwood City School District   *In U.S.:* since adolescence
    in Redwood City
    Address: Redwood City School District
                815 Allerton St.
                Redwood City, CA 94063
    Phone: (415) 369-3759 (work)

25. **Yolanda Ledon Torres, M.A.**
    Child Care Consultant
    Self-employed in Pasadena
    Address: 495 California Terrace
             Pasadena, CA 91105

    Born: California
    Parents Born: Mexico

26. **Gil Villagrán, M.S.W.**
    Child Welfare Social Worker
      and Coordinator
    Family Resource Center and
      Nuestra Casa Youth Project
    Address: Santa Clara County Social Services Agency
             1725 Technology Drive
             San Jose, CA 95110
    Phone: (408) 441-5626 (work)

    Born: Mexico City (Federal
      District), Mexico

    In U.S.: for 41 years

27. **Graciela H. Ybarra, B.A.**
    Resource Teacher
    Address: 500 Chiquita Ave., Apt. 15
             Mountain View, CA 94041
    Phone: (415) 966-1305 (home)

    Born: California
    Parents Born: Mexico (mother)
      and Texas (father)

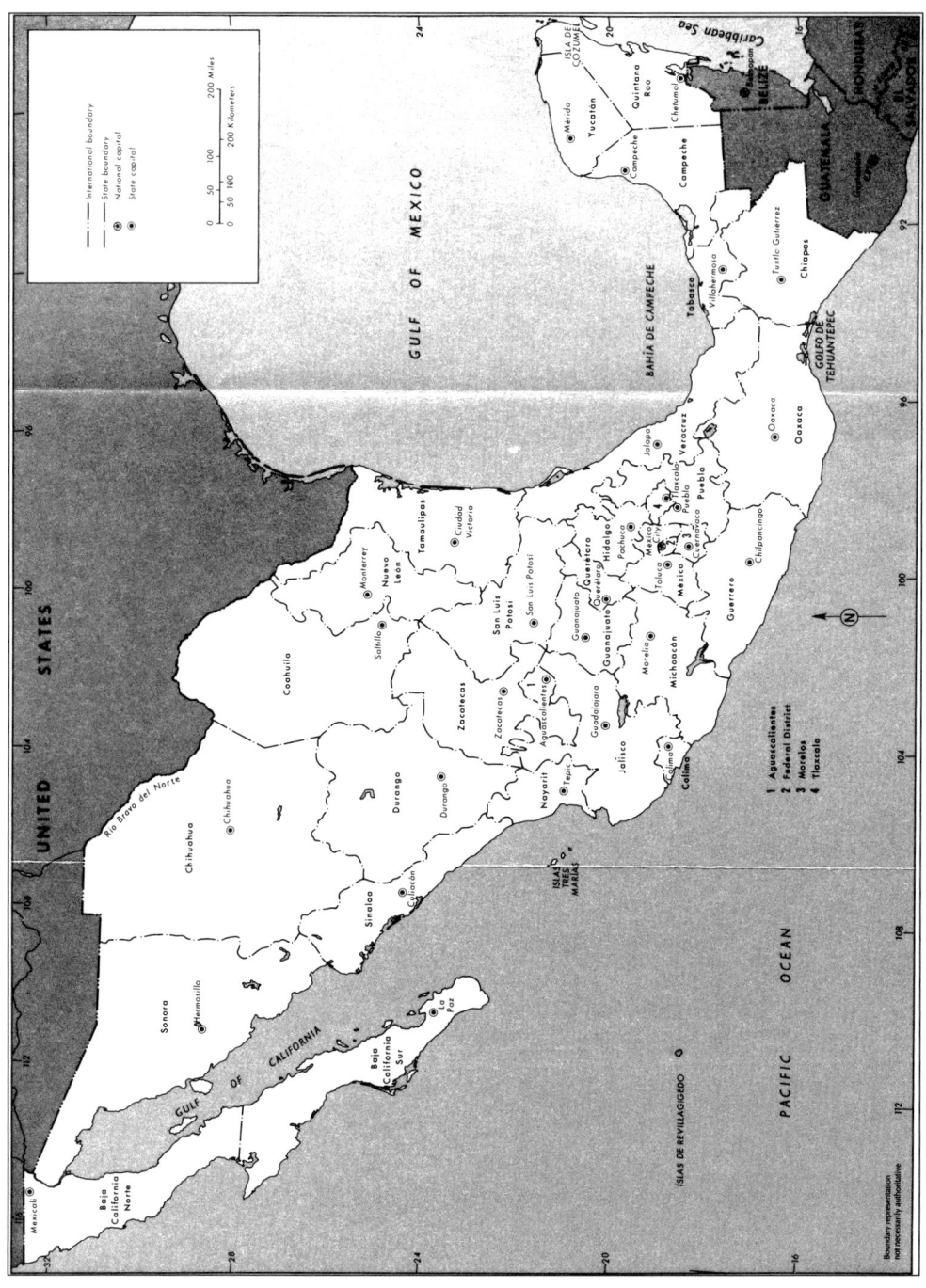

Reprinted from *Mexico—A Country Study* ed. by James D. Rudolph. Washington, D.C.: Secretary of the Army, U.S. Govt. 1985.

Map of Mexico and Its States

(Pronunciation Guide in Alphabetical Order)

1. Aguascalientes [AH · gwahs · kahl · YEHN · tays]
2. Baja California Norte
   [BAH · hah · kah · lee · FOHR · nyah NOR · teh]
3. Baja California Sur
   [BAH · hah · kah · lee · FOHR · nyah soor]
4. Campeche [kahm · PEH · cheh]
5. Chiapas [chee · AH · pahs]
6. Chihuahua [chee · WAH · wah]
7. Coahuila [ko · ah · WHEE · lah]
8. Colima [ko · LEE · mah]
9. Durango [doo · RAHN · gch]
10. Guanajuato [gwah · nah · HWAH · toh]
11. Guerrero [gehr · REH · roh]
12. Hidalgo [ee · DAHL · goh]
13. Jalisco [hah · LEES · koh]
14. México [MEH · hee · koh]
15. Michoacán [mee · cho · ah · KAHN]
16. Morelos [moh · REH · lohs]

17. Nayarit [nah · yah · REET]
18. Nuevo León [NWEH · bo leh · OHN]
19. Oaxaca [wah · HAH · kah]
20. Puebla [PWEH · blah]
21. Querétaro [keh · REH · tah · roh]
22. Quintana Roo [keen · TAHN · ah roh]
23. San Luis Potosi [sahn · LWEES poh · toh · SEE]
24. Sinaloa [see · nah · LOH · ah]
25. Sonora [soh · NOHR · ah]
26. Tabasco [tah · BAHS · koh]
27. Tamaulipas [tah · mah · oo · LEE · pahs]
28. Tlaxcala [tlahs · KAH · lah]
29. Veracruz [veh · rah · KROOZ]
30. Yucatán [yoo · kah · TAHN]
31. Zacatecas [sah · kah · TAY · kahs]

Distrito Federal (Federal District)
[dee · STREE · toh feh · deh · RAHL]

Appendix D

Suggested Readings

History and Current Conditions

Atkin, S. *Voices from the Fields: children of migrant farmworkers tell their stories.* Boston: Little, Brown and Co., 1993.

Flores, B. *Chiquita's Cocoon: the Latina woman's guide to greater power, love, money, status, and happiness.* New York: Villard Books, 1994.

Hall, D. *The Border: Life on the Line.* New York: Abbeville Press, 1988.

Martinez, E. (ed.) *500 Years of Chicano History in Pictures.* Albuquerque, N.M.: Southwest Organizing Project, 1991. [(505) 247-8832]

Meier, M. and Ribera, F. *Mexican Americans/American Mexicans: From Conquistadors to Chicanos.* New York: Hill and Wang, rev. 1993.

Moore, J. and Pachon, H. *Hispanics in the United States.* Englewood Cliffs, N.J.: Prentice-Hall, 1985.

Rudolph, J. (ed.) *Mexico—a country study.* Washington, D.C.: U.S. Govt., Dept. of the Army, 1985 (out of print but available in libraries)

Westridge Young Writers Workshop. *Kids Explore America's Hispanic Heritage.* Santa Fe, N.M.: John Muir Publications, 1992 (a book for children)

Developing Cross-Cultural Competence

Lieberman, A. Culturally Sensitive Intervention with Children and Parents. *Child and Adolescent Social Work, 7,* 1990, 101 - 120

Lum, D. Toward a Framework for Social Work Practice with Minorities, *Social Work, 27,* May, 1982, 244 - 249

Lynch, E. and Hanson, M. *Developing Cross-Cultural Competence: a guide for working with young children and their families.* Baltimore, MD.: Paul H. Brookes, 1992.

Storti, C. *The Art of Crossing Cultures.* Yarmouth, ME.: Intercultural Press, 1990.

Culture and Childrearing

Clark, A. *Culture and Childrearing.* Philadelphia: F.A. Davis Co., 1981 (out of print, available in college libraries)

McAdoo, H. (ed.) *Family Ethnicity: strength in diversity.* Newbury Park, CA: Sage Publications, 1993.

Phinney, J. and Rotheram, M. *Children's Ethnic Socialization: pluralism and development*. Newbury Park, CA: Sage Publications, 1986.

Werner, E. *Cross-cultural Child Development*. Monterey, CA: Brooks/Cole Publishing Co., 1979 (out of print, available in college libraries).

———

Buriel, R. Mercado, R., Rodriguez, J. and Chavez, J. Mexican-American Disciplinary Practices and Attitudes Toward Child Maltreatment: A Comparison of Foreign- and Native-Born Mothers. *Hispanic Journal of Behavioral Sciences, 13,* 1991, 78 - 94.

Gutierrez, J. and Sameroff, A. Determinants of Complexity in Mexican-American and Anglo-American Mothers' Conceptions of Child Development. *Child Development, 61,* 1990, 384- 394.

Martinez, E. Child Behavior in Mexican American/Chicano Families: Maternal Teaching and Child-Rearing Practices. *Family Relations, 37,* 1988, 275 - 280.

Martinez, M. Family Socialization among Mexican Americans. *Human Development, 29,* 1986, 264 - 279.

Moreno, R. Maternal Teaching of Preschool Children in Minority and Low-status Families: a critical review. *Early Childhood Research Quarterly, 6,* 1991, 395–410.

Olvera-Ezzell, N., Power, T., and Cousins, J. Maternal Socialization of Children's Eating Habits: Strategies used by Obese Mexican-American Mothers. *Child Development, 61,* 1990, 395 - 400.

Powell, D., Zambrana, R., and Silva-Palacios, V. Designing Culturally Responsive Parent Programs: A Comparison of Low-Income Mexican and Mexican-American Mothers' Preferences. *Family Relations, 39,* 1990, 298 - 304.

Rueschenberg, E. and Buriel, R. Mexican-American Family Functioning and Acculturation: A Family Systems Perspective. *Hispanic Journal of Behavioral Sciences, 11,* 1989, 232 - 244.

Zepeda, M. Selected Maternal-Infant Care Practices of Spanish-Speaking Women. *Journal of Obstetric, Gynecologic and Neonatal Nursing,* Nov/Dec 1982, 371–374.

Culture and Child Care

Delgado, M. Providing Child Care for Hispanic Families. *Young Children, 35,* September, 1980, 26 - 32

Gonzalez - Mena, J. *Multicultural issues in infant care*. Mountain View, CA: Mayfield Publishing, 1992.

York, S. *Roots and Wings: affirming culture in early childhood programs.* St Paul, MN: Red Leaf Press, 1991.

Special education and ethnic minorities

Condon, E., Peters, J., and Sueiro-Ross, C. *Special education and the Hispanic child*. New Brunswick, N.J.: Teachers' Corp. Mid-Atlantic Network, 1979.

Cummins, J. *Bilingualism and special education: issues in assessment and pedagogy*. San Diego, CA: College-Hill Press, 1984.

Harry, B. *Culturally Diverse Families and the Special Education System,* New York: Teachers College Press, 1992.

Harry, B. Making Sense of Disablility: Low-Income, Puerto Rican Parents' Theories of the Problem. *Exceptional Children, 59,* 1992, 27 - 40.

Health care issues with Latino families

Abril, I. Mexican-American Folk Beliefs: how they affect health care. *American Journal of Maternal Child Nursing,* May/June, 1977, 168 - 173.

Anthony-Tkach, C. Care of the Mexican-American Patient. *Nursing and Health Care ,* October, 1981, 424 - 428.

Berlin, E. and Fowkes, W. A Teaching Framework for Cross-cultural Health Care. *Western Journal of Medicine, 139,* 1983, 934 - 938.

Clement, D. Border Crossings: Refugees Travel Difficult Route to Health Care. *Minnesota Medicine, 75,* 1992, 24 - 29.

da Silva, G. Awareness of Hispanic Cultural Issues in the Health Care Setting. *Children's Health Care, 13,* (1), 1984, 4-10.

Gums, J. and Carson, D. Influence of Folk Medicine on the Family Practitioner. *Southern Medical Journal, 80,* (2) 1987, 209 - 212.

Maduro, R. Curanderismo and Latino Views of Disease and Curing. *Western Journal of Medicine, 139,* 1983, 868-874.

Marsh, W. and Hentges, K. Mexican Folk Remedies and Conventional Medical Care. *American Family Physician ,* 37(3),1988, 257 - 262.

Mayers, R. Use of Folk Medicine by Elderly Mexican-American Women. *Journal of Drug Issues, 19* (2), 1989, 283 - 295.

Poma, P. Hispanic Cultural Influences on Medical Practice. *Journal of the National Medical Association, 75* (10), 1983, 941 - 946.

Rodriguez, J. Mexican-Americans: Factors Influencing Health Practices. *The Journal of School Health,* February, 1983, 136 - 139.

Schreiber, J. and Homiak, J. Ch. 5 Mexican Americans in *Ethnicity and Medical Care.* Harwood, A. (ed.) Cambridge, MA: Harvard University Press, 1981.

Trotter, R. and Chavira, J. Curanderismo: An Emic Theoretical Perspective of Mexican-American Folk Medicine. *Medical Anthropology* 4 (4), 1980, 423 - 479.

Waxler-Morrison, N., Anderson, J., and Richardson, E. (eds.) *Cross-Cultural Caring: A Handbook for Health Professionals in Western Canada.* Vancouver, B.C.: University of British Columbia Press, 1990.

Werner, D. *Where There is No Doctor: a village health care handbook,* Palo Alto, CA: Hesperian Foundation, rev. 1992.

Resources

Parenting Education Curricula - Designed Specifically for Latinos

1. **Avance** (Family Support and Education Programs)
   301 S. Frio, Suite 310, San Antonio, TX 78207
   (210) 270-4630

   Gloria G. Rodriguez, Ph.D., President

   AVANCE has been nationally recognized for establishing a successful family intervention program for hard-to-reach families with special emphasis on serving Hispanic families. The Avance intervention model begins with families of infants and young children. Services are comprehensive in scope, community based, preventive in nature and provided in a sequential manner to children and parents. The Avance program is offered in the home, school, and in centers, some of which are located in public housing projects. For 20 years, direct services have formed the core of the Avance Intervention Model for hard-to-reach families. The center-based 9-month intensive parent education program serves low income families with their children three years of age and under. Parents attend weekly parenting classes. Monthly home visits are made to each participant for observing parent-child interactions.

   Avance also provides an adult literacy education program, fatherhood services, Even Start, economic development services, child abuse and neglect intervention services and a comprehensive child development program (CCDP). In addition, Avance conducts research on the conditions and factors associated with poverty and other social/economic problems in high-risk communities and it operates a national training center to share and disseminate information, material and curriculum to service providers and policy makers interested in supporting high-risk Hispanic families.

2. **Cara Y Corazon** (Parent Education/Family Strengthening Program)
   15865-B Gale Avenue (Suite 1004), Hacienda Heights, CA 91745
   (818) 333-5033

   Jerry Tello, Program Developer and Trainer

   Cara Y Corazon (Face and Heart) is a parent education/family strengthening program developed to work with parents and families who have been raised in an alcohol/drug dependent and/or oppressive home environment. The concepts of Cara Y Corazon are indigenous concepts that formulate the basis for "La

Educacion" (character development) which for Latino families is a fundamental principle for appropriate living. The Cara reflects the values of *dignidad* (dignity) and *respeto* (respect) and the Corazon reflects the values of *confianza* (interdependent, intuitive bonding) and *carino* (love, acceptance). A person who has a good sense of "La Educacion" (character) has a balanced sense of Cara Y Corazon, incorporating the four values in their interaction with the world. In an alcohol, drug dependent, or oppressive family environment, it is these four values that are traumatized and ultimately cast parents who have come from these environments as high-risk for inappropriate parenting. Utilizing either an eight or twelve week format, the Familia program incorporates an interactive learning process to cover the following areas:

1. Conocimiento (Who are We?)
2. Mi Familia, Mi Corazon (My Family, My Heart)
3. Guiando el Camino, La Educacion (Guiding the Journey, Character Development)
4. Regalos y Cargas (Gifts and Baggage)
5. Valores con Valor (Values with Meaning)
6. Creciendo y Apprendiendo (Growing and Learning)
7. Padre y Maestro (Parent and Teacher)
8. Ceremonia y Tradicion (Ceremony and Tradition)
9. Conocimiendo, Mi Familia (Getting to Know My Family)
10. Raices de Entendimienta (Roots of Understanding)
11. Integracion; Bailanda a Diferentes Ritmos (Dancing to Different Rhythms)
12. Movimiento; Celebrando Family (Celebrating Family)

After completing the Familia Program, the participants are encouraged to participate in one, or all, of the support groups. This program also offers extensive facilitator training and guides.

3. **MELD** (Programs to Strengthen Families)
   123 North Third Street, Suite 507, Minneapolis, MN 55401
   (612) 332-7563

   Joyce Hoelting, Resource Development Coordinator

MELD's goal is to enhance the confidence and competence of parents by providing relevant information that is easily understood in a very supportive atmosphere. MELD programs bring together parents with common needs. The groups meet for two years - time to learn, grow and become friends while solving problems and creating a healthy family. Experienced parents volunteer to facilitate groups. These parent group facilitators are carefully selected, trained and supported by a trained MELD professional in each community.

MELD helps communities and individuals realize that positive parenting behaviors can evolve when parents get valuable information and emotional support. A powerful support system develops in MELD groups that helps parents solve problems together. MELD believes that there is no one right way to raise a child. It encourages respect and appreciation for the uniqueness of each individual.

MELD's inclusive, respectful and accepting philosophy is warmly received by many kinds of parents.

Its administrative and programmatic practices promote cultural inclusiveness. When reaching parents in new cultures, MELD partners itself with agencies and professionals who know and are trusted by parents.

MELD has a program for the Mexican and the Mexican-American Family. La Nueva Familia comes complete with materials for parents and trainers; also there is a helpful baby book and journal and child development posters celebrating the Latino culture. MELD offers an extensive program of training for facilitators.

4. **Los Ninõs Bien Educados**
   (a Parent Training and Skill Building Program)
   CICC, 11331 Ventura Blvd. (Suite 103), Studio City, CA 91604
   (800) 325-CICC

   Lupita Montoya Tannatt, Ph.D. and Kerby Alvy, Ph.D., Coordinators.

This parenting skill-building program was developed especially for Spanish-speaking and Hispanic-origin parents. It is respectful of the unique traditions and customs of Hispanic families and it is sensitive to the variety of adjustments that are made as Hispanic families acculturate to life in the United States.

Los Ninõs Bien Educados is based on child rearing research with Hispanic families, the recommendations of Hispanic educators and mental health authorities, and adaptations of parenting skills that have been found to be helpful for parents of all ethnic and social class backgrounds.

The program is built around the value of raising children to be "bien educados", i.e., well-behaved in a social and personal sense, as well as educated in an academic sense. It explores parental definitions of what constitutes "bien educados" and looks at how these definitions get expressed in traditional family and gender role expectations of children, and traditional age expectations. From this cultural framework, it teaches parents a wide variety of strategies and skills for promoting and maintaining those child behaviors that they define as constituting "bien educados" and for reducing those that they see as reflecting "mal educados." The program consists of 12 three-hour sessions. CICC can arrange to teach a one-day seminar for parents or provide facilitator training. Materials are also available for purchase.

5. **PIQE** (Parent Institute for Quality Education)
   6306 Riverdale Street, San Diego, CA 92120
   (619) 285-9905

   Patricia Mayer, M.S., Executive Director

This program teaches Hispanic parents to become partners with the school system educating their children. The program teaches parents to assume a role that is visible, audible, and participatory in the education of the child and how to get involved as well as stay involved. As this is so different from the expectation in

Latin American schools, parents need to be taught these new roles. The program, conducted in Spanish, consists of six classes, each 90 minutes. Besides the concept of becoming a "comadre" with the school principal in the education of their child(ren), the topics include culture conflicts, communication skills, discipline, self-esteem, drug abuse, and higher education.

This program has been participated in by 25,000 parents in San Diego and Los Angeles since it was founded by Vahac Mardirosian in 1987. It is strongly supported by the public schools and through private donations.

Training for other professionals is currently available in California through the Institute's main office.

6. **CEDEN** Family Resource Center (Parent-Child Program)
    1208 East 7th Street, Austin, TX 78762
    (512) 477-1130

    Emily Vargas Adams, Ph.D., Director

This bilingual and multicultural program was designed to serve high-risk and developmentally delayed children, principally from low-income homes whose parents have many needs. Program materials are also very useful for parents of low-risk children. The program serves infants and children, to 36 months of age, their parents, siblings, and extended families with comprehensive, integrated and developmentally appropriate services. CEDEN also offers an extensive prenatal education program.

Program goals include: reversal and prevention of developmental delays; improvement of health care and nutritional status; improvement of parenting skills and home settings; and achievement of family self-sufficiency.

CEDEN has developed bilingual materials for others to use in parental education programs, parent-child programs, teen parent programs and other programs as well. It also offers training workshops and advisory services.

7. **Family Focus for School Success** (a program of education for families)
    815 Allerton Street, Redwood City, CA 94063
    (415) 365-1550

    Jean Anthony, M.S., Coordinator for Family Support Services

Family Focus for School success is a comprehensive early intervention effort (preschool through 3rd grade) designed to provide individualized parent/family education and support for low-income members of the Hispanic community in Redwood City, California. There are three main goals for Family Focus: 1) to improve the socio-economic competence of parents and children involved in the program; 2) to improve the school adjustment of students at risk of school failure; and 3) to improve the school achievement among those children served by the program.

Family Focus is a three-pronged program; it includes three distinct, yet integrated service delivery models:

    A. **Home Education:** home intervention service for preschool-aged children who have a high potential for failing school because of complex environmental factors which cannot be mitigated without external support. Weekly, individualized home visits utilize a year-long curriculum which is reflective of current thinking about early childhood education and development as well as community needs.

    B. **Mental Health:** school-based mental health service program for kindergarten through third grade students and their families. Students are referred by their classroom teachers. This is an interagency effort between the school district and county mental health.

    C. **Family Resource Centers:** School based centers which link families with their children's school very early in the child's school career.

    The curriculum for the Home Education Program is currently being prepared for national distribution.

Latino Organizations *

  1. **National Council of La Raza**
    810 First Street N.E. Suite 300, Washington D.C. 20002 - 4205
    (202) 289-1380

    Raul Yzaguirre, President and CEO

    Mission: "Serves as an advocate for Hispanic Americans and as a national umbrella organization for 150 formal "affiliates" - community-based organizations. . . . NCLR seeks to create opportunities and address problems of discrimination and poverty in the Hispanic community . . ."

  2. **Center for U.S.–Mexican Studies**
    University of California, San Diego
    10111 North Torrey Pines Road
    La Jolla, CA 92093-0510
    (619) 534-4503

    Wayne Cornelius, Ph.D., Director

    Mission: The Center for U.S.–Mexican Studies was established in 1979 and quickly became the leading U.S. institution of advanced scholarly research, training, and public service devoted entirely to Mexico and U.S.–Mexican relations. Each year the Center brings together many of the world's leading authorities on Mexico, representing all social science disciplines and history, to address the full range of problems affecting economic and political relations between Mexico and the United States. The Center also studies the history, economy, political system, and social structure of Mexico; aspects of the U.S. economy and U.S. public pol-

---

*This is a "starter" list of well-established Latino-focused organizations in the areas of health, education, social services, parent education, mental health, and policy-making.

icy that affect Mexico; and Mexico's economic interactions with Japan and other Pacific Rim countries.

Through its program of visiting research fellowships, the Center makes a unique contribution to the training of a new generation of specialists on Mexico. Through its annual Summer Seminar in U.S. Studies, the Center also trains promising young social scientists, public officials, and journalists from Mexico and other Latin American countries to teach, do research, and report on the United States.

3. **The Tomás Rivera Center**
   710 North College Ave.
   Claremont, CA 91711
   (909) 625-6607

   Harry Pachon, President

   Mission: Dedicated to promoting the well-being of the Latino population of the United States through the improvement of the nation's policies and programs, The Tomás Rivera Center conducts rigorous, policy-relevant research, evaluates the effects of governmental and corporate practices on Latinos, and serves as a non-partisan source of information, analysis, and ideas on the Latino population for the policymaking community. The Center convenes leaders and scholars to define the challenges facing Latinos as well as to suggest approaches to meeting those challenges through policies and programs. Furthermore, the Center addresses critical policy issues by sponsoring informative, substantive, timely forums and through publication of pertinent data, analyses, and informed perspectives.

4. **Latino Issues Forum**
   1535 Mission Street, San Francisco, CA 94103
   (415) 552-3152

   Guillermo Rodriguez, Jr., Director for Research and Policy

   Mission: This is a public policy and advocacy institute "dedicated to advancing policy concerns from the Latino perspective. LIF's primary focus is on the broader issues of access to higher education, economic development, health access, regional development and telecommunications issues."

5. **COSSMHO**
   National Coalition of Hispanic Mental Health
      and Human Service Organizations
   1501 16th Street N.W., Washington D.C. 20036
   (202) 387-5000

   Jane Delgado, Ph.D., President and C.E.O.

   Mission: "... transfer of knowledge to help improve the planning and delivery of health, mental health, and human services to Hispanic families, children, youth, elderly, and other special populations.

6. **Association of Mexican American Educators, Inc. (A.M.A.E.)**
   634 So. Spring Street, Suite 1015, Los Angeles, CA 90014
   (209) 782-7193

   Carmen Cortez, M.A., State President

   Mission: The mission of the Association of Mexican American Educators, Inc. is to ensure equal access to a quality education at all levels for the Mexican-American/Latino students where cultural and linguistic diversity is recognized and respected. We advise state/local boards and legislators, administrators and faculty and work in partnership with the community and parents for the benefit of our students.

   A.M.A.E.'s vision is that it will assert its position as the leading educational rights advocate for Mexican-American, Chicano and Latino students, educators and parents. A.M.A.E. will work towards obtaining equal access to a quality and equitable education for our students. A.M.A.E. will embrace the entire educational community in a coalition which strives for the educational advancement of our youth and which prepares them for social, political, and economic justice in a culturally diverse America.

7. **National Association for Bilingual Education**
   1220 L Street N.W., Suite 605, Washington D.C. 20006
   (202) 898-1829

   James Lyons, Executive Director

   Mission: Ensuring that language-minority students have equal opportunities for learning the English language and for succeeding academically; involving language-minority parents in the process of schooling and in public policy decisions affecting them and their children; identifying and publicizing exemplary bilingual education programs; promoting and publishing scholarly research in the fields of language education and multicultural education; increasing public understanding of the importance of language and culture in education; and fostering the establishment of national language policies which meet the needs of a pluralistic society in an era of global interdependence and competition.

8. **Hispanic Association of Colleges and Universities**
   4204 Gardendale, Suite 216, San Antonio, TX 78229
   (210) 692-3805

   Laudelina Martinez, President.

   The Hispanic Association of Colleges and Universities (HACU) is a national organization representing Hispanic-serving institutions (HSIs) of higher education —those nonprofit, accredited colleges and universities where Hispanics constitute a minimum of 25 percent of the total enrollment at either the graduate or undergraduate level. (Membership is by institution, not individual).

   Mission: Promote the development of member colleges and universities:

improve access to and the quality of post-secondary educational opportunities for Hispanic students: meet the needs of business, industry, and government through the sharing of resources, information and expertise.

9. **National Hispanic Medical Association**
   Morrisania Diagnostic and Treatment Center,
   1225 Gerard Ave., Bronx, NY 10452
   (718) 960-2793

   Luis Estevez, M.D., President

   Mission: A coalition of Hispanic physicians interested in improving health care by participating in public policy reform.

10. **Mexican American Physicians Association**
    4201 Medical Drive, Suite 280, San Antonio, TX 78229
    (210) 692-9344

    Edmundo O. Garcia, M.D., President

    Mission: Dedicated to increasing the representation of Hispanics in the health care field and increasing the accessibility of health care throughout Texas.

11. **California Hispanic-American Medical Association**
    1030 South Arroyo Parkway, Suite 220, Pasadena, CA 91105
    (818) 799-5456

    Gustavo Alza, M.D., President

    Mission: Professional seminars to educate and sensitize Hispanic and non-Hispanic physicians who are interested in the Hispanic patient; programs to assist medical students to choose their area of specialty and the practice setting that suits them best; publications to communicate its membership's collective voice to the Hispanic and non-Hispanic physicians, medical universities, and other medical societies; and free referral services for the Spanish-speaking and Hispanic populations seeking specialty physicians throughout California.

12. **National Association of Hispanic Nurses**
    1501 16th Street N.W., Washington D.C. 20036
    (202) 387-2477

    Sarah Torres, R.N., Ph.D., F.A.A.N., President

    Mission: Strives to serve the nursing and health care delivery needs of the Hispanic community and the professional needs of the nurses. It is committed to work toward providing equal access to educational, professional and economic opportunities for Hispanic nurses.

13. **The Association of Chicana-Latina Nurses**
    P.O. Box 3176, San Jose, CA 95156
    (408) 683-4631

    Conception Macias, R.N., President

    Mission: The association believes that the Chicana/Latina nurse should: create a role for herself as an advocate of quality health care in the Latino community; create an awareness among other health professionals of the Latino's special health care needs; collaborate with existing health organizations to encourage their involvement in issues that relate to health access for the Latino community; and stimulate interest among Chicano/Latino youth to enter the health professions and encourage the upward mobility of those already in the profession.

14. **Latino Coalition for a Healthy California**
    1535 Mission Street, San Francisco, CA 94103
    (415) 431-7430

    Carmela Castellano, J.D., Executive Director

    Mission: Governed by a policy committee of Latino health services researchers, providers, public health officials, economists and academics, the mission of the coalition is "to empower the Latino community by identifying health care needs and advocating for solutions to the health care crises in local, state and national arenas."

15. **National Hispanic Psychological Association**
    Box 0611, Arizona State University, Tempe, AZ 85287-0611
    (602) 965-1352

    Andres Barona, Ph.D., President

    Mission: to promote the psychological welfare of Hispanics in the U.S. and secondly to promote the training and development of Hispanic professionals in the mental health fields.

16. **Latino Social Work Network Inc.**
    P.O. Box 374, 11718 Barrington Court, Los Angeles, CA 90049
    (310) 206-3844

    Juanita Chavez, M.S.W., A.C.S.W., President

    Mission: The Latino Social Work Network (L.S.W.N.) of California, Inc. was formed to advance Latino social work practice, and to advocate policies that improve access of quality professional social work practice by the Latino community. L.S.W.N. of CA, Inc. also provides an organizational framework whereby Latino social workers can exchange ideas, and participate in professional development.

17. **Latino Caucus of Family Resource Coalition**
    200 South Michigan Avenue, 16th Floor, Chicago, Illinois 60604
    (312) 341-0900

    Layla Suleiman, Latino Caucus Coordinator

    Mission: The caucus now has over 200 practitioners and advocates working with Latino families, all "...committed to the principles of family support and to addressing cultural diversity and language differences within the context of family support..." The Latino caucus is committed to serve as the link between the Family Resource Coalition, the national organization of parenting educators, and the Latino communities of this country.

18. **Hispanic Institute for Family Development**
    1740 Cleveland Avenue, San Jose, CA 95126
    (408) 288-7014

    Josie Romero, L.C.S.W. , Executive Director

    Mission: to provide its members (who are highly trained professionals with expertise in serving Hispanic families) and other professionals "with educational and training opportunities which expand their clinical and cultural proficiency."

19. **Hispanic Women's Council of Northern California**
    255 North Market St. Suite 244, San Jose, CA 95110
    (408) 288-2227

    Carmen Johnson, President of the Board of Directors

    Mission: To improve the status of Hispanic women through education, career and leadership development activities; to empower them to fully participate and contribute to the social, economic and cultural structure of the region, and to become role models for the upcoming Hispanic young leaders of the next century. The Hispanic Women's Council of Northern California was inspired by the Hispanic Women's Council Inc. founded in 1973 in Los Angeles.

About the Author

B. Annye Rothenberg, Ph.D. is a Child/Parent Psychologist and Director of the Child Rearing Education and Counseling Program at the Children's Health Council in Palo Alto, California. She received her Ph.D. from Cornell University in Child Development and Child Psychopathology. She is a nationally recognized expert on parenting education and guidance for parents of young children. Dr. Rothenberg is also a leader in training professionals in education, health care, and social services to provide more effective guidance to parents and help increase parents' skills in understanding and raising their children.

Dr. Rothenberg is the senior author of *Parentmaking: A Practical Handbook for Teaching Parent Classes about Babies and Toddlers* (Menlo Park, CA: Banster Press, 1983; revised, 1995)—an award-winning parenting education curriculum; and the new *Parentmaking Educators Training Program: A Comprehensive Skills Development Course to Train Early Childhood Parent Educators (birth to 5)*—a book and videotapes package (Menlo Park, CA: Banster Press, 1993).

Dr. Rothenberg is herself from an ethnic minority and has had a long term interest in ethnic minorities and the differing values and styles of family life and child rearing practices. She is the mother of a 24 year old son, Bret who has brought her much *naches* [NOKH·ess: joy and pride (in Yiddish)]. This book is the first in what is expected to be a series of contributions to this important area.

Understanding and Working with Parents and Children from Rural Mexico

What professionals need to know about child-rearing practices,
the school experience, and health care concerns

B. Annye Rothenberg, Ph.D.
with the views of twenty-seven Latino professionals

This book is about the fastest growing minority in the U.S.—the Mexican population, particularly the many who immigrate from rural and semi-rural Mexico. It speaks to you through the words of the real experts, the many Latino professionals we interviewed who work extensively with families from Mexico. Written by Dr. Annye Rothenberg, child/parent psychologist and author of the nationally-acclaimed *Parentmaking* books and videotapes, she has found a unique way to bring her expertise and that of many Latino professionals to give you an exceptional learning experience.

This book tells you about life in rural Mexico—which is where the majority of Mexicans coming to the U.S. are from. It tells about real peoples' adjustments to a new country and explores child-bearing and child-rearing practices, including information on how children and adolescents are viewed, talked to, played with, and disciplined. The reader will also learn about the experience for Mexican children and their parents of going to school in the U.S. You will learn some of the keys to more satisfying use of health care services by Mexican families including details on folk medicine and ways to integrate folk healing methods with those of Western medicine.

Understanding and Working with Parents and Children from Rural Mexico is filled with very important and little known insights about these families. Throughout the book, many practical suggestions are made to help professionals become more welcoming and successful in their work with Mexican families. You will be fascinated and educated by what you learn in *Understanding and Working with Parents and Children from Rural Mexico.*

Already highly acclaimed by leading Latino and Anglo colleagues, *Understanding and Working with Parents and Children from Rural Mexico* is a *must* for all professionals working with families from rural Mexico—whether they are nurses, early childhood educators, social service workers, educators/special educators, mental health clinicians, or physicians.

285 pages • Quality Paperback • 7″ x 10″ • ISBN 0-9642119-0-4
$22.50 for a limited time (Publisher's list price $27.50)
The CHC Center for Child and Family Development Press
P.O. Box 7326 • Menlo Park, CA 94026 • **(650) 369-8032**
www.bansterpress.com

- -

Order Form

Please send me _____ copy(ies) of *Understanding and Working with Parents and Children from Rural Mexico* by Dr. B. Annye Rothenberg at $22.50 plus $3.00 each for packing and shipping on prepaid orders. (CA residents, add $1.85 sales tax)

Name _____

Organization _____

Address _____

City _____ State _____ _____ Zip _____

$_____ enclosed. If not completely satisfied, I may return the handbook in saleable condition within 10 days for a full refund. (Customer pays return shipping.)

☐ Send me information about the Parentmaking training materials for family guidance professionals.

Mail to: **CHC Center for Child & Family Development Press**
P.O. Box 7326
Menlo Park, CA 94026